EVERYBODY'S SON

EVERYBODY'S SON

★ ★ ★ A NOVEL ★ ★ ★

Thrity Umrigar

HARPER

An Imprint of HarperCollins*Publishers*

This is a work of fiction. Names, characters, places, and incidents are products of the author's imagination or are used fictitiously and are not to be construed as real. Any resemblance to actual events, locales, organizations, or persons, living or dead, is entirely coincidental.

HarperCollins books may be purchased for educational, business, or sales promotional use. For information, please email the Special Markets Department at SPsales@harpercollins.com.

FIRST EDITION

Designed by Bonni Leon-Berman

Library of Congress Cataloging-in-Publication Data has been applied for.
ISBN 978-0-06244224-6
17 18 19 20 21   LSC   10 9 8 7 6 5 4 3

God have mercy on the man
Who doubts what he's sure of
—BRUCE SPRINGSTEEN

ACKNOWLEDGMENTS

Thank you, Rachel Dissell, for your generous help in explaining the family court and foster care systems to me. Thanks, Subodh Chandra, for your prompt reply to my query about the U.S. Attorneys system.

Thank you, Pat D'Sousa and Peggy Veasey, for your friendship, and profound gratitude to your parents for welcoming me into their home during those long-ago Christmas trips to Georgia that had such an impact on my life.

I am lucky to work with the finest of colleagues at Case Western Reserve University. Special thanks, Cyrus Taylor, for your enthusiastic encouragement and support.

I am beyond grateful to my brilliant and alarmingly hardworking agent, Daniel Greenberg, and to my wise and wonderful editor, Gail Winston. Thank you, Gail, for your sensitive and thoughtful edits.

To my extended HarperCollins family—thank you for the attention and care you bring to my books. Michael Morrison and Jonathan Burnham, so proud to know you.

To my readers: You are the ones who breathe life into my books. I am more grateful than you can know.

Thanks to my friends, too numerous to mention by name. You sustain, nourish, and challenge me.

As always, thank you, Eust, Gulshan, and Homai, for being my forever people.

And Dad, missing you still. Always will.

EVERYBODY'S SON

PROLOGUE

On the seventh day, the boy broke the window.

It had been sealed shut by a coat of paint applied years earlier, and after several futile attempts to open it, he picked up the nearest dining room chair and heaved it against the glass.

Even though it happened during the quiet of a Saturday afternoon in May, no one appeared to have heard. No heads stuck out from their own window to examine the source of the shattering, no feet hurried to the apartment where the boy had stayed alone for seven days.

It was a miracle, really, that he had survived. Outside, the worst heat wave in a decade was raging, and when the police got there, they reported indoor temperatures of ninety-five degrees. The electricity had been cut off four days earlier. If there had been food in the refrigerator, it surely would have turned moldy. As it was, he had finished eating whatever little was in the fridge—a few slices of pizza and two hot dogs. The rest of the time he had survived on bags of potato chips, crackers, and candy bars.

Still, he had not sought help. Nobody could understand why not. When the police asked if he hadn't wondered whether his mother was dead, struck by a car, maybe, or worse, he had simply stared back at them with those big amber eyes. The officer suspected that this was not the first time he had been left alone while his mother went scouring for drugs, but the boy was noncommittal. "She told me she'd be back" was all he said. And so he had waited.

Waited. In the tiny one-bedroom apartment that had no air-conditioning and only one ceiling fan that could not operate with the power off. Waited in the apartment with the dead fridge and food running out and no television to watch.

Even when he smashed the window of the first-floor apartment and tumbled out onto the tiny patch of lawn outside, what greeted him was the indifferent world. No middle-aged woman walked over to see what the commotion was. No elderly neighbor appeared curious about the shards of glass sprinkled on the grass and the cement walkway. The young punks hanging around the housing project didn't look up from their self-absorbed jousting to see the young boy dripping blood from where the broken window had sliced his left leg.

In the end, it was the blood that saved him. The cop in the cruiser who patrolled the Roosevelt projects was used to spilled blood in this neighborhood. But even from a distance, he could see how fragile and vulnerable the young boy looked. And yet he was walking, walking away from the desolate brick buildings, as if searching for something, dragging his left leg along. Something about the boy's posture, frail but resolute, made the officer leave the air-conditioned comfort of his cruiser and step out into the blistering heat. "You okay, sonny?" he asked, but he knew the answer even before he finished the question.

It all happened quickly after that. The call for the ambulance. The call to Children's Services. A short hunt for the mother. Turned out she was in a crack house less than three blocks away. When they found her, she was passed out and half-naked, semen caked on her thighs. A pipe lay on her chest. They arrested the other two women and four guys in the house and confiscated multiple drug paraphernalia, along with two thousand dollars' worth of crack cocaine.

When she came to, she asked repeatedly for her baby boy. Swore that she'd intended to go out only for a hit and return home straight away, but Victor, her drug dealer, had raped her and kept her doped up. She'd locked the apartment door from the outside because the housing project wasn't a safe place for a young boy to be alone. Hell, she did that even if she went to the food pantry. All the mothers did this to keep their babies safe, ask any of her neighbors. The cops ignored her mewing. There was nothing here that they hadn't heard or seen before. It was 1991. There was a crack epidemic raging across the country. A few towns over, the rich white kids were snorting cocaine. But here, in the inner city, it was a goddamn jungle. Filled with animals like this disheveled, wild-eyed woman who had left her son to bake in a locked apartment in the middle of a heat wave.

If they had their way, if they had any goddamn power, which they didn't, of course, they'd lock up the bitch forever. Make sure she never got to hurt that poor kid again. But as it was, they knew she'd walk free in a couple of months. And so they shook their heads and drank their beer and shot some pool until they could forget about her, her and her ilk, people who seemed to exist only to make their goddamn jobs even goddamn harder.

BOOK ONE
June 1991

CHAPTER ONE

The room where he was to meet the boy was painted a cheery blue, its walls covered with posters promoting the county's foster care program, but David Coleman barely noticed any of it as he walked in, escorted by the social worker. He was too nervous. The two men made their way to the maroon couch, and David eased his lanky frame onto it. They made small talk for a few seconds, and then the social worker looked at his watch and stated the obvious: The boy was late.

The older man nodded. His right hand fluttered for a moment and automatically made its way to his front pocket, where he typically kept his pack of cigarettes, but then he remembered. He had quit smoking three months ago, a promise to Delores on their wedding anniversary.

Delores. It seemed wrong that she was not beside him now. She'd had a terrible migraine the previous day, but still, he'd been shocked when she'd begged off this morning. Becoming foster parents in their mid-forties hadn't particularly been her idea, but he was here today in large part in an attempt to wipe out the sadness that had taken root in her eyes for the last five years—ever since . . .

Ever since The Calamity. He'd be embarrassed to say those words out loud, but that was how David thought about it, what had happened to them that night five summers ago. He knew that bringing another child into their home could never change what had occurred, that in the pristine, close-knit community where they lived, they would always be the Colemans, the cursed couple who had suffered the unthinkable. But still. Even if all he could do was turn the sorrow that had taken root in Delores's eyes into a smudge, something faint, rather than a live, burning thing, it would be worth it.

And could there be a more deserving case than the boy he was scheduled to meet, the boy who was running late? Neglected, abandoned, the son of a junkie, a woman whose case was being heard by his colleague, Superior Court Judge Robert Campbell. Quite a coincidence, really, that this was the boy they were offering him. Not that he'd needed to hear about the boy's situation from Bob. It had been in the newspapers, how the poor kid had fended for himself for seven miserable days until he finally broke out. That was a month and a half ago, around the time David and Delores had completed their training to become foster parents. In fact, one of their workshops had been on how to take care of a black child. David had felt mildly uncomfortable as the speaker gave them pointers on how to groom black hair and how to understand black English. And really, what would've been the odds of them landing a black foster kid, given the racial makeup of their county? But they'd sat through it, and now David was thankful, although he hoped Delores remembered the section on black hair better than he did.

The social worker was talking, and David forced himself to listen. The young man—his name was Ernest, and David thought he'd never met a man so perfectly suited to his name—was asking whether David had any last-minute questions about Anton.

"I don't think so," David replied. "I think we're okay."

"Yes, well. It's just that . . . I don't want you to think . . ." Ernest looked at David for a minute and continued, "He's a really good kid. You'll see. I mean, it's too bad it didn't work out with his current foster parents. It's not his fault, really. We never should've placed him with a family with five kids. After what he's been through, he needs extra attention. And the Brents just couldn't . . ."

David smiled. "Are you this strong an advocate for all your clients?"

Ernest looked pained. "Well. Yes. I mean, I try." His face brightened. "But Anton is special. You'll see." There was a short silence and then Ernest said, "They should've been here by now. Mr. Brent was to have dropped him off half an hour ago. I'll go see what's taking so long."

"Okay." David smiled again. "But they're not really that late, you know. I don't mind waiting."

He watched as Ernest walked to the door, reached for the knob, and then looked back. "Judge Coleman?" the younger man said. "I . . . I just want to say . . . I'm a huge fan. I think you've done a fine job on the bench. And I'm awfully glad you're taking in Anton." Inexplicably, Ernest blushed. "That is, I think you'll hit it off. I mean, it's a good match. So many of these kids . . ."

"Thank you." But inwardly, David felt weary. Just once, especially on an occasion as fraught as this one, he would like to be anonymous, just Joe Schmo the electrician, say, looking to foster a kid. Anyone but Judge David Coleman, whose father had been a U.S. senator for almost twenty-five years, whose grandfather had been a much decorated admiral in the U.S. Navy. Anyone but the man whose son's death had made the papers all over this small northeastern state. He shook his head, a gesture so slight as to escape the younger man. David had spent his entire life in the public eye. It was wishful thinking to believe that things would be different now. "Thank you," he said again. "Appreciate it," and he nodded in a gesture that was at once humble and dismissive.

Ernest straightened. "Be right back," he mumbled.

Alone in the blue room, David felt a tightening in his chest that he recognized as nervousness. He should've insisted that Delores come with him. In an attempt to tamp his restlessness, he rose to his feet and paced the room. Was something wrong? Could the boy's current foster family have changed their minds and decided to keep him? From what he had read in the boy's file, that didn't seem likely. Or could some relative have come out of the woodwork to claim him? As far as he knew, before Children's Services had placed Anton with the Brent family, they had contacted his only available kin, a grandmother in Georgia. But the woman, legally blind and of little means, had been unable to take him in. What would that feel like, David wondered, being rejected by your only blood relative after spending seven harrowing days in a dangerously hot apartment while your mother was cavorting with her junkie friends? He stopped his pacing as another thought struck him: What if this abuse was only the tip of the iceberg? What else had this poor child endured? Would the damage be too severe, too lasting, for him and Delores to handle?

And then there was the race thing. The boy had grown up in the Roosevelt projects, and shuddering, David remembered touring them with Pappy, then still a senator. What would Anton think when he saw his new home in Arborville? His new school? David and Delores had been so surprised when they'd offered the boy to them. Yes, there was a dearth of black foster parents, but still. The only dark faces in the tree-lined, affluent town belonged to janitors and the street-cleaning crew. Though wait, there were now two black cops on the Arborville police force, weren't there?

Delores had balked when David first mentioned the call from the county. "What do we know about raising a black child, David?" she'd protested. He had put up a brave front. "For crying out loud, Dee," he'd said. "It's 1991. If the Spelmans can adopt a child from China, why the heck can't we foster a black kid for a few months? Until they figure out what to do with him?"

David ran his hand through his hair as he recalled how he'd gotten on his soapbox. He'd fed Dee some bullshit line about how it was time to walk the walk, how this was a chance for people like them, to whom so much had been given, to give back. The old noblesse oblige bit. He'd believed everything he'd said, but he had also felt a sense of unreality as he'd said the words. Delores had looked at him dubiously, her lower lip jutting out. But she hadn't fought back. She rarely did anymore. He suspected she'd given in for his sake, thinking mistakenly that this was something he wanted. But he knew the truth—he was doing this for her. Giving her something she didn't know she needed. Not that this could take the place of James, obviously. Nothing ever could. But here was the thing: Delores had been a fabulous mother. Fabulous.

David shook his head swiftly, unwilling to let the image of James's mangled body nestle there. He wouldn't think of his dead son. Not today. To the best of his ability, he wanted to go into this new venture clean, openhearted, and unburdened by the past. And above all, to do it for the right reasons. This was an opportunity to give a damaged kid a stable home.

He looked around for a phone, but there was none in the room. He would've liked to call his wife, to inform her that nothing had happened yet, that he wouldn't be home for at least another hour or more. She would be anxious to know. She had promised to make dinner for tonight, something simple—salad, baked chicken, and potatoes. Ice cream for dessert. He had felt a twinge of excitement when he'd run to the store for ice cream this morning, and then a twinge of apprehension when he'd realized he had no idea what flavor the boy liked. He'd picked up a pack of the Neapolitan, deciding to hedge his bets.

He heard the door open and spun around to see the boy walk in with the social worker. Ernest had his arm around his young charge, but David was struck by the boy's tentative posture. David took a few steps toward where the pair stood and, suddenly aware of his great height, stooped from the waist as he stuck his hand out. "Hi there," he said gently. "You must be Anton. I'm David."

"Hi." The voice was weak, barely audible, and David felt a stab of disappointment. But then the boy tilted his head up, and David's breath caught in his throat. Anton's skin was golden, almost luminous. His large amber eyes dominated a beautiful, slender face. When those eyes landed on David, he felt—there was no other way to say it—privileged, as if some rare bird had alighted on his shoulder. But he was also acutely aware of the guardedness with which Anton Vesper was looking at him.

"It's good to meet you." David smiled. "Finally."

Anton looked up at Ernest for guidance. The man gave the boy a slight nudge. "Go on," he said, pointing to the couch. "The two of you can chat for a few minutes. I'll be back to check on you soon, okay?"

David waited until Ernest had left the room to ease himself down on the couch beside the boy, who stared resolutely ahead, as if hoping David would disappear. David had seen defendants in court who had seemed less upset by his presence. And he'd never had to take one of them home.

"Was there a lot of traffic getting here?" he asked.

The boy shrugged. "Some."

David nodded, unsure what to say, feeling ungainly and old. Again, he wished Delores was here. She'd know what to say to this boy, how to ease his apprehension.

"You know why I'm here, right?" David said. "You're . . . I . . . we're hoping you'll come live with us for a while. My wife was sorry she . . ."

Anton turned toward him. "I wanna go home," he said loudly. "To *my* home. To my mam."

David had witnessed some version of this impulse for all the years he'd been in the legal profession. People seldom acted in ways you'd expect them to. Wives returned to abusive husbands, husbands forgave their cheating spouses, and children always, always loved their parents, no matter how shitty their behavior.

"I understand," he said. "Of course you do. But . . . for right now, it's not possible. So the real question is, do you want to go back with

Mr. Brent? Or come home with us, where you'll have your own bedroom and stuff?" He forced a laugh. "I should tell you, my wife's a terrific cook."

He waited for a response, but there was none. Anton simply stared ahead as if, now that he'd stated his intentions, he could withdraw into himself again.

"Anton." David lightly touched the boy's shoulder. "Listen. I can imagine how hard this is. And I understand how scary it must feel. But all I'm asking is that you give us a chance, okay? Let's just—"

"Are you the guy who did it to my mam?"

"What? Did what?"

"Are you the judge who locked Mam away?"

"What? Oh. No. God, no." The relief that he felt was palpable. And there was no way he was going to admit to his friendship with Bob Campbell, or the fact that he had run into Bob at the club just days after Juanita Vesper first appeared before him, and the older man had vented his disgust at the irresponsible, child-breeding vermin clogging his courtroom day after day. "No, no." David shook his head. "Uh-uh. That was another judge. Not me."

Under his hand, he felt Anton's shoulder relax. "Well, can you let her out?"

David sighed. "Anton. I can't. It's not my case, you see." He gave the boy a sidelong glance and decided to plunge ahead. "Also, your mommy did a bad thing. We need to make sure—"

"She made a mistake. She said she was sorry."

David was about to respond when he thought the better of it. This is a young boy, he reminded himself, a scared, traumatized child about to go home with a stranger. A white male, to boot. Cut him some slack.

"So what do you like to do, Anton? You play any sports?" he asked.

Anton flashed him a look that he couldn't decipher and fell silent.

"Basketball? Baseball? Soccer?" Eyeing the unresponsive boy, David felt a desperate need to get a response. "Cricket? Lacrosse? Polo?" he continued, hating himself for his meanness.

There was a brief silence and then Anton said, "I know what cricket is."

David sat up. "You do? Wow."

Anton nodded. "I saw a movie about it once, I think."

"Really? What movie?"

"I dunno."

"Well, I have a friend who is English. He can teach you, if you're interested." David had no idea why he was saying this. God help him if Anton remembered this conversation later.

"I hate the English."

"You do? Why?"

"They bombed Earl Harbor."

David opened his mouth and then shut it. Anton was talking to him. That was the main thing. The history lessons would have to wait.

"Well, then, I guess you're not learning cricket. You have a favorite sport?"

Anton shrugged again. "I play soccer."

"I bet you're good."

"Pretty good," Anton said matter-of-factly. "I'm probably the second best player at school, after Reggie."

"We'll have to make sure you practice a lot this summer." David rose from the couch, nudging Anton to his feet in the same movement. "Come on, kiddo. Let's go get your things."

"I need to leave a note for Mam so that she knows where to find me."

"Okay." Resisting the urge to check his watch, David walked toward the door and opened it. As he had suspected, Ernest was hovering in the hallway. "Anton needs to leave a note for his mom," he said deliberately. "Do we have any paper and pencil? And an envelope, maybe?"

Ernest met his eye. "Yeah, sure," he said, and hurried away, only to return with the stationery and a pencil.

They left the boy in the room to write his note and went into Ernest's small office down the hallway. Ernest handed David a backpack with Anton's belongings and went over last-minute instructions. Eyeing the meager backpack, David felt a combination of sadness and excitement. How little this boy possessed. And how much they could provide for him. He was glad it was a Friday afternoon. They would take Anton shopping for clothes and shoes tomorrow.

After ten minutes, David raised his eyebrows at the increasingly talkative Ernest, and as if on cue, the younger man said, "Let's go find out if he's done." They walked back into the blue room to find Anton licking the envelope. On it, he had written, "For Mam. Love, Anton."

The boy turned solemnly to face Ernest. "Can you give this to my mam when she comes for me? And can you tell her where to come get me?"

Ernest looked even more earnest than usual. "Sure will." He gathered Anton into a hug. "Bye, Anton. You be good, you hear?"

"I'll try." Anton's voice was small and muffled against Ernest's waist.

David swallowed. "Come on, kid," he said gruffly. "Let's get you home and settled."

THEY MADE DESULTORY small talk during the ride home. Mostly, Anton looked out the window and David tried to see the world through his eyes. They drove down streets with discount stores and payday loan services and pawnshops. They drove past neighborhoods with boarded-up houses, which later gave way to small middle-class ranch houses with tiny but well-tended front yards. It took forever, it seemed, to get to Arborville, where the trees stood taller and greener, the streets were wider, and million-dollar homes rose proudly atop manicured lawns as big as golf courses.

"Wow," Anton said as they passed a house with an enormous fountain in the front yard. "Where are we?"

"Almost home."

"It looks like Disney World."

David smiled. Then frowned. Anton was right. Compared to where he came from, Arborville did seem like Disney World, a magical place built out of cotton candy and fairy dust. How difficult would this transition be? And what if it didn't work out? What if Anton misbehaved, threw things around, refused to eat, or punched another kid, as he had with the Brents'? David was forty-four years old, Delores a year younger. Could they cope with a nine-year-old boy, a boy who had undergone unspeakable trauma? A boy who had no incentive to try to fit into their world, focused as he was on returning home to his mom?

David's heart was heavy as he turned onto his street. But just then Anton squealed. "Look," he said. "There's a woman who's walking a *cat*."

David glanced out of the window. "Oh yeah," he said absently. "That's Ruthie. She lives on our street. She's walked that thing since it was a kitten."

"Cool. I never seen that." Anton turned in his seat to take one last look. "I love kitties. Do you have one?"

"No. Do—did you?"

"Nope. Mam wouldn't let me. She has allergies."

A laugh exploded from David's mouth. A crack addict, a woman who smoked poison into her lungs, couldn't have a cat because of her allergies. What a crazy, jumbled-up world this was.

"What? Why you laughing?" Anton asked as David pulled into the driveway.

David shook his head, unable to explain and not wanting to upset the boy. He pulled the keys out of the ignition, went around to the other side, and helped Anton out. "Well," he said. "This is it. This is home."

He watched as the boy's eyes grew large, saw the incomprehension on his face, followed by apprehension. "This is your house?" he said. "You live here with your wife?"

David felt his face flush. "Yup."

"You guys got any kids?"

Wrong time for this question, because David knew Delores would be out to greet them any minute. He reached over and squeezed the child's shoulder. "Anton," he said. "We will talk later. But come on, I want you to meet my wife."

He took the boy's hand in his, aware of how cold and sweaty his palm was. He could feel Anton's fear transmitting itself like a current of electricity through the length of his own arm. His heart ached in sympathy.

He had maybe thirty seconds before Delores appeared. Facing the boy, David got down on one knee, as if making a marriage proposal. "Anton," he said, "I know you're scared. Don't be. You will be okay. I will take care of you. I promise."

For the first time since they'd met earlier in the day, the boy looked directly into the man's eyes. He opened his mouth to say something, but just then, the front door opened and they heard Delores say, "Well, hi there."

Embarrassed to be caught in this position, David gave her a quick wave and then pretended to tie Anton's shoelace. When he looked up, the boy was giving him a knowing look, as if he understood what David was doing. Something transpired between the boy and the man. Then David got up and the two of them walked into the house, feeling closer than they had a moment earlier, bound by the first shared lie of their life together.

CHAPTER TWO

David and Delores stood whispering in the kitchen, their heads bent toward each other. "Honey," Delores said, "you gotta go back in there and stop him. He's had three pieces of chicken, and he's now on his second bowl of ice cream. He's going to be sick."

David shook his head. "I can't. I don't want him to be self-conscious about anything he does. Besides, the kid needs fattening up."

"But hon—"

"Nine-year-old boys eat a lot. You've just forgotten . . ." The words were out of his mouth before he could take them back. He bit his lower lip. "I didn't mean . . . It was just a slip of . . ."

For a moment, Delores's chin wobbled, but when she looked at him, her eyes were blank. "Well, if you don't say anything to him, I will." She moved toward the doorway separating the kitchen from the dining room and then looked back. "And since I have to play the heavy, you have to load the dishwasher."

He watched in apprehension as she entered the dining room, sat down next to Anton, and pulled his dessert bowl away from him. "I think that's enough for one evening, kiddo," she said. "You've eaten enough ice cream to sink a ship."

David cringed at the firmness in Delores's voice. To his surprise, the boy giggled. "My mam says the same thing."

"Well, she's right." Delores's voice was matter-of-fact, with not a trace of the judgment or indignation that David felt every time he heard Anton mention his mother.

"One time we went to Dairy Queen and I ate so many scoops, I got a tummyache."

"Well, we don't want any tummyaches tonight. Right?"

"Yes, ma'am." Anton sounded subdued, but he cast a bashful look at Delores, and they smiled at each other.

Unbelievable, David said to himself as he began loading the dishwasher. Delores was unbelievable. Crisis averted. Thank God.

He strained to hear what they were chatting about in the dining room but couldn't. When he walked back into the dining room, Delores rose. "Well, kiddo," she said briskly, "we've all had a long day. I still have a headache, and you must be tired. Let's have you brush your teeth and get into bed, yes?"

Anton shook his head vigorously. "Uh-uh. I'm not tired. Can I watch TV?"

Delores looked at David, but before he could respond, she said, "Not tonight. You need to rest."

"But I'm not tired. At home, Mam lets me watch TV any time I want."

For the first time since he'd brought Anton home, David saw Delores purse her lips. "We have different rules here, Anton. And we can discuss those tomorrow. But first, let's get you changed."

Without warning, the boy burst into tears. "I don't *want* to stay here," he said. "I wanna go home."

David looked uncertainly at his wife, who flashed him a warning look. I'll handle this, the look said. "I'm sorry, sweetheart," she said, not sounding sorry at all. "But that's not an option. Now, come on, let's go up to your room."

The boy flung a look of hatred at Delores. "It's not my room. It's not my house. You're not my mom. I'm going home."

"Okay," Delores said heavily. "Okay. You wanna go home? Fine. You can go tomorrow. We'll drive you back to Children's Services tomorrow morning. But tonight we all have to go to bed."

Her words startled Anton enough that the crying decreased in volume. "But I . . . don't want to . . . go to Children's Services," he said between sobs. "I . . . miss my mom."

"Oh, honey, of course you do." In one graceful movement Delores leaned toward the sobbing boy and embraced him. "And I'm sure your mommy misses you, too."

Anton raised his head to look at Delores. "Jon said Mam left me alone because she hates me."

"Oh, baby, that's just not true. Who's Jon?"

"One of the kids at Mr. Brent's house. My foster brother."

David had a flash of insight. "Is that the kid you punched?"

It pleased him to no end that Anton looked embarrassed before he nodded. "I just wanted him to shut up," he mumbled.

"I don't blame you," Delores said loudly. "I'd have punched him, too."

It was exactly the right thing to say. Watching the look on Anton's face, David knew that immediately. How did she do it, Delores? How did she always know how to reach deep into a person's wounds and drain the muck that festered there?

"Listen," she was saying, "I want you to remember what I'm telling you now. Your mommy loves you. She always will. And your mom didn't leave you. She just . . . got held up somewhere. You understand? You know how sometimes you don't want to do something bad but you just do? Well, grown-ups do that, too. They make mistakes. So your mommy made a mistake. But she would never, ever not love you, Anton. I promise."

His wife and the boy were staring solemnly at each other, as if sharing some unspoken language, and David suddenly felt like the third wheel. He cleared his throat. "Well, okay. Hey, do you have some clothes to sleep in tonight, sport? Tomorrow we'll go buy you some clothes, okay? Would you like that?"

Slowly, Anton turned toward David, his amber eyes sparkling from his earlier tears. "Okay," he said, and rose from the table.

David waited on the bed in Anton's room as the boy used the attached bathroom. When he came out, he was wearing a Michael Jordan T-shirt and blue shorts. "You like him?" David asked, pointing to the T-shirt.

"I love him," Anton breathed.

"Me, too," David said. "Maybe we can go see him play sometime."

Anton threw him a sly look, as if he had caught David in a lie. "He's in Chicago."

"Sure." David shrugged. "But he plays elsewhere, too, right? So we can maybe catch him at an away game sometime."

Anton's eyes grew wide with excitement and disbelief. But then his face fell. "That nice lady said she's taking me to Children's Services in the morning."

David patted the bed. "Come sit here." He turned slightly to face the boy. "Anton. Here's the deal. We would like it very much if you would stay with us for a while. If you'd let us be your foster parents and let us take care of you. So what do you say, sport?"

"What about my mam?"

"Your mom will always be your mom. But you can spend some time with us, right? Just until your mom can . . . get back on her feet." Even as David said this, the thought of the boy returning to a life of poverty and addiction produced a chalky feeling in his mouth.

But no time now to parse his feelings, because he was flooded by a sudden memory. His first day at Phillips Exeter. Away from his parents for the first time, friendless, unfamiliar with the routine of a boarding school, he couldn't have felt more alone if he'd been marooned on the moon. And scared. Lord, he'd been scared. Everything that had previously seemed routine—whether or not to raise his hand in class, whether to tell a joke to a group of boys—now had to be thought through and analyzed. He had walked around terrified, lonely, cut off from the world, until Connor Stevens, who had already been there for a term, had befriended him, picked him up like a stray puppy and rescued him. Then everything had changed.

"Hey," David said. "I've been there. I know what you're going through. But listen, it'll get better, okay? We'll have fun this summer, okay? Can you just hang in there a bit? You know, just give us a chance?"

When Anton smiled, it lit up his face like the morning sun. David felt anew the shock of his beauty. Unbidden, the lines from Yeats's "The Living Beauty" entered his mind:

> *From beauty that is cast out of a mould*
> *In bronze, or that in dazzling marble appears*

He ran his fingers through the boy's cropped hair, realizing it was the first time he'd ever touched black hair. How soft, how familiar, how organic it seemed, like wool on a lamb, this thing that they all feared so.

He heaved himself up from the bed. At the door, he lingered. "Listen. Our room's right next door to yours. If you're scared or can't fall asleep, you just call for me, okay?" He waited until Anton nodded. "Good night, Anton. Sweet dreams."

" 'Night."

David closed the door behind him and decided he would go into the library and have a drink before going to bed. It had been a long, emotional day.

It was only after he had poured himself the cognac that he realized it was the first time in five years he'd been able to enter James's old room without thinking about his dead son. He had been angry when, three years ago, Delores had insisted on reclaiming the room, packing away James's football trophies and his size-twelve shoes. David had argued against taking down the posters of the Clash and the Bangles and packing up James's books, seeing no reason why he couldn't afford himself the momentary comfort of entering his son's room and reliving the memory of James lounging in the bed reading *The Grapes of Wrath* or sitting at the small wood desk beside the window. But even after Delores had stripped the room clean of its possessions, the memories lingered. After she got the walls repainted, David still knew exactly where the *Abbey Road* poster had hung, the precise spot from where the Rolling Stones had stuck out their tongues at him.

Life is what happens to you while you're busy making other plans. Did anyone know the truth of that line from "Beautiful Boy" better than he and Delores? Five years ago life had happened with such swift brutality that it had nearly claimed them along with their son. But here was the strange thing. Tonight he hadn't thought of the room as James's. Anton, with his shabby backpack and his fraying Michael Jordan T-shirt, had already made it his.

CHAPTER THREE

They were standing in their bedroom, careful to keep their voices low. "Are you crazy, David?" Delores hissed. "How can you take the risk? It's not fair to Anton."

David gritted his teeth. "We've been over this again and again. I told you, Connor's gonna be one of fifty other guests. Anton won't even know he's there. You know how big this shindig is each year."

"But what if?"

"You think the kid has a clue what's going on? All he knows is that his mom is already in jail. I bet he doesn't even know about the sentencing."

Delores frowned in a distracted way. "Speaking of which. I don't know how he's going to manage at school, David. He's going to lag behind something fierce. You know I'm working with him day and night, but his spelling and grammar are terrible. It's like they taught him nothing at his previous school."

David grimaced. "Yeah, well. That's what the combo of a druggie mother and a crappy school system buys you. Our tax dollars at work. Hell, he might have done better going to school in Bangladesh."

"And his general knowledge is outrageously bad. He told me yesterday that President Bush bombed Iraq to find and kill Hitler. That's . . . that's mind-boggling."

David gave a short laugh. "See? History is obviously not his strong suit." He put his arm around Delores's waist and pulled her close. "And you're worried about him realizing that Connor is prosecuting his mom? He's a kid, honey. He'll never make the connection."

"But David . . ."

He stroked her cheek and gave her a light peck on the lips. "Dee. Stop worrying. Connor's my oldest friend. Jan's like a sister to you. What are we going to do? Never see them again because of Anton?"

"I suppose you're right." She picked off a piece of lint from his shirt. "I hope we haven't bitten off more than we can chew, David. I honestly don't know if I'm cut out for this foster parenting thing."

"Dee. You're just stressed out. It's going to be fine."

But Delores looked unconvinced. "I'm so concerned about school, David. I only have another month to catch him up, and I don't know if I can. I mean, he's very bright, but a new school's going to be hard enough without—"

"I know," he said quietly. "I'm worried, too. He's probably also going to be the only black kid in his class. Think we should send him to private school instead? So he can get more individual attention?"

Delores rolled her eyes. "Like there's a difference between public and private schools in this bourgee town. Hell, our test scores are actually higher and our student-teacher ratio is better than the private schools'. We must be one of five school districts in the whole damn country that can claim this."

They looked at each other ruefully. "We have almost a month to bring him up to speed," David said at last. "If kids can come here from Laos and Cambodia without a word of English and become National Merit scholars within a few years, surely Anton can learn to read and write proper English in his own country." He ran his index finger across his wife's lips. "Besides, he has the most brilliant and patient teacher in the state."

She gave him that crooked smile. "I'll try, honey. But I ain't no miracle worker." She moved away from him and began to rummage through her dresser. "I tell you what, though. He's a natural at math. Just an innate ability, I suppose. That kid could give me math lessons."

"Thank God for small mercies."

In the three weeks they'd had Anton, none of David's initial concerns had been realized. Sure, the kid had occasional meltdowns and bouts of homesickness, but that was to be expected. For the most part, Anton appeared to be adjusting well. He was polite and grateful when they bought him new clothes, ecstatic when David bought him a pair of Air Jordan sneakers. For a young boy, he was surprisingly neat in his personal habits, much neater than James had been at that age. He made his own bed in the morning and, since last week, had taken to clearing the table after dinner. Delores had wanted to protest the first time he did this, but David stopped her. "He feels comfortable enough to do this, honey," he'd said. "It's his way of belonging. Let him."

But for all of these graces, David knew that the worst lay ahead of them. Delores was right—school loomed, an unknown meteor that could, at any moment, smash their newly constructed, peaceable lives to bits. For the last three weeks, they had shuttered themselves from the outside world, giving their family a chance to find a new equilibrium. Now that was about to end. He and Delores had always had a large social circle. Both of them had endured lonely childhoods, raised as only children in patrician, genteel families with workaholic fathers, and because of this, they had each sought out a different kind of life once they left home. David and Delores had married young, forced to by David's father, Senator Harold Coleman, after Delores became pregnant in college. (David had often wondered if he and Delores would have married so young had she gotten pregnant just a few years later, after *Roe* v. *Wade* had legalized abortion.) As it was, they couldn't be out partying or dancing the night away like their friends, so they entertained at home. And once Connor had married Janet six months later, then started his own family, the Colemans and the Stevenses had been inseparable, spending major holidays together, even vacationing together except when the Colemans were visiting the senator at his vacation house on the Cape.

David glanced out the window. It was still light outside. He slipped out of his bedroom and knocked on Anton's door. He remembered how surprised the boy had been the first time he'd rapped on the door for permission to enter. Hadn't his mom done the same? David had inquired. Anton had looked at him incredulously for a second. "No," he'd mumbled. Then, as if he had somehow betrayed his mom by this admission, the boy had added a little defensively, "My mam let me have the bedroom. She slept on the couch."

But now Anton responded with a matter-of-fact, "Come in," and David poked his head in.

"Hey, fella. You want to shoot some hoops?"

The boy grinned. "Sure."

The first time he and Anton had played together in the driveway, David had been self-conscious, wondering if the steady thud of the ball reminded Delores of the ferociously competitive games he and James used to play. But Delores had not reacted, and as the weeks went by, David relaxed. Anton was a steady, focused player, but he was not competitive, and David refrained from talking trash with him, the way he used to with James.

They played until it grew dark outside and their T-shirts were damp with sweat. When they finally looked up, they saw the two glasses of lemonade Delores had left on the steps leading to the back of the house. David and Anton sat side by side on the stone steps, sipping the drink.

"This is so gooood," Anton said. David giggled. "What? Why you laughing?"

David shook his head. "I don't know."

"Who should I ask?" Anton said, putting his hand on his hip and sounding exactly like Delores.

"Hey. That's Dee's line. Come up with your own."

A slight breeze rose from the grass and cooled their damp T-shirts. Summer, David thought. A hot evening with a cool breeze. Lemonade. A game of hoops with his son. Life didn't get better than this.

He caught himself immediately. Anton was not his son. Anton was someone else's son, a borrowed gift he would soon return. His own son, his blood, his legal heir, was dead.

Anton pulled at one of the hairs on David's knee. "David," he said, "I don't want to go to the party tomorrow."

David was struck by the contradiction—the intimacy of Anton's unconscious gesture, juxtaposed by the distancing act of calling David by his first name. Other foster children called their foster parents Mom and Dad, he and Delores had learned during their training. But not Anton. At least the boy didn't call him Mr. Coleman. As for his wife, Anton and Delores had come up with a good compromise. The boy called her FM, for foster mom and for, as Anton had put it with a giggle, FM radio. The code name was ironic, playful—and did not betray James in any way. It worked for Delores.

David focused his attention on Anton. "Why not, buddy?" he said, keeping his tone light. "It's a fun party. Lots of food, lots of games for kids."

"But David." Anton's voice was urgent. "I won't know anyone there."

He turned slightly to look at the boy, but Anton was staring straight ahead. What did he see, David wondered, in this lush, manicured lawn with the azalea bushes, the flower beds, the pond with the exotic fish?

"I know. But here's the thing. These people—many of them, anyway—are our friends. And you are now part of our family. So you have to get to know these people, right?"

"But David. I'll be gone soon. Soon as the judge lets my mam go home."

Before David could control his body, he stiffened. That's how Anton saw himself, as a guest. It didn't matter what he or Delores said or did or felt. He tasted the bile in his throat and felt a sudden bitter detachment from the boy sitting next to him. What difference did it make? Beyond a new wardrobe and some nice table manners, what could they provide Anton? Why was Delores breaking her back trying to improve his diction, his spelling and grammar? Let the boy wallow in his ignorance, let him believe that Hitler and George Bush were mortal enemies. Anton was right. Chances were his mother would be home in no time, long before he and Delores could combat the damage done by his lousy education, his absent father, his worthless mother. David, of all people, understood sentencing guidelines for child endangerment—hell, she could serve as little as four to six months. Even if Bob tacked on the drug possession charge, she would still be out in no time.

He shook his head. Anton was staring up at him, his mouth slightly open, a scared look in his eyes. Lord, he must look a sight. What had Anton read on his face? He had no business taking out his frustration on the boy.

"David," Anton whispered, "I'm sorry. I'll go to the party with you."

He forced his face into a smile. "Only if you want to, Anton." Then, "Though I think you'll have a great time. And I'll be by your side all afternoon. Okay?"

"Okay," the boy said.

David forced himself to not hear the unease in the boy's voice. But his heart was heavy as he rose to follow Anton into the house, where he could almost feel Delores's disapproval at dragging the boy to a party where he would come face-to-face with his mother's prosecutor.

CHAPTER FOUR

The first few days were fine. He had worried when his mother didn't come home that first night, but then he remembered that a year ago she had stayed away all night, and when she returned home the next day, she had given him a dollar bill for being a brave little boy. And besides, it was kind of fun, staying up and watching TV all night long, munching on potato chips and the cheddar cheese left over from the visit to the food pantry at the beginning of the month. The power was still on then, so the apartment was cool and the fridge humming.

The trouble started on the fourth day, when the power went off and the heat began to rise. He had wanted to call the power company, like he'd heard his mother do, but she hadn't paid the telephone bill in a couple of months, either, and so the phone was dead. Besides, what could he say? That he was alone at home? And get her into trouble? He still remembered when the cop had come to their apartment after he'd missed school for a week. Mam had been home that evening, and Anton had hated how she'd acted around him. It had made him feel small and angry in a new way, to see her act like this, like she was a little kitten begging for a saucer of milk. Watching the cop look around their small, shabby apartment, his lip curled with disgust, listening to him lecturing his mother as if she were a bad girl, had made Anton want to break something. It was funny, what the cop had made him feel—invisible and yet hyperaware of his flushed body in a whole new way.

So no, even if he could have, he wouldn't have called the power company. Or anyone else. She would be home soon. He would stay in place, like "The Boy Who Stood on the Burning Deck," which was his favorite poem in the whole world. When the apartment got too hot, he dunked his head under the cool water of the kitchen faucet. When he began to run out of food, he simply drank more water to fill his belly. He played on his Nintendo Game Boy until the batteries died. Every day he clung to the thought that this would be the day she would return home.

Until the afternoon of the seventh day, when he woke up from the couch in a sweat, shivering with the conviction that his mother was dead. He had no idea what had introduced this thought in his head, but he knew it was true. His mam was dead and he was trapped inside an apartment with two windows, both of which were sealed shut. No use trying the front door—when she went out, she always locked it from the outside to keep the punks who hung about the apartment complex from breaking in.

He looked around the living room in a panic. He had to find her. Find out what had happened to her. Already he was unsure of how many days had passed since she'd left him. Was it twelve? Or four? He was losing count.

Tears streamed down his cheeks as he tried to lift the painted-shut window, grunting. He thought of punching out the glass but then spotted the dining chair, and before he could think, he was lifting it and smashing it against the pane. He hadn't anticipated how easily the glass would shatter or into how many pieces. It exploded like a bomb. But the main thing was the chair had made a hole large enough for him to heave himself out of. In his haste, he didn't notice the big shard of glass lodged in the wooden frame, but once it cut open his thigh, he noticed it for sure. For a few moments, the pain was so severe that he thought he would pass out. He wanted to sit down on the lawn, but there was glass everywhere. So he began to walk. The trail of blood that followed him made him want to vomit, but then he remembered his dead mam, and he knew that if he could just make it to his friend Terry's house a few buildings away, his dad would help him find her body.

★   ★   ★

Anton woke up with his heart pounding, and for a second he was back in that hot apartment, waking up on the couch with the cold realization that his mother was dead. Slowly, as he realized where he was, that terrible, icy feeling of dread eased away. He pushed the tiny button of the Timex watch that David had bought for him, and the digital screen glowed red in the dark. It was three in the morning.

Ever since they'd brought him here, he was waking up at this time. No matter how tired he was—whether he had helped his foster mom in the yard or shot hoops with David in the evening—he would awaken at this hour, his thoughts racing, his heart pounding. He had never known this middle-of-the-night fear until the Children's Services folks had removed him. In his old life, he had not been afraid of the gang members prowling his neighborhood or of the bullies at school. Everybody had pretty much left him alone. Even the cops who patrolled the projects ignored him because he didn't get into trouble. Mostly, he stayed home with his mam, the two of them eating a hot dog or a cheeseburger together when she got home from her job at the Tip Top, where she stocked shelves. After dinner, they watched TV or he did homework. Sometimes Mam had her friends over, and she'd ask him to go to his bedroom while they partied in the living room. He didn't like those friends and he hated Victor, the guy who sold drugs to his mam, but he wasn't scared of them. In fact, he liked the sound of their merriment because it broke up the everyday quiet and dullness of their life.

She was a good mom. That's what he'd tried telling the social worker and the cops, but they had just patted his head and nodded in a way that he could tell meant they weren't listening to him. He knew she'd done wrong to leave him locked up at home for so long, and that made him angry. He knew it was wrong for her to do the drugs, that she should Just Say No like the huge billboard across the street from the housing project said. She'd made a bad mistake, for sure, he understood that.

But what he didn't get was why it was anyone's business but his and his mam's? Even Ernest, the social worker who he liked so much, acted like it was okay for them to take him out of his own home. And that it was okay for some old judge, who didn't even *know* them, to put Mam in jail. It scared him terribly, to think of her in jail, along with thieves and kidnappers and gang members. She was so tiny. What if someone bullied her in jail or hurt her? It would be the fault of that old judge, who didn't even *know* her.

Even without food and power, he had felt safer in his own apartment than he did in this big old house, where he got lost sometimes. And the people here—they were okay, they were nice, even, but he was a little afraid of them. The lady, FM, she was nice to him, made him corn on the cob every day after he'd told her he loved it. And even though he sucked at reading and still made spelling mistakes and all, she was patient with him, unlike Mrs. Rose at school, who rolled her eyes every time she returned a test to him. Yeah, he liked FM, especially after Maria, the cleaning lady, told him that FM's son, James, had died in a car accident. His mam's brother had died in a car wreck when she was little, and sometimes, when she talked about him, she still cried. That was who she'd named him after, her older brother. His uncle Anton. So he knew how sad FM must feel, and he let her teach him grammar and spelling even though they were boring, because she probably missed teaching her own boy.

David was nice too, but every time he bought Anton something—

like the watch—he looked at him in a burning way, like he wanted something back. Like last night, when he'd mentioned going home to his mam soon and David's face had grown funny. David was a judge, too, so how come he couldn't free his mam? Then he could go back home and they could stop buying him clothes and stuff and go to their stupid party by themselves.

Anton turned onto his side and looked out the window into the dark. When he was little, his mam used to read *Goodnight Moon* to him every night, as they snuggled in bed together. It was the only book he'd ever owned, and they had kept it until last year, when he'd been invited to a birthday party for a four-year-old kid in the neighborhood, and since there was no money in the house, his mam had made him give the book as a gift. He'd hated her then, but tonight, Anton dug his thumbnail into his index finger as punishment for having been angry with her. When he saw his mam again, he was going to beg her to stop doing the drugs, and he knew that if he asked real nice, she would stop. Because she was a good mom and she loved him.

Maybe if he had a fever, they'd leave him at home and he wouldn't have to go to the party. That was the other weird thing about being here—they never left him home alone, not even for ten minutes. In his apartment, he was alone often—when he skipped school or when his mam had to work Saturdays, or when she ran errands to buy bread or milk or drugs. He liked being by himself. He would watch television or play games on his Nintendo Game Boy that Mam had bought him for his birthday. That was back when she still had money, before she started spending most of it on Victor and the drugs.

Here, they allowed him to watch only an hour of TV. It was just like being in jail. FM even chose what books he could read, and they were *not* comic books. Where was his Game Boy now? Who had it? His head pounded at the thought of Maurice who lived next door stealing his video game. He hated Maurice.

Blinking back his angry tears, Anton flung the sheets away from his sweaty body and turned over again. If only he knew how to make his way home, he could run away. He missed his neighborhood, with its noise and excitement. On a warm summer night, he'd fall asleep to the sounds of squealing tires and crying babies and engines gunning and the loud laughter of the young men who gathered on the streets outside his window. This house was as silent as a grave. Probably the dead boy, James, was buried in the basement. Anton shivered at the thought. And nobody in this town looked like him. Except for his old school principal and one other teacher, he hadn't known any white people. He had never really seen blue eyes up close until David. Looking into his eyes made Anton feel like he was drowning in an icy lake.

Even the barbershop in town was as quiet as a library, so different from the noisy, teasing, swearing place back home. FM had taken him there two days ago and the man had made a big fuss over never having cut hair like his, until Anton had felt his cheeks flush. In his old neighborhood, nobody even noticed him beyond a casual "Hey, Anton. Wassup, man?" Here, he was stared at wherever they went, like he was in the circus.

Would there be any black kids at the party? He'd wanted to ask David but had felt embarrassed. He knew how much they wanted him to like them and their house, how they were cooking special foods for him, buying him shoes and stuff, and he was trying to be polite, like his mam always taught him, but he was beginning to get impatient. When was she coming to get him? When were they taking him back home? Every time he tried asking, David's face got weird. And in any case, it was no use trying to talk to them. Any time he said anything, they were always correcting him. Any time he asked them for something, FM would say, "It's 'ask,' honey, not 'ax.'" And turned out the word was "impatient," not "inpatient," as Anton had always said. And "supposedly," not "supposably." Everything he had ever known, it seemed, was wrong.

He checked his watch again. He'd get up real early in the morning the day of the party and make his way into their kitchen. He knew where FM kept the onions in a hanging basket. He would steal one and return to his bedroom. A kid at school had once told him that if you placed an onion in your armpit for an hour, you'd get a fever. Anton hated being sick, but it would get him out of going to the party. He'd spend the time alone, watching TV and maybe eating some ice cream. He knew where they kept that, too.

CHAPTER FIVE

David was so thrilled with how good the boy looked. In his pale blue Hawaiian shirt and khaki shorts, his new haircut, and brand-new Keds, Anton shimmered. His golden skin shone like copper in the late-July sunlight, and it made him look tanned and fit, as if he had just stepped off a sailboat at the Cape. Less than a month with them and already Anton looked radiant, the picture of good health, so different from the timid, frail kid David had picked up from Children's Services. Delores was wrong. This kid would be fine at school. No, not just fine. He would thrive. David would make it happen through the sheer force of his will. Anton just needed what all kids needed: Good food. Sunshine. Clean air. Education. Exercise. Discipline. Love. All the things that he and Delores were uniquely qualified to offer. He felt giddy, filled with a sense of possibility, as he looked out on the backyard to where Smithie's annual summer party was going on full swing.

David glanced at his watch. Damn Connor for being late, as usual. Anton seemed to be holding his own among the other kids here, but most of the children were either a few years older or younger. Connor's son, Bradley, was Anton's age, and David was hoping the two boys would hit it off. If Connor and Jan ever showed up, that is. It was a running joke between them—Connor had landed at Exeter early, a full term before David. For everything else, he had come late.

Don Smith, the host of the party, came up behind him and smacked him lightly on the back. "You having a good time, David?"

"As always, Smithie."

"Then how come your glass is empty?"

David grinned. "A little too early to get drunk, don't you think?"

"Bullshit. It's never too early." He stood next to David and took in the scene before them. "That's the little boy you took in?"

"Yup." Inwardly, he cringed. Don made it sound like they'd adopted a stray.

"So how's it working out?"

"So far, so good." David was aware that he was being evasive, but he didn't care to discuss Anton with Don.

His fears were realized the next second. "Well, bully for you," Don said. A brief pause and then "My mother, God bless her, always warned me against this sort of thing, y'know, adoption and such. Said you never knew what you were bringing home. Other people's messes and all that."

David felt his temper flare but tamped it down immediately. This is just Smithie being Smithie, he reminded himself. Originally from Oklahoma, Don had built one of the most successful insurance businesses in the state, but he prided himself for his lack of polish. As his business slogan said, "What You See Is What You Get."

"Well, we're just fostering him. But you're right. It's not for everybody," David said vaguely.

Don nodded. "That's right. Different strokes for different folks." His eyes narrowed as he squinted into the backyard. "He's pretty light-skinned, for being colored. Hell, he could pass for Lebanese or something."

This time David didn't hide his annoyance. "Really, Smithie? *Colored?* What is this, 1954?"

Don chuckled. "Relax, David. I'm just a dumb old Okie from Muskogee, you know. I ain't no blue blood like yourself."

Despite himself, David grinned. "Knock it off. I've known you too damn long for the I'm-just-a-poor-redneck routine to work."

Don poked him in the ribs. "You got my number." They stood quietly for a minute. "So, changing the subject here. Rumor is that Michaels is going to retire from the appellate court next year. If that happens, the governor will have a seat to fill. What do you think?"

David glanced at Don. "What do I think about what?"

"Come on, David. You haven't gotten this far by playing coy. You know we all have big plans for you. Want me to put a bug in the governor's ear? I'm having dinner with him next month."

David hesitated. He knew that Don was a big donor to the Democratic Party and was on friendly terms with Richard Tufts, the current governor; and he was too busy a man to waste his time on idle promises. But did David want to move up to the appellate court? He knew what his father would say. Pappy would be incredulous that he was even debating this. "Never look a gift horse in the mouth," he always said.

"Let me think about it," he said.

"Okay. But don't think for too long. You know some of your fellow judges would be chomping at the bit for this offer."

"I know. I don't mean to be ungrateful. Thank you, Don."

The older man leaned in toward David. "Your father was always a friend of the insurance industry when he was senator. I never forget a favor. And you're going to go far. Everybody knows that. If I can be a stepping stone, I'd be proud to help."

"Thank you," he said again. It always made him uncomfortable to be compared to Pappy or to be reminded of whom he had helped as senator. Not to mention the expectation that David would follow in his footsteps. David had chosen the legal profession to escape that pressure, believing that he didn't have the temperament for the deal-making and glad-handing that had come so easily to Harold Coleman. But it was a small state, and many assumed that David would eventually enter the family business. Hell, many residents still had not forgiven his dad for stepping down from the Senate because he had gotten fed up with the partisan bickering during the Reagan years. David knew that they expected him to atone for what they considered to be the senator's folly by running for office himself someday.

"Uncle David!"

He spun around to be greeted by the full force of Bradley Stevens racing down the wooden porch to run smack into him. "Oof," David grunted. "You almost knocked me over, Brad."

Bradley looked up at him with a grin. "Sorry."

David rubbed the boy's back affectionately. "You remember Connor's son, right?" he said to Don, who nodded. "Where's your dad?" he asked, but before Bradley could reply, Connor came out of the house, a highball in his hand.

"Smithie," he said, putting his arm around the older man. "Sorry we're a little late."

Don glanced approvingly at Connor's glass. "At least you're not wasting any time with the libations." He smiled. "Unlike your prissy girlfriend here."

The three men laughed. "So where is he?" Connor asked after a second. "Anton?"

"Over there." David pointed with his chin. He glanced around quickly, making sure Delores was still in the house. "Come on," he said, deciding that it was foolish to not introduce Anton to his best friend. "You and Bradley should meet him."

Connor shot David an inquiring glance. "You think that's a good idea?" he murmured.

David looked him in the eye. "I do." He kept eye contact with Connor until the latter finally looked away. "Okay," Connor said, shrugging.

"Excuse us for a moment, Smithie," David said, and the two men stepped off the porch. Bradley followed them across the lawn to where Anton was playing with some younger kids. "Anton," David called as they approached, and the boy stopped midsentence and ran up to them.

David stood behind Anton with his hands on the boy's shoulders. "Anton," he said, "this is my friend Connor."

"Hey there," Connor said, smiling. "This is my son, Bradley."

"Hi," Anton said shyly, keeping his eyes on Brad.

The two boys stood looking at each other until David gave Brad a nudge. "Anton's new here. How about you introduce him to your friends?"

"Sure." Brad flashed Anton a disarming smile. "Come on."

They waited until the boys had run off together before Connor turned to David. "Well, this is a new one for me. Can't say I've ever socialized with the child of someone I'm prosecuting."

David shrugged. "What're you gonna do? Just the luck of the draw that I got him."

"Yup. A little awkward, though."

Connor was right, of course, but David felt a worm of irritation crawl under his skin. "Well," he said lightly. "Here we are."

But Connor wouldn't drop it. "Be a bit awkward if someone saw me here with the kid. Or if he—"

David made a dismissive sound. "Connor. Stop it. You're sounding just like Dee. She didn't even want to come today because of you." He made a sweeping gesture with his hand. "Look around you. You're at a party with sixty other people. I've known you since we were twelve.

What are we supposed to do? Not be friends because of this situation? As for Anton, don't worry. He still thinks the president of the United States flies his own plane."

Connor smiled. "That's funny. Okay. Sorry. How've you been?"

"Great. Busy. The boy has kept me on my toes. But he's a great kid, really."

"Glad to hear. I heard from the mother's lawyer just yesterday. Looks like she's ready to cop a plea."

David felt the flutter in his heart. A plea bargain meant a lesser sentence. Anton was going to get his wish after all. He waited to compose himself before he spoke. "So what's the deal?"

Connor shrugged. "Well, we're offering to drop the drug possession charge. So that leaves only the child endangerment."

David did not attempt to hide his disgust. "So that's, like, what? Six months?"

"Probably."

David curled his upper lip. "Figures."

"What?"

He shook his head and turned to walk away, a sour feeling in his stomach. "Forget it. Just forget it."

"David. What's the matter?"

He swung back on his heels and turned to face Connor, his face flushed and sweaty. "I'll tell you what's the matter. You're going to uproot Anton from the only chance he's ever going to have to make something of his life, and put him back in that . . . filth." He leaned in and jabbed his finger in Connor's face. "You know what's going to happen, right? A year from now she'll do exactly the same thing again. Except this time the boy may be dead."

"Wait a minute—"

"No. You wait a minute. You think six months in the slammer is going to change anything? Straighten her out? You know better'n that."

"David. For Christ's sake. Lower your voice. And get your finger out of my goddamn face." Connor waited and then continued, "You know how crowded our jails are, better than anyone. Jeez. I don't get this. You've always advocated rehab for first-time offenders and—"

"It's different this time, Connor."

"What's different? The fact that you're fostering the woman's kid? The entire legal system should change because of this?"

David's voice was low but quivering with anger. "Fuck you, Stevens."

Connor's mouth went slack with shock. "I don't believe this. I just don't believe it. What the . . ."

Out of the corner of his eye, David could see people glancing in their direction. He was making a scene, and that was the last thing he wanted. He looked around for Anton and Bradley, but the boys were safely out of earshot. He felt a pang of remorse when he saw the stunned look on his friend's face. "I'm sorry," he said. "I truly am." He swallowed. "I'm just tired. Very tired." He put his hand on Connor's shoulder and then turned away before his friend could respond. "I'll see you later, okay?"

As he walked back toward the house, he struggled to regain his composure. Delores was right. Coming to the party had been a mistake. He should've kept his distance from Connor until the whole legal matter had been resolved. Maybe he wasn't cut out to be a foster parent after all. During the training sessions, the caseworkers had repeatedly stressed the importance of not getting too attached to their wards, had reminded them that the majority of foster children were returned to their parents. Less than a month in and he had already forgotten this. Which was why Connor's words had affected him so. Sure, it was a screwed-up legal system that valued parental rights over the welfare of the child. But then who was he to know what was best for Anton? His track record as a father wasn't exactly great—he had not even been able to keep his only child from being killed.

Stop it, he said to himself. Get a grip. Find Delores. She'll know what to do.

He entered Don's living room and spotted Delores immediately. She was sitting on the couch with Connor's wife, Jan, who looked up as he walked in. "Hey, handsome," she said, grinning. "We were just talking about you. Seen my husband yet?"

David had no choice but to go up to them and dutifully kiss Jan on the cheek. "Yeah, he's outside."

"So what're you doing in here?" Jan seemed to notice something was amiss. "Hey. Are you okay?"

"Yeah. Just been in the sun too long," he lied. He glanced at Delores, who was shooting him a skeptical look. "Can I talk to you for a second, honey?"

Delores rose to her feet immediately. "Sure."

They found a relatively quiet spot in one of the bedrooms. "What's the matter?" Delores asked. "You look awful."

He shook his head and found himself on the verge of tears. "I don't know." He stared out the window for a second. "I just had a nasty exchange with Connor. I was rude to him, I'm afraid."

"About Anton?" she asked sharply.

"Yes."

She sighed. But she was too much of a class act to say "I told you so."

"The mother wants to plea-bargain. She'll be out in about six months."

"So?"

"So . . ." But what could he say to Delores? That he loved having a young boy in the house again? That he'd wanted Anton to stay with them a little while longer? That he was irrationally, unreasonably angry with his friend the county prosecutor for following the law?

"David." Delores took a step forward and touched him lightly on the arm. "Honey. He's not our child. We're just . . . his temporary custodians. We knew that going in. And you know how much he misses his mom."

"But—"

"It doesn't matter what she did. She's his mom. Don't you get that? It's . . . it's biology."

She was right. She was right. They would have to give him up soon. If they were lucky, Anton would maybe finish one semester of school here before returning home. And if that was the case, David didn't want to waste another moment at this party, didn't want to share Anton with people like Connor, who hadn't even wanted to meet him in the first place. "Let's get out of here," he said to Delores. "You were right. We shouldn't have come."

"Oh, David. Don't be like this. Go make up with Connor. I don't want to leave yet."

"No, it's better if he and I don't talk until this whole business is sorted out." He bent to kiss the top of Delores's head. "Let's stay for another half hour and then go, okay?"

They walked out of the room and Delores was nabbed by Patti Schik, who lived two streets down from them and whose husband was president of the local chamber of commerce. David headed to a corner of the lawn where a group of kids were playing cornhole. "Uncle David," Bradley said excitedly as he approached. "We're winning."

"Who's we?"

"Anton and me." Bradley grinned. "He's pretty good."

And as if to prove his new friend right, Anton landed the bag in the hole. He glanced up and smiled shyly at David, who beamed back.

"Hey, let's switch teams," said Joshua, one of the other players.

"No way," Bradley cried.

"But that's not fair. You guys will just keep winning if—"

"Boys, boys," Anton said in the pseudo-serious tone of a teacher while flapping his hands like a bird. "No fighting. There's enough of Anton to go around."

David stared at the boy incredulously for a moment and then guffawed. Anton was a ham. Who would've known it?

As the other boys tittered appreciatively at Anton's performance, David glanced at his watch, rethinking his earlier plan to leave early. Anton was so obviously blossoming in the company of the other children. David felt a rush of affection for Bradley, who had effortlessly included the new boy in his circle of friends. Much as Bradley's father had included him in a different time and place, he reminded himself, and felt another twinge of remorse for making Connor an easy target for his frustration and fear.

Don came up to him again and thrust a beer into his hand. They stood silently watching the boys play, and then, without warning, Don grabbed one of the beanbags from Joshua and began tossing it himself. "Come on, David," he yelled. "Best of ten."

David was aware of Anton's gaze on him as he played. His heart swelled when he heard the boy's "Yay, David" each time he scored. He knew that it would behoove him to let the older man win, both for his obligations as a guest and because of the promise that Smithie had dangled before him, but found that he couldn't. Anton's pride in him carried the day, and it was the sound of Anton's victory whoops that rang in his ears rather than Don's hearty "Good job, David. I'll whup your ass next time."

"Yeah, yeah, yeah," David said. Good humor restored, he decided they didn't need to rush home after all. "You hungry, bud?" he asked Anton, who nodded. "Good. Let's go get you some food."

He walked back toward the house, flanked by Anton and Bradley. "We have a pool," he heard Bradley say. "You should come swim."

"I don't know how," Anton confessed, and David tensed, preparing himself for a wisecrack or, worse, an expression of incredulity from Bradley. But Brad only said, "I'll show you how." David looked down at the red-haired boy in admiration. Connor and Jan had raised one terrific kid.

"Can I go to Brad's house?" Anton asked, tugging at David's sleeve, and he hated himself for answering with a noncommittal "We'll see."

They found Delores, and she led Anton to the enormous buffet table. David tried to look at the banquet, with its conspicuous excess, from Anton's eyes. What did it feel like to go from eating moldy cheese from a food pantry to this? Not for the first time, he admired the child's equanimity, how he appeared to take things in his stride. Anton actually was better-behaved as he stood in the buffet line than many of the other children. David wondered if Delores was aware of it, too, the nobility that resided in this little boy whom fate had delivered to them.

"David." Jan had come up behind him so quietly, he hadn't heard her. "Connor told me that you were pretty upset earlier." He opened his mouth to apologize, but she shushed him. "I just want to say that if I were in your shoes, I'd be pretty upset, too." She leaned in toward him, and he could smell the alcohol on her breath. "I'm sick and tired of spending our tax money on these people," she said. "As far as I'm concerned, they should lock the bitch away forever and let you keep that poor child."

He took an involuntary step away from her. He loved Jan, but he was repulsed by what she was saying. He had been in the legal profession long enough to know that human behavior was complicated and unpredictable and that justice always had to be tempered with mercy. But she was looking at him expectantly, as if she wanted his gratitude for siding with him against her husband. Unsure what to say, he looked down at her and muttered, "Thanks."

Before she could say another thing, he squeezed her shoulder, smiled, and stepped away to join his wife. "Hi," he said softly, wishing he could burrow in to Delores and get away from all these people whom he had known and liked for years but who today were getting on his nerves. "Will you be ready soon?"

"You're not eating?"

"I think not. It's too hot."

"Everything okay?"

"I think so . . . Jan is drunk."

They exchanged a look. "Fifteen minutes," Delores said. "And we'll leave. Go say our goodbyes to Don and his wife."

He walked around the enormous house looking for his host. Twice he spotted Connor, but each time both men looked away. He finally found Don ensconced among a group of local businessmen. "Thanks, Don," he said. "Great party."

"You're not leaving?"

"Afraid so. Delores has a bad headache."

"Aw, shit. That's too bad." They spoke for a few more minutes, and then David excused himself from the group.

"Don't forget what we talked about," Don called, and David gritted his teeth as he walked away. "I won't," he said without looking back.

It wasn't until the three of them were in his car and heading home that David felt his body relax. Looking at Delores in the passenger seat and Anton asleep in the back, he smiled to himself. Screw Connor, Jan, Don, the whole lot of them. He knew that Anton was on loan to him for a very short while. He was bound and determined to enjoy every second they had together.

CHAPTER SIX

David was in his chambers, catching up on some paperwork, when there was a light, perfunctory knock on his open door. He looked up to see his colleague Bob Campbell. "You busy?" Bob asked.

"No, no, come on in," David said as he capped his pen and rested it on the pile of papers on his desk. "I'm happy to take a break."

"Good." Bob lowered himself onto the wooden chair across from David. "Haven't seen you much these past few weeks."

"Yes, well." David felt embarrassed. "Some of that is deliberate. I just thought it was better if we kept our distance until, you know, the Vesper case was resolved."

There was an expression on Bob's face that David couldn't quite read. "Ah. I figured as much. Well, we don't have to worry about that anymore."

David stretched his arms above his head and leaned back in his chair. "Meaning?"

"Meaning, it's over. I sentenced her this morning."

A sudden heaviness came over David as he stared at Bob, who stared back, the small eyes under his dark, bushy eyebrows blinking rapidly. "Aren't you going to ask me what the sentence was?" Bob asked at last.

David shrugged. At this point, he had reconciled himself to the matter. Four months or six, what did it matter? Anton would be back home, either way, before his mom had any realistic chance at rehabilitating herself.

But then a sliver of doubt entered his mind. The Family Division of the superior court, where Bob presided, was located on the sixth floor of the courthouse. His office in the Criminal Division was on the fourth. This was no ordinary drop-in. Bob had clearly made an effort to come see him.

"Are you going to tell me?" David asked. "Or is there some—"

"Two and a half," Bob said abruptly.

David gripped the edge of his desk in an attempt to control his fury. "That's ridiculous," he snapped. "I've handed out sentences for animal abuse that were longer than that."

Bob stared at him from under those expressive eyebrows. "Years."

"What's that?"

"Two and a half years. That's what she got."

David couldn't trust himself to speak. He tried to, but his mouth moved wordlessly.

Bob grinned, clearly pleased with the impact of his words. "Wow, Dave. Never seen *you* speechless before."

David's head felt cloudy, even as a ray of happiness kept trying to pierce through. "How? I thought . . . Didn't Connor agree to the plea bargain?"

"Sure. And it got her to plead guilty. Saved the court a lot of time and money." Bob scowled suddenly. He has the most mercurial face, David thought absently. "Her plea bargain was with the prosecutor's office," Bob continued. "But I'm the goddamn judge. Nothing in the law says I couldn't give her the maximum sentence."

David felt as if air were being pumped into his lungs and he could breathe normally for the first time in weeks. He had been waiting for the other shoe to drop, had been grieving the imminent loss of Anton ever since Don Smith's party. "Was Connor upset?"

Bob looked at him incredulously. "Upset?" He rose from his chair, walked the few paces to shut the door to David's office, and sat down again with a thump. "He was thrilled. If he was upset about anything, it was about upsetting you at that party."

"You heard about that?"

"David. Please. It's a small community. Everybody who was at that party was talking about how wonderful it was to see you and Delores looking happy again. In any case, I saw Connor at the club soon after, and he said he regretted the plea bargain. Well, I told him right there and then that he was making an awfully big assumption—that I would go with the lower end of the sentencing guidelines." Bob smiled broadly.

David leaned back in his chair, stunned by what he was hearing.

Bob raised an eyebrow. "Well? Have I truly rendered the Honorable David Coleman mute?"

He knew he should say something, pump Campbell's hand and thank him. He knew that was what the burly man across from him was expecting. But David felt cold and removed, as if watching himself and Bob from a distance. He had an urge to tell Bob that he had made a terrible mistake, that a law greater than the one they both practiced had triumphed—the law of unintended consequences. He had quarreled with Connor, yes, but once he'd calmed down, he had accepted the decision. He had not wanted anyone to intercede on his behalf and corrupt the law, this law that he had embraced precisely because it was so much cleaner and more clear-cut than the family business of politics; he did not want to be the recipient of Bob Campbell's largesse or pity; did not want Connor to compromise his ethics in order to salvage the friendship with his best friend. And yes, he didn't want a poor, uneducated black woman to be railroaded by a bunch of white guys with law degrees, to be cheated by a legal system that she and her ancestors had played no role in designing; or to be robbed of her own child by duplicitous means. He wanted Anton, yes, but not like this. Never like this.

But how could he say any of this to Campbell without earning his contempt and enmity? How could he prevent some part of his heart from reacting with joy, from believing that, in denying justice to Anton's mother, a greater justice had been done? The world belonged to the young, he had always believed that, and what if locking the woman up for a little longer gave Anton a chance to shine, gave him and Delores more time to rub off the grime of poverty and bad nutrition and a failed education? Who could claim that this was a lousy trade—that instead of lying half-dead in a crack house, Anton's mom would instead spend her days in jail, where there was at least a reasonable chance that she could get clean and, by doing so, give her son a shot?

Bob Campbell cleared his throat. "Whatsa matter, David? You look like you've seen a ghost. Connor and I—we'd expected a different reaction."

David looked up. His eyes were misty. "No. Sorry, Bob. No, of course I'm happy. I just . . . It's a lot to take in."

Bob rose to his feet with a grunt. "Well, if that's your happy face, David, I'd hate to see your sad one." He stuck out a beefy hand. "See you around."

David mustered up a grin and shook Bob's hand as heartily as he could. "Thanks again, Bob. Really. Thanks."

★   ★   ★

David left work early that day, but instead of going home, he drove to a nearby park. He wanted to walk along the mulched pathway beside the lake but decided against it for fear of running into someone he knew. Instead, he sat in the Audi with its tinted windows and peered out at a pair of squirrels chasing each other. It was the first week of August. Anton would be starting at his new school in twelve days. David and Delores would work extra hard to make sure that he was ready. Everything was different than it had been just a few hours ago. Two and a half years. Now there was a real chance to have an impact on the boy's life, to create changes that would last a lifetime.

Connor. David didn't want to wait until he got home to thank him. He pulled out of the parking lot and drove to a restaurant at the corner of Hive and Broad where there was a phone booth. David dialed Connor's direct line. "Joanne, it's me," he said to Connor's secretary. "Is he in?"

"Just a minute, Judge Coleman," she said, putting him through.

He held the phone, not knowing which should come first—his apology or his thanks. As it was, Connor made the decision for him. "Hiya," he said. "You talk to Bob yet?"

David swallowed the lump that formed in his throat. Connor sounded so excited—for him. He knew how seriously Connor took the law and what it must've cost him to talk to Bob Campbell. "I did. Connor, I . . . I don't know what to say."

"There's nothing to say. In any case, it was up to Bob to determine whether to accept the plea or not. And however it came down, it's in the kid's best interest."

So that's how Connor would justify it to himself—not as a favor for a friend but as a service to a young boy who deserved better than the cards fate had dealt him. That was a story they both could—would—live with.

"I'm sorry for my reaction at the party. I . . . You just caught me by surprise."

There was a brief silence and then Connor said, "David. Let's not do this. We don't need to talk about this again. The only thing I ask is you don't ever let slip to Anton that I prosecuted his mom."

"I'm fine with that." David's voice was husky. He didn't deserve a friend like Connor. He never had.

"So go home and celebrate. Go home to your wife and your . . . family."

"Okay. We'll see you guys soon, right?"

"Right-o."

David hung up, got in his car, and drove directly home. Delores and Anton were at the kitchen table, a bunch of biology textbooks scattered around them. David bent down to kiss his wife, rubbed Anton's back in greeting, and then said to Delores, "Can I talk to you for a moment?"

"I'll be right back," she said to the boy. "Keep reading."

"Can I get a glass of chocolate milk?"

"Anton," she said warningly. "I'm hip to your procrastination. If you haven't finished this chapter by the time I get back . . ."

The boy grinned. David marveled at how easily the two of them got along. Would he ever have as close a relationship with Anton?

As they left the kitchen, he took his wife's hand and led her to the far end of the house, to the guest bedroom. He shut the door.

She shot him a look. "David, if you're . . ." she started, and he shook his head. "No. Not that. Would love to, but—"

Without warning, her face crumbled. "Well, what, then? Is it bad news?"

He knew exactly what she was thinking, her mind flying back to that awful night when he'd received the phone call from the police and entered their bedroom unsure of how to form the words that he knew would destroy her life forever. She was remembering how he'd come up behind her, turned her around, held her by both shoulders, and sat her down on the bed.

"No, no, no," he hurried to reassure her now. "Honey. It's not bad news. Not at all. It's terrific news, actually."

"Spit it out."

"It's . . . well, they sentenced Anton's mom." He heard Delores exhale loudly, as if whatever he was about to say would be anticlimactic, but he ignored her. "They gave her two and a half years in prison."

"Oh my God. That poor woman. Is that normal? I mean, isn't that excessive?"

Why did she not understand what he was telling her? Instead of celebrating the news, why would she concern herself with a drug-addled woman she didn't know? "What this means is . . ." he began.

". . . that poor Anton is going to be separated from his mother for more than two years." She turned to face her husband. "You said you had good news?"

He stared at her blankly. Was she being deliberately obtuse? Or was this one of those celebrated communication failures between men and women?

"Is that a rhetorical question?" he asked.

"What?"

"To state the obvious, the good news is that Anton gets to live with us for the next several years without any of us having to look over our shoulders. We can provide him with a great education, a loving home, and a . . . a stable family life."

"I see." Delores didn't bother to hide her sarcasm. "So it's good news for us. And shitty news for Anton."

"I can't believe you said that."

She shrugged. "Why? It's true, isn't it?"

His knees buckled. In order for this to work, he needed Delores on his side. How could she not see that this was in everybody's best interest? "Baby," he said urgently. "Think of what this means for him. What opportunities we can provide him."

Delores looked him squarely in the eyes. "I'll only say this once. So you better listen good." Her lower lip quivered a bit, but she held his gaze. "Anton is not James. He never will be."

He flinched as if she had slapped him. "That's the lowest thing you've ever said to me."

"I know that's how it comes across. But that's not how I mean it. I'm not trying to hurt you, David. I just want you to understand what's going on. To see what you're doing."

He tilted his head back defiantly. "This isn't about me. It's about helping an innocent child."

"Are you sure, David? Are you sure about that?"

He forced himself to maintain eye contact. "Yes."

She looked at him for a full minute, and then, as if she'd come to a decision, she nodded. "Good," she said as she moved away from him. "Then *you* break the good news to him."

WHICH HE COULDN'T do, of course. Not that day. The next day, Saturday, he took the boy with him to the video store, where he allowed Anton to pick out three action movies, groaning inwardly at the thought of having to sit through them. After they got back in the car, he stroked the boy's hair gently and told him he had some bad news: His mom was going to stay in jail for a while.

A tearful Anton turned to face him. "For how long, David?"

David understood now what Delores had tried telling him, and his heart was genuinely heavy when he said, "I don't know, son. At least until after Christmas, okay?" And then, to punish himself for his earlier thoughtlessness, he added, "You must miss her a lot?"

In reply, Anton said, "Can I just go to my old apartment and get my things?"

"Afraid not, son."

Anton nodded. After a few minutes, he turned away from David and looked out the closed window of the air-conditioned car. His right hand curled into a fist, and for a split second David thought he was going to attempt to smash the window. Instead, Anton tapped on it with his knuckles. Twice. Then he stared straight ahead.

And David had the strangest feeling that Anton had just tested the boundaries of his freedom and found that it extended only as far as the plushness of this car. It wasn't just Anton's mom they had locked away, he realized. Anton, too, was in a jail that he hadn't chosen.

CHAPTER SEVEN

They said this was a school, but maybe they were fooling him. This didn't look like no school he'd ever been to. There were no buckets collecting rainwater in the classrooms. Nobody was shoving anybody against the wall in the hallways. And all the windows were closed because the whole building was air-conditioned, and you could actually hear what the teacher was saying instead of the sounds of traffic horns and police sirens.

The building itself wasn't one of those crumbling brick structures that said "school." Rather, it was shaped like a spaceship or something, with a curved roof and slanted walls inside. And instead of an ordinary blackboard, the classroom had a whiteboard upon which the teacher wrote with a marker.

FM had walked him to the principal's office this morning, and the lady, Mrs. Johnson, had escorted him to his first class. The other students were already there, talking and joking with each other. "There you go, Anton," Mrs. Johnson said at the door. "This is your classroom. Your teacher will be here in a moment."

He stood quietly for a second, trying to still the churning in his stomach, feeling their eyes upon him as he walked to an unoccupied desk. These kids seemed so different from the boisterous classmates at his old school. Although these kids also talked loudly and were clearly happy to see each other after the summer, they were not shoving each other around, as he and his friends would've done. It was as if the air-conditioned air and the carpeted floors had muffled some essential trait that Anton recognized as childhood.

The first period was social studies, and their teacher was a nice-looking lady called Ms. Green. Her eyes searched the room until they fell on him and she smiled, and Anton had the odd and self-conscious feeling that she had been looking for him. Instead of smiling back, he looked down at his desk, hoping her eyes would glide away from him. And so he winced when he heard her say, "We have two new students this year, class. One of them is Natasha, who is from Russia. The other is Anton, who is from . . . around here. I hope you will make them feel welcome."

Natasha, a petite girl with blond pigtails, leaped to her feet and waved quickly to the other students, who then looked expectantly at Anton. Feeling the heat of their expectations, he rose grudgingly to his feet. "Hiya," he mumbled before sitting down again.

"Great," Ms. Green said brightly. "Now, does everyone know where Russia is?"

Maybe it was because he was in the act of settling back into his chair when she asked the question. Maybe it was nervousness. Whatever the reason, Anton heard himself say, "In China?"

Natasha's response was immediate. "China's a different country, silly," she snapped, and the class giggled.

He knew that. He was pretty sure he knew that China was a different country. Why, then, did he think that Russia was in China? And what had made him open his mouth during the first class of the first day at a new school where he didn't know anybody? And where everybody was now laughing at him, and a strange girl who looked like a Barbie doll had called him silly? Anton was mortified.

"It's an easy mistake to make," he heard Ms. Green say, and he loved her for it. "They're both Communist countries, after all, although Russia's president is trying to change that. Now, who knows another name for Russia?"

"The Soviet Union," several of the students yelled, and Anton felt a wave of fear. How come his classmates knew so much? How come he knew so little?

The rest of the morning was full of surprises and challenges. Anton was delighted to receive what looked like brand-new textbooks for each of his classes. At his old school, the books often had torn or missing pages, or were so covered with the scribbles of former students that it was difficult to read the text. He held his breath as he turned the pages, secretly reveling in the new-book scent, even as he noticed that the other kids didn't seem nearly as impressed as he was.

After the embarrassment in social studies, he didn't dare raise his hand during the other morning periods, not even during math, when he was pretty sure he knew the correct answers. However, he noticed that Natasha, despite her heavily accented English, spoke up several times. And that all her answers were correct. A new feeling entered his body—shame. Something was wrong. This was why David and FM had spent so much time ruining his summer by making him do homework. But why did he know so little compared to all these other students, with their cheerful voices and their ready laughter and hands shooting up in the air before the teacher had finished asking the question? Was it true that white people were smarter than black people? If so, why had FM brought him to this school? And why was she always telling him how clever he was, how quickly he picked up on new things? Because it was true? Or because—Anton felt a sob gather at the base of his throat—it wasn't?

At lunch, he bought himself a hamburger and fries with the money FM had given him, then carried his tray to an empty table at the far end of the cafeteria. He noticed that Natasha was sitting with a group of girls at one of the tables, but it didn't occur to him to be hurt by the fact that no one had invited him to sit with them, relieved as he was to be by himself. He bit in to the burger and thought it was the best thing he had ever tasted. He remembered the insipid, stale food he ate daily in the school lunch program at his old school and fought the urge to gag at the memory. This cafeteria looked like a restaurant in a movie, compared to the dingy, dirty, crowded lunchroom where he had eaten so many nasty meals.

He was dipping the fries in ketchup when a group of four male students approached him. "Hey, can we sit here?" one of them asked and, without waiting for an answer, set his tray next to Anton's.

The four boys settled in, and then the first one turned to him. "I'm Jerry," he said. He was a tall, gangly kid with braces.

"Anton," he said with his mouth full.

"Atom?"

"No. Anton."

"Oh. Pleased to meet you, Anton-io," Jerry said. The other boys giggled. "See? I told you he was Italian."

Anton stopped chewing. "I'm not Italian," he said indignantly.

"No, you're Jewish."

"Huh? No, I'm not."

"That's right. You're An-ton. From An-twerp."

Another boy piped up, "Hey. You said, 'An twerp.' Get it? An *twerp*."

He knew that they were mocking him, but he didn't even know what Antwerp was, so it was hard to respond. He looked down at his plate, his appetite suddenly gone.

Jerry was apparently not finished with him. "Well, where are you from?"

Anton looked around helplessly. "From here," he said finally. "I'm American."

Jerry grinned triumphantly. "Oh. I thought you were a Russian. From China."

At his old school, he would've pushed the boy hard, but here, Anton was afraid to. Jerry was laughing, and there was something mean about his laughter. It reminded Anton of when he was younger and would occasionally go with his mother to the grocery store where she worked. The store manager would pat his head and say that he was cute, but he always kept his eyes on Anton. Mam said it was because Mr. Hudson thought all black boys were thieves.

Anton eyed his half-eaten burger, unsure whether to stay or to leave. If he left, where would he go? He knew there was a playground outside where they were expected to go after lunch, but he also knew that no one would invite him to join their games. He was debating his next move when someone poked him from the back and said, "Hi, Anton."

Anton saw the jolt of surprise in Jerry's eyes before turning his head to see Bradley Stevens. Anton's heart leaped with joy. But before he could respond, Jerry said, "You know Anton?"

Brad's tray was empty, but he set it down across from Anton, waiting wordlessly until the boy occupying that spot scooted down the bench. As Brad sat down, he turned to Jerry and said, "Yeah. We're friends. Why?"

The "why" hung in the air, packed with a hidden challenge. In the second that it lingered, several things happened—Jerry heard the dare and backed down from it; the other boys shifted and rearranged their allegiances; and Brad Stevens, with his mop of red hair, sharp features, and compact, fearless body, became Anton's lifelong friend. Although he couldn't quite take in everything that had just occurred, Anton felt the overpowering sense of having been saved, and he understood that Jerry had just been demoted from emperor of the lunch table to court jester.

He remembered now that FM had told him yesterday to look for

Brad during lunch, but in his nervousness, he had forgotten. In any case, Anton looked from under hooded eyes as Brad now held forth, mimicking his new teacher, stealing a french fry from Anton's plate, quoting a limerick he had learned that had them all hooting. The burger tasted good again, and for the first time all day, Anton felt the faintest sense of belonging. Still, he didn't trust himself to speak, awed as he was by his companions' verbal nimbleness, their choice of words. At his old school, there was a lot of verbal jostling, but it was different—rougher and yet more intimate. Here, the wordplay was cooler, the jokes more sophisticated, the humor less obvious. It bewildered Anton, but it also excited him, as if he were about to learn a new language.

Brad waited until Anton finished his burger and then stood up. "We have about twenty minutes. Wanna go play soccer?" It was a general invitation, but he was looking directly at Anton, who smiled and nodded.

They put away their trays, and the six of them walked together toward where the glass doors of the cafeteria led to the outdoors, Brad and Anton heading the procession. Anton noticed that several girls called out to Brad, but he barely seemed to notice them.

They played for fifteen minutes, and all that time, Anton felt like he was under the shadow of a large shady tree, one that offered him protection from the hot glare of everybody's curiosity. Brad passed to him constantly, forcing Anton to keep his attention focused on the ball, until his muscle memory kicked in and he began to play his natural game. Then his lithe body sliced through the August heat, and even though he was sweating and flushed, he felt clean and laser-sharp as he chased the ball and maneuvered around the other kids, who suddenly looked thick and clumsy.

"Wow," one of the boys said after they were done. "Where'd you learn to play like that?"

Anton simply shrugged and mumbled, "I don't know," but Brad beamed with pride and smacked his friend on the back.

In what seemed like seconds, word got around the playground that the new boy was a killer soccer player, and other kids wandered up to them as the bell went off and they began to stream into the building.

YEARS LATER, WHEN he would remember nothing else about that first day in school, Anton would remember this tableau: Brad puts his arm around Anton's shoulder as the final bell rings and they push open the glass doors and enter the school building, two confident nine-year-olds who have just conquered the soccer field. The air-conditioned air that greets them is as sweet as a drop of dew on their flushed faces. Behind them, the chatter of the other students is already muted as they enter the building. They stand together for a second, and then Brad says, "I wish we were in the same classroom. Anyway, see you tomorrow?"

It is the casualness of the "See you tomorrow?" that makes the other boy blink back the embarrassing tears that sting his eyes. In it, there is a promise, not just of friendship but of something else—a promise of continuity, an acknowledgment that today was not an aberration.

And so, when Anton takes his seat, he is not thinking about Russia or China. His head is swimming with the tantalizing possibility that he has made a new friend.

CHAPTER EIGHT

The boy was flailing. Floundering. Failing. Fucking up. Whatever you called it, the fact remained—Anton was not doing well at school. Delores was beside herself. She and Anton were spending longer hours at schoolwork, staying up well into the late evening. Every few weeks, she drove to school to meet with his teachers. Nothing was helping. In fact, he was regressing. David had tried talking to Anton repeatedly about whether something was wrong: Are the teachers mean to you? Are the other students teasing you? Do you miss your old school friends? To each question, Anton would shake his head.

In late October, Anton came home with a D in math. A frantic Delores met David at the door when he came in from work. "That's it," she said. "There's no way he gets a D in math. This boy is a whiz. I tell you, he's just not applying himself."

It had been a long day at the courthouse, and David was exhausted. "What do you want me to do?" he asked.

"I'm gonna homeschool him," Delores said. "That's the only thing I can think of."

"What does that do? How does it help?" He put his hand on his wife's shoulder, but Delores shook it off. "I don't know," she snapped. "You have a better idea?"

He did not, not right then, but after they'd finished dinner and he'd retired to his study while Delores and Anton sat at the kitchen table going over homework, an idea presented itself. He rose from his chair and went back into the kitchen. He stood in the doorway and watched them for a second, took in the panic on Delores's face, the sullenness on Anton's.

"Okay," he said to them both. "Here's what we're doing. We're gonna take a quick family vacation this weekend. We leave for New Hampshire Friday afternoon."

As he could've guessed, Delores frowned. "And how is Anton going to get his homework done?" she said. "He's already behind."

Anton came to life. "Yay," he cried. "Where're we going, David?"

"To a ski lodge," he said. "To ski."

The boy's face fell. "I don't know how," he mumbled.

David grinned. "That's why we're going. You're going to learn to ski."

He ignored the fact that neither Anton nor Dee was thrilled. He had a plan, and he intended to execute it. Delores was wrong. Homeschooling would only isolate Anton, would reinforce whatever self-doubts he harbored. The secret to success, David believed, was success.

THEY TOOK TO the slopes early on Saturday morning, and the air was cold and thin. Anton had grumbled about waking up early, about leaving the warmth and comfort of the lodge, about being fed a light breakfast of hot chocolate and oatmeal. Still, his mood had recovered once he put on the jacket Delores had bought for him and slipped into the skis that they'd rented. He enjoyed being pulled up by the rope tow to the beginner's slope and breathed in deeply as the three of them stood at the top of the hill, admiring the bluish mountains in the distance. He also listened intently as David gave him his first lesson.

The first time he landed on his back, Anton looked so nonplussed that David and Delores burst out laughing. Anton was a good sport and laughed, too, as David offered him a hand and helped him back onto his feet. He was eager to try again, and David could see the competitiveness in his eyes as smaller kids flew gracefully past. But again and again, he landed on his butt, his feet tangled up in the skis, and his face began to burn, although it was hard to say whether it was from the cold or embarrassment.

The seventh time Anton tried, he managed to ski downhill a few paces before his right ski somehow got under the left one and he flipped over and landed on his side. A boy with long brown hair streaked past, and David heard him jeer, but by the time he reached Anton, the young skier was long gone. "Your weight distribution was wrong," David started to say, and then he noticed the tears streaming down Anton's face. "Hey, hey, hey," he said as he bent down. "What's wrong, you hurt?"

Anton shook his head no but made no effort to lift himself off the snow. Delores skied down to where they were. "What happened? Anton, sweetheart, are you all right?" The boy shook his head. "Well, come on, then," Delores said. "We gotta get you out of the way of other skiers."

David watched as his wife helped the boy to his feet and dusted the snow off his parka. "Come on, honey," she whispered, holding him to her side.

"He called me a loser," Anton whimpered.

"Who? Who called you a loser?"

"That boy with the long hair. On his way down."

"Oh, honey. He's just being mean. Don't let him get you down, okay?" She turned Anton toward her, one hand on each shoulder. "How about we go get more of that hot chocolate?"

Anton wiped his nose with the back of his gloved hand and nodded. "Sure."

"What the heck? We've barely been out on the slopes," David said. "How's he going to learn if—"

They both scowled at him and spoke at the same time.

"I don't want to learn this stupid game."

"David. I can't believe how insensitive you can be at times." Delores grabbed Anton's hand. "We're headed back to the lodge. You can join us later if you like."

"I don't believe this."

"Believe it."

After they left, David went to the advanced slope and skied alone for two hours. Skiing had always centered him, calmed him down, but today he felt a slow burn as he played over what had just transpired, how easily Anton had called it quits, how effortlessly Delores had enabled him. He had always been proud of Anton, of his strength and equanimity, but today, for the first time, he was embarrassed. The boy was a quitter. No wonder he was failing at school.

When he returned to the ski lodge, he found the two of them in the lobby by a roaring fire, hunched over a Scrabble board. Normally, the sight would've filled him with a deep contentment, but now it simply irritated him. He had brought them here so Anton could learn to ski, not so they could sit by the fire like a couple of dowagers. His plan had been to give Anton a sense of accomplishment that could then expand into his schoolwork. Self-esteem was all the rage these days, and David agreed, of course, that in order to accomplish something, one had to have self-esteem. But unlike contemporary educational beliefs, his was an old-fashioned one—that self-esteem had to be earned, not bestowed.

They both looked up as he stood glowering before them, but if Delores noticed his bad mood, she didn't comment on it. Instead she said, "Hi, honey. I'm teaching Anton to play Scrabble. You wanna join?"

He shook his head. "You guys go ahead."

He sat watching them play a few turns, and his irritation grew. Anton was forming words like "cat" and "yes," small, juvenile words that scored him minor points. The worst part, David fumed to himself, was that Anton didn't seem the least bit perturbed by his low score. David intervened a few times, helping the boy form a larger word, but Delores made warning eyes at him, as if afraid he would embarrass the boy. The true embarrassment, he wanted to say to her, was the mediocrity of Anton's ambition. But he kept his mouth shut and, after another fifteen minutes, mumbled that he was going upstairs to take a hot shower.

Predictably, he and Delores got into a fight that afternoon while Anton was taking a nap. "You're too hard on him," she cried.

"And you're too soft," he replied. "You think you're protecting him, but you're not."

She gave him a scathing look. "You can be such a ripe old bastard at times," she said, turning her back on him.

He was still stinging from that insult when he offered to take Anton into town to see *The Mighty Ducks* that evening. Delores begged off, pleading a headache, and he was glad. They exited the gates of the resort and made the left turn onto the rural two-lane road that led into the center of town, Anton chattering away about the movie, which many of his classmates had already seen. This is going to be the highlight of his weekend, David thought, this is what he'll brag about when he returns to school on Monday. Without knowing it, he hit the brakes, bringing their car to a halt. Ahead of them, the sun was setting, inflaming the sky with color. Trees glowed scarlet and gold all around them. For a moment, they had the road entirely to themselves, and then another car appeared in the opposite lane, slowing down as it passed them. Still David sat, his foot on the brake. "Hey," Anton said softly. "What's wrong, David?"

What was wrong was he was taking the boy to the movies. With his shitty academic performance and his entire life at stake, David was taking the boy to the movies. As if nothing were the matter. As if something awful hadn't happened on the slopes earlier today. As if failure were an option.

He put the car in drive and in one fluid motion made a U-turn, careful to avoid landing in the ditch on either side. Anton let out a yelp. "Hey. What you doing, David? Where're we going? You said we was going to the movies."

"We were," he corrected absently. "We *were* going to the movies." He glanced at the boy, who was looking at him in confusion. "But we're not. I'm sorry. We're headed back up to that ski slope."

"I don't wanna," Anton screamed. "You promised. I don't want to be in that old snow. It's cold. And it's dark. It's too scary."

"Yup." David nodded. "You're right, buddy. It is scary. Any time you learn something new, it's scary. Getting hurt is scary. Falling is scary. Being up there in the cold and dark is scary. Yup. I get that."

"Then why—?"

"You know what's scariest of all? Failure. That's the real scary thing. The real monster is failing. Being a quitter. Proving that boy right. You know? The one who called you a loser? That's the true scary." David took his eyes off the road and glanced at Anton. "And that's something I cannot allow."

"David, I can't—"

"You can. You will. Even if it means we stay on those slopes all night long. But Anton, I promise you this: By the time you come down that hill tonight or tomorrow, I don't care when, you will do it on your own two skis."

DELORES HAD GONE to bed by the time they entered the room at eleven P.M. But the sound of their celebratory laughter woke her up. "How was the movie?" she asked sleepily, and then looked confused when Anton yelled triumphantly, "We didn't go."

"What?" She looked at David. "You took him to dinner or something?"

David grinned broadly. "Yup. If you consider popcorn and hot chocolate dinner." He sat at the edge of her bed. "We went back. To the
slopes." He saw her mouth begin to form a protest and laid his hand
on her cheek to stop her. "It's okay. Anton learned to ski tonight." He
reached out with his other hand to pull the boy toward him. "Isn't that
right, buddy?"

Anton's cheeks were flushed and his eyes shiny. "I did it. David
taught me. And we're gonna go again tomorrow morning, FM. You
should come." He flung his arms open theatrically. "I loooove skiing."

"I don't believe it," Delores said wonderingly.

"Believe it."

"And tomorrow I'm gonna kick that boy's ass," Anton shouted. He
threw them a furtive look. "Oops."

"Anton. Language," Delores corrected, but David squeezed the boy
even tighter. "That's the spirit," he said.

He waited until Anton fell asleep and then got into bed to talk to
Delores about what had transpired. "Have you heard of something
called the broken windows theory?" he asked, and when she shook her
head, he explained. "It's all the rage now. It basically says that if you
nip crime in the bud—you know, zero tolerance for minor crimes like
vandalism and such—you prevent bigger problems." He stopped for a
moment, feeling a little sheepish. "What I'm thinking is we try something like that at home. Except instead of punishing crime, you reward
success." He saw that Delores was puzzled. "See, I think that success
begets success. I'm hoping that the more accomplished Anton feels in
one area, the more confident he'll feel in school."

Delores looked at him wistfully. "I wish it were that simple, hon. But
the fact is, he's over his head. He's gone from one of the worst schools in
the state to one of the best and—"

"So we should expect the worst from him?" he said curtly, cutting her
off. "You're saying that his past should dog him his entire life?"

"You're twisting my words."

He turned his head to look at the sleeping boy. In the dark, all he could see was the rise and fall of Anton's chest. For a second, he wondered if Delores was right. What he was trying to do with Anton was to implement Pappy's theory of success—a theory formulated by a white wealthy aristocrat to experiment on his only son. It had worked with him. And it most certainly had worked with James. But was there any guarantee it would work with a boy from the inner city? Stop, he chided himself. You're overthinking it. All you've done is teach the boy to go down the hill a few times, for Christ's sake. For all you know, Anton will unravel on the slopes tomorrow.

He held Delores's hand. "Sorry," he said. "That was unfair. Well, we're not going to solve this tonight." Still holding her hand, David kissed his wife good night and turned off the light.

But even in the dark, he was aware of Delores looking at him with her big, wary eyes.

He needn't have worried. Anton had retained everything that he'd learned the night before—how to shift his weight between the skis, how to handle the poles, how to turn, how to stop, even how to fall and get up after a fall. What was most impressive was Anton's desire to get to the top of the slope and ski his way down again and again; he stood impatiently in the line for the rope tow, grumbling about how long it took to get his turn. And after his fifth time down, he was pestering them to take him on a harder course.

"I can't believe it," Delores kept saying. "How could . . . ? I can't believe this is the same kid."

David's voice was husky with pride. "But it is." He took his eyes off Anton for a second to look at his wife. "This kid . . . he's special. And the worst thing we can do is lower our expectations for him." He raised his hand, following Anton's descent with one pointed finger. "I know how bright Anton is. All we've got to do is push him."

Delores squeezed David's arm. "You win this round, Judge Coleman." Then, with her eyes searching his face, her voice pleading, she said, "But David. He's just a boy. Remember that. Please."

"Come on, Dee. I know that." He paused and then decided to take the plunge. "I was wondering. Do you think I should pitch in with the homework? I could work with him for an hour after dinner each night, if you like." He saw the aggrieved look on her face and added hastily, "Only if you think it'll help, of course."

She was quiet for a long time, and he braced himself for an argument. Instead she said, "That's fine. If you wish."

His jubilation was tempered by the realization that the old Dee would not have let him win this easily. James's death had changed her, perhaps irrevocably. "Well, we can try," he said. "Just for, you know, a few weeks."

She nodded. After a few seconds she pulled away from him wordlessly and skied down to meet Anton at the bottom of the hill. And David was left alone on his perch at the top of the hill, overlooking the vast whiteness all around him, a solitary emperor of snow, unable to hold on to the feeling of jubilant satisfaction that he'd experienced just a few minutes earlier.

CHAPTER NINE

The squeals and shouts from the pool where eight preteen boys and girls were splashing and playing drifted back to the deck where the two men sat in their Adirondack chairs.

"I hope Jan's not regretting offering to host Anton's birthday party," David said dryly.

Connor waved his hand dismissively. "We'll soon be closing up the pool for the season. May as well use it before then."

September 18, 1993. Hard to believe, but Anton was twelve years old today. David peered from the screened-in porch to see the boy jump feet-first into the pool, his scrawny body exploding the water like a bomb. It was unimaginable that a little over two years ago, the kid had been afraid of the water.

David turned to glance at Connor, who was stretched out on his chair, his arms folded behind his head. "I think Brad has helped Anton acclimatize to his new life more than Delores and I have. Without Brad, I'm not sure . . ."

Connor acknowledged the compliment with a quick nod. "He's a good kid. But Anton's been good for him, too. You know, Brad will always be Gerard's kid brother. This has given him a chance to shine a bit."

David smiled. "Guess befriending helpless waifs is a Stevens family tradition. One for which we Coleman boys are most grateful."

He caught himself immediately: Anton was not a Coleman. In fact, in a few more months, he would be reunited with his mom, and all David could do was hope that some trace of what they'd taught him would see him through the rest of his life.

As if he'd read David's mind, Connor said, "I need to prepare Brad for the fact that Anton will be—leaving. He's going to be pretty heartbroken, I imagine."

David sighed. "Brad and me both. And Delores, of course."

Connor shot him a sympathetic look. "I know, buddy. And I'm sorry."

"Don't be. You, of all people . . . you've made the last two years possible. And they've been great years."

"So do you think you will do this again? Foster another kid?"

Would he? He didn't know. Perhaps he'd feel the same connection with another child, though he thought that was unlikely. From the moment David had met Anton, he had felt a bond. In his reticence, his self-control, Anton had reminded David of himself. And Anton was smart, his intelligence unsullied by his past circumstances. He had come to them covered with the dust of ignorance. All they'd had to do was blow off that dust. The boy's natural aptitude for math should've hinted at his raw intelligence, but his appalling lack of general knowledge and his lousy grammar had hidden the truth from them for months. They had hit the jackpot with this kid.

"Well?" Connor asked again. "Will you?"

David scratched his nose. "I have no idea. I'm sure we're going to need some time to recover from . . . from losing Anton."

Connor nodded. When he spoke, his voice was so soft that David had to strain to hear him over the hooting and yelling from the pool. "You know, in all these years, I've never said this. But thank you. Thank you for never resenting the fact that Gerard survived the crash and James did not." He turned his head toward David, and his eyes were wet. "I can't tell you how guilty I've felt about it over the years, David. It tears at me even now, the randomness of it. And yet . . ."

"Hey, hey." A shocked David reached for Connor's hand. "What do you mean, resent it? My God, I'd have to be a monster to do so. On the contrary, we've always been so grateful that Gerard survived. It was the only silver lining to that horrible night."

David watched in wonder as Connor struggled to control his emotions. He had thought that he knew Connor as well as he knew anybody. And yet he hadn't suspected the burden that Connor had carried all these years. He and Delores had been so devastated by their own loss that they'd never considered how horrible it must've been for the Stevenses, feeling as though they were not entitled to the pure, unmitigated joy and relief that comes from a child's escape from tragedy.

"Connor," he said urgently. "I can't believe you've been carrying this around. It's nobody's fault. It was just dumb luck, pure physics. The oncoming car hit James's side, that's all." He lightened his tone. "Are you listening to me, you crazy Irishman? This is just Catholic guilt, that's all."

Connor sighed and nodded. "Thanks." He reached into the cooler beside him and pulled out two bottles of Coors. He opened them and handed one to David, who fisted a few peanuts into his mouth before he took a swig. A light breeze blew into the porch, carrying with it the scent of the Heritage roses that Jan had planted along the side of the house. "Nothing like a cold beer on a late summer's day," David said. He glanced at his friend. "Are we okay? You need to talk more about this?"

"We're okay." Connor looked straight ahead. After a moment he asked, "So how's work?"

David exhaled heavily and rubbed his eyes. "The pace is just relentless."

"That's the life of an appellate judge," Connor said teasingly but with unmistakable pride.

"Yeah. Most days I feel like killing Smithie and the governor for making this happen. Not necessarily in that order, either."

"You know what they say about paying your dues. Besides, it's a good stepping stone," Connor said.

"For what?"

Connor shot him a look. "Don't play dumb. You know you're gonna run for public office one of these days."

David gave a short laugh. "Everybody seems to know this but me. What am I running for? Dog catcher? The school board?"

"One of these days there's going to be an open senate seat. Or the governorship. They'd be yours for the taking."

"Oh, really? And what exactly are my qualifications? Hell, I didn't even run for class president in high school. You're the one who should run."

"And if I had your good looks and family name, I would." Connor shifted in his chair and fixed his gaze on David. "Any race you enter, you'll be in the top tier based on name recognition alone. That means something, David."

David felt the faint but familiar stirring of anger. "Yeah, what it means is that I would be elected for all the wrong reasons." He pointed toward the laughing boys in the pool. "You're wrong, Connor. What our country needs is not people like you and me running shit for another hundred years. What it needs is a meritocracy—and that means people like Anton, who come from nothing but become something."

"In case you haven't noticed, Anton's twelve years old. A little too young to run for political office. So you may have to serve as a place-holder while we wait for him."

"Touché." David grinned appreciatively as he pushed himself off the chair. "I'm hungry," he announced. "You coming in, or are you gonna sit here all afternoon hatching Machiavellian plots about my future?"

They went into the kitchen to where Jan and Delores were baking appetizers and assembling a fruit salad. "There you are," Jan said. "Can you guys grill some hot dogs for the kids?"

David popped a mini quiche into his mouth. "What about the rest of us?" he asked. "Why do we have to eat cucumber sandwiches while the kids eat real food?"

Delores smacked his hand. "Because you're watching your cholesterol, remember? Now go get the grill going."

The men carried the platter of hot dogs to the deck. "These will be done in no time," Connor muttered as he lit the grill. He stepped onto the lawn and yelled, "Food's almost ready. Time to get out of the pool."

Like wet puppies, Bradley and his friends spilled out of the pool and headed for the deck. "Hey, hey," Connor shouted. "Use those towels to dry yourselves off."

"Why?" Anton said, his eyes flashing gold as he looked up at Connor with an impish grin. "We're only going to get wet again."

Connor held up the spatula with mock menace. "Because I said so," he said, lunging to grab Anton by the waist.

"Okay, okay," the boy squealed, trying to escape Connor's grip.

Watching Anton and Connor horse around, David felt a stab of happiness so sharp that it registered as pain. He loved that Anton was comfortable around Connor's family; it mitigated the fact that after two years, Anton persisted in calling him David. Always he pretended not to notice, even while wondering who else did.

The children went off to dry themselves, and it was from this feeling of pleasure-pain that David spoke. "Man, if I were his mother, I'd give him up. If I saw the change in him, what progress he's made, I'd never block his way. Only a selfish woman would do otherwise."

"What are you saying?" Connor asked.

"Nothing." David shook his head sharply to dismiss the thought forming there. "Forget it."

There was a long, awkward silence. Then Connor said, "You want me to see if I can talk to her?" His face was red from the heat and the beers.

David looked up with a start. "No. I mean, how can you?"

Connor shrugged. "I don't know. But anything's possible."

Hope, thin as a thread, sharp as a fishing line, cut into David's heart. "But what could you say? And why would she? I mean, she obviously didn't care enough about him to . . ."

"I wouldn't say that," Connor said slowly. "She was pretty distraught about losing her kid. I think she loves him very much."

Did David imagine the chastisement he heard in Connor's words? He wasn't sure. He suddenly felt flushed, mildly nauseated, the heat of the afternoon, the smell of meat sizzling on the grill, the stale taste of beer in his mouth, all making him feel a little out of sorts. "Well, there you go," he said. "She'd never give him up. Why would she?"

Connor shrugged and went back to tending to the grill. After a few moments, David wandered indoors. He was upset at himself for doing exactly what he'd promised himself he wouldn't do two years ago. Then he'd sworn that he'd live in the moment and enjoy every bit of his life with Delores and Anton without letting the knowledge of its finiteness cloud his joy. He still had five months left with Anton. That would have to do.

After lunch, he went out in the heat to watch Anton do a series of backflips into the pool. *Well, she can't take that away from him*, he thought. *For the rest of his life, he'll know how to dive.* And watching him knife through the blue water, *Or that. He'll know how to swim, forever.* And a few hours later, when Anton told a joke whose sophistication David knew would've eluded him just a few years earlier, he thought, *He'll always have this great sense of humor. Even though she won't understand it.* He felt a sneering contempt for the woman, and a kind of triumph, for his would be the invisible hand that had shaped her son.

It wasn't until they had been home for a few hours and he was pouring himself a drink in his library that David recognized that his resolve to accept the situation with Zenlike equanimity was insincere. Biology is destiny? Bullshit. To believe this would be to condemn Anton to the Dark Ages. The true crime, the true bigotry, was to condemn this bright, effervescent boy to the darkness of his mother's home. David remembered how the boy had stayed alone in the apartment with the power cut off, and it suddenly seemed like an apt metaphor for the opaqueness of his former life. There had been nothing valuable or graceful about that life. A broken woman had been raising a broken child. How long before he, too, would've fallen prey to the vice of her addiction? How long before he would've picked up a pipe or a needle? How long before she would've traded her son, with his luminous beauty, to a drug pusher in exchange for a hit?

The brandy tumbler shook in David's hand, and he set it down with a bang on the walnut side table that had belonged to his great-grandmother. Absently, he stroked its dark polish. He could trace his family back at least six generations. Not everyone could, he understood that. But Anton didn't even know the name of his own father. The boy's grandmother had been unwilling to take him in. And he was supposed to believe in the sanctity of the biological family unit? The social workers, the family courts, the whole system was wrong, their assumptions faulty.

He sat up in the plush armchair, his body jolted by a sudden thought: Perhaps, just perhaps, he had another birthday gift to give Anton. And it would be the best one yet.

CHAPTER TEN

David sat alone in the conference room with the lights turned low. Smithie was out in the reception area, waiting for the van to pull up. David had arrived twenty minutes ago and Smithie had let him into the nondescript single-story building, which housed one of his satellite offices. He had escorted David to the conference room, with its one long table, and then gone again to the foyer to await the van.

Now, as he sat at the head of the empty table, his elbows on the armrest of his chair, his fingertips joining to form a triangle, an image flashed before his eyes—Michael Corleone in *The Godfather*. That's who he felt like, restless, agitated, packed with an explosive energy. God, that was a good movie. When James was in high school, he and David had watched the original and the two sequels over the course of a weekend, a male rite of passage. He had been so thrilled that James had loved the movies as much as he did.

His mind began to wander. Who would his son have turned out to be? What would he be doing if he were still alive? He yanked it back. He needed to focus his full attention on the task ahead. He heaved his briefcase up on the table. This well-worn leather briefcase, a gift from his father on his thirtieth birthday, had held so many things over the years—legal briefs, files, his checkbook. But never had it held something that had the power to change the course of all their lives.

SHE LOOKED DIFFERENT than he had anticipated. Seeing her diminutive form in the chair, looking into the big round eyes that held no hostility, just fear, he felt a pang of remorse. For over two years he had demonized this woman in his head. In his imagination he had bulked her up, made her loud, brash, vulgar, and trashy. He realized now what he'd been doing—he'd tried to make her an opponent worthy of his contempt and disgust. But the woman sitting across from him was tiny, even girlish. She had a birdlike face whose most salient feature was those big light-brown eyes. A pigtail hung from either side of that face. Her eyes were clear as water, with none of the jerky shiftiness that he associated with drug users. She was apparently clean, drug-free.

And yet for all of its mystery, the face looked deeply familiar. David stared at her, trying to make sense of this, and the realization jolted him. Of course. She looked like Anton. Or rather, the other way around. But whereas Anton had a beauty that dazzled, the woman did not arrest your attention. What she had was—David groped here for a way to categorize—a kind of country charm. Yes, that was it. Despite her hard living, Juanita looked like the southern country girl she once was. There was nothing brutal or hard about this face. In fact, he found himself liking her.

Maybe this was a sign that he ought not to go ahead with what he had come here to do. Maybe another way was possible—David closed his eyes for a brief second as he laid out a different scenario: Perhaps he and Delores could help this woman when she got out less than three months from now. If they could get her a job, if they made sure she attended a recovery program, if they paid for Anton's education at a private school, they could ensure that the boy had a good future. This woman was not a hardened criminal or a lost cause—he had enough judicial experience to trust his instincts about this. He could help her, which was the same as helping Anton.

He opened his eyes to see the woman watching him closely, and something about the intensity of her gaze, the fact that she had caught him in a moment of weakness, annoyed him. How soon before the woman had an unsavory boyfriend? How soon before she quit a job and went missing? He reminded himself what the recidivism rates were for crack cocaine addicts. The path to hell was paved with good intentions. He would not risk Anton's future for a moment of sentimentality.

He pulled himself up to his full height and looked at her gravely. "Do you know why you're here? Do you know who I am?"

"No, sir."

He swallowed. He had no idea how Connor had made this happen, what strings had been pulled, which warden had been involved, in bringing the woman here late in the evening in an unmarked van. They had approached Smithie only a week ago for his help with a meeting place, knowing he could keep a confidence, and true to form, he had agreed without asking too many questions. Connor had wanted to use a proxy to get a message to Juanita Vesper. But David had refused, knowing that nobody else could make his case for him. He was taking an awful risk, he knew, with this clandestine meeting. But he also knew that the very recklessness of such an encounter, its sheer improbability, would protect him. Now, as he eyed the woman sitting beside him, he felt his face soften. How terrifying it must be for her, being whisked out of prison without explanation and brought to an empty office building where she had been greeted by an unknown white man and was now sitting across from another. Did she think she was being kidnapped? He could see the tremor in her lower lip, how frightened she was and how she was fighting to keep her composure. This was apparently another trait Anton had inherited from his mother.

"I'm David Coleman," he said, his voice gentle. "I'm Anton's foster dad."

The woman's face brightened, as if it had been flooded with light. "Anton," she said. "Lord have mercy. How is he?"

Her response was so genuine and spontaneous, it warmed his heart, destroying the last of his defenses. Delores had been right. This was mother love that he was witnessing. The pleasure that she derived from hearing Anton's name made the encounter feel egalitarian, both of them united by their love and concern for the boy.

"He's fine," he said. "Actually, he's more than fine. He's thriving."

Juanita nodded matter-of-factly. "He's very smart," she said, tapping the side of her head. "Takes after his dad, I guess."

He looked at her, surprised. He hadn't expected her to know who Anton's father was. "You know him?" he blurted out, and then blushed as she fixed him a look. "I mean, who is he?"

She tightened her lips in a way that reminded him of Delores. "He was a doctor," she said shortly. "But he's crossed over."

"Crossed over?" he said stupidly.

"He's passed."

He wanted to ask more questions but held himself in check. Juanita's eyes had gone opaque and her face was shuttered. And really, what did it matter? Far more important to get to the business at hand.

He opened his mouth to speak, but she got there first. "Is he here?" she asked, looking out into the dark hallway. "Anton? He's come to see me?"

"What? Oh. God, no. No, he's not here." And then, for a reason he never understood, he added, "He didn't want to come."

Juanita's eyes flickered as she absorbed the blow. She swallowed once and then said, "He's still angry at me?"

David shrugged. "He's upset," he said vaguely.

"That's why he's never come to see me in jail? Or write to me?"

"He wrote a few times, didn't he?" David remembered that Delores had made Anton write a few letters in the early days, so that he could stay in touch and also practice his spelling. But the letters that came back from prison, David had intercepted, over Delores's vociferous objections. As time went by, he had managed to convince her that it was in the boy's best interest to keep the letters from him.

"A few times. But when I wrote back, there was no answer."

What was it that he was hearing in Juanita's voice? Suspicion? Hurt? Doubt? Whatever it was, he had to move her away from this line of questioning. Nip it in the bud.

He cleared his throat as if preparing to render a judgment in court. "Ms. Vesper," he said, "you can't really blame the boy for being angry, can you?"

"No, sir." She shook her head vigorously. "Can't blame him at all." Her voice grew plaintive. "But I says I was sorry so many times. He still never wrote back."

Anxious to change the subject, he reached for his briefcase and pulled out a folder. "On a happier note, here are some pictures of Anton today." He had deliberately chosen photos that showed Anton in places and activities that would be alien to the woman sitting next to him—Anton at the helm of Pappy's sailboat at the Cape last summer; Anton in his red ski jacket, staring directly at the camera; Anton posing with Brad and three of their friends, all of them dressed in chinos and polo shirts.

He heard her gasp as she flipped through the pictures. "That's my baby boy? He looks so grown." She looked up at him. "You've done gone and kidnapped my son." But she smiled as she said it. "Sweet Jesus. He looks like a . . . a—" She cut herself off.

But David heard what she hadn't said: He looks like a young prince. A handsome young prince.

He sat back in his chair and surveyed her, the last of his hesitation gone. "Yes, we've been fortunate. We—my wife and I—have been able to give young Anton a very good life. Frankly, it's a life that other children, well, other children can only dream of." He looked at her with slight hostility, as if defying her to contradict him.

Juanita folded her hands in a gesture of humility. "Thank you. I will always be grateful. I worry day and night about my son. You know, when you're in prison, every thought you have is an ugly one. So much evil in this world."

David bit down on his tongue to keep from saying the obvious: You weren't so worried when you left your son home alone during a heat wave. He was surprised to find that his earlier liking of this woman was dissipating. How curious, he thought, but then he realized why. Juanita and he could never be friends. They were natural rivals. Whether the woman was aware of it or not, they were competing for the same prize.

He gathered the photographs from her, shuffling them as if they were playing cards. Just as he was about to place them back in the file folder, she asked shyly, "Can I have one?"

He hesitated, not wanting to leave a paper trail from this illicit meeting, but then he looked at her again, small and pitiful in the office chair, and he thought, Who will ever know? Who will ever believe her? And so he smiled and pushed the photographs back toward her. She chose the one of Anton on the ski slopes. "Baby boy," she murmured, still clenching the picture. "I'm counting the days before I see you again."

It stuck in David's craw how effortlessly, how dumbly, this woman assumed that she would reclaim her son even after seeing visual proof of how Anton had bloomed under David and Delores's care. Did she really think that love would conquer all?

As if she had read his mind, she said, "You've done a lot for my son, Mr. David. I'm not gonna let you down." She looked at him earnestly. "I've been clean for two years. I've started a Bible study group. Prison's been good for me. I lost my boy once, and praise be to God, he ended up with someone nice like you. But I swear, I'll never risk losing Anton again. Never again."

He'd heard some variation of the same speech in court too many times to be particularly impressed by her words. Juanita was obviously sincere, but good intentions meant squat when faced with the temptation of a highly addictive drug. She'd be lucky if she stayed clean for six months once she was out of prison.

He shifted restlessly in his chair as he glanced at the wall clock above the woman's head. She still had the long drive back to the prison. It was time to cut to the chase. "Ms. Vesper," he said, leaning forward. "Let's talk candidly, shall we?" He paused, taking in her puzzled look. "It's about Anton, of course."

★　★　★

David lay in bed, careful not to express his mental agitation in the movement of his body, for fear of waking Delores. It had gone well. About as well as he could've expected. He had won. At least he thought he had. He had gone through too much, had risked too much, for any other outcome to be possible. Pulling an inmate out of prison to meet with her surreptitiously? If word got out, he would lose his legal license. And needless to say, the ensuing scandal would destroy any political aspirations he might have. The worst of it was he would take Smithie and Connor down with him. He had taken the biggest gamble of his life, and he'd done it because the payoff was so enormous. So it had to work. Had to.

Anyway. It was done. Almost done. He had gotten Juanita Vesper to see what he saw so clearly. He had painted a picture of what he could do for her son. And to give the woman her due, she appeared to get it. The magic word had been "college." When he'd said that he could afford to send Anton to whatever college he chose, anywhere in the country, he had heard her involuntary gasp, and her eyes had shone with a sudden light. He felt a begrudging respect for her then. Did she know how much one year of a good college cost? he'd asked her, and she'd shaken her head. When he'd told her, she'd said, "That's more money than I earn in three years."

And so he had pressed home his advantage. Told her that Anton was now taking piano lessons, was on the swim team, had excelled in science class. That he could take French in high school if he wanted. She had listened to him with her mouth open, as if hearing a fairy tale.

But she was still unsure, resistant to the idea of losing her son forever, and even though he understood her resistance and respected her for it, it made him impatient. And afraid. So he had said it. Said the cruel lie even though each word was like hitting her in the face with a mallet. He could literally feel her absorbing each blow, reeling from it, getting weaker and weaker. He persisted because a strange thing happened—the more he spoke, the more he believed what was coming out of his mouth. If a lie could ever be the truth, then this was it. And when he was done, she disappeared behind her own face, was swallowed up whole, and the devastation he'd wrought was so perfect that he had to look away. He stared at the ceiling, not daring to look in her direction, and finally, after God knew how long, she whispered something he didn't catch. When he looked at her, she nodded quietly and said she'd think about what he'd said, think about it real serious. That she wanted what was best for her Anton. And then she thanked him again for what he was doing to help her son.

David turned his head slightly to gaze at his wife. He was glad that Delores had been asleep by the time he'd gotten home. She would have picked up on his agitation, and he didn't want to answer her questions tonight. If Delores ever found out what he'd done, she would leave him. Of this, he was sure. And there was always the chance that Juanita would not give up Anton without a fight. David had to step lightly now, find a way via long distance to keep up the pressure on Juanita until she actually turned custody over to the state. Perhaps Connor, with his vast contacts in Children's Services, would know how to proceed? Or should they simply give Juanita a few days to think things over and allow her to make the first move? The woman had seemed nearly convinced by the time she got back into the van, she really had.

David rolled carefully onto his side. He stared at his wife's face, which even in repose carried the sadness that had claimed it from the moment she had found out about James. Closing his eyes, David imagined what it would be like to have Anton with them forever. Would the promise of that permanence finally wipe some of that anxiety off Delores's face? Or would it create a new anxiety? Fostering a child had mostly been his idea, but tonight he was suddenly unsure why Delores had acquiesced. Had she agreed only to please him? Or was having a child in the house something she also desired for herself? David sighed. How was it possible to love Dee as much as he did and yet not know the answers to these basic questions? He remembered the awful days immediately following James's death. He had needed his wife so desperately to keep him from going under. And Dee had been there for him, she really had. But when he'd tried rescuing her back, she had spurned him, walled herself off. Something new—a formality, a guardedness—had crept into their marriage.

He would be so much more careful with Anton. With James, he hadn't been vigilant enough. The two boys and their dates had eaten at their house before leaving for the prom, an elaborate steak dinner that Delores had prepared. David had taken several pictures of the four of them, kids he'd known their entire lives, looking hilariously adult and heartbreakingly young in their tuxedos and gowns. And just before they left for the prom, he had made James promise not to drink and drive. Stupid, stupid him for not thinking about the other drivers out on prom night.

His left leg began to twitch, and he forced himself to take some deep breaths. A new beginning, he said to himself, and the thought comforted him enough that he said it again. A new beginning. A new beginning. Please, God, a new beginning.

And with that, David Coleman fell into a fitful and troubled sleep.

CHAPTER ELEVEN

It took Juanita three weeks to make up her mind to relinquish custody. David could scarcely believe the news when he got the phone call from a caseworker at Children's Services. Before hanging up, he broached the subject of a permanent adoption, and the woman at the other end of the phone sounded pleased.

Anton was over at a friend's house, so David broke the news to Delores soon after he got home, careful to leave out the part about adoption.

"I don't understand it," Delores kept repeating. "Something must've happened to that poor woman in jail. I mean, why would a mother willingly give up her child? It doesn't make sense, David."

He grimaced. "That's what addiction does, honey," he said. "It dulls even the maternal instinct. I've seen it happen a thousand times."

"I mean, I don't know how much she knows about how Anton is doing." Delores's voice was incredulous. "What if he was unhappy with us? How could she abandon him like that, without even making an effort to see him?"

"Well, she did it once, didn't she? Abandon him?" He heard the strange, harsh note in his own voice. "You think a few years in the slammer will change that?"

Delores turned to him, shocked. "This news is going to break the little fella's heart. So what do we do?"

David focused his pale blue eyes on a spot beyond his wife's shoulder, afraid to look her in the face. "I don't know," he mumbled.

Delores sighed and reached for his hand. "To tell you the truth, I was looking forward to getting our life back," she said. "Don't get me wrong—I've grown very fond of Anton. I don't regret what we've done to, you know, help him. But it's hard, taking care of someone else's kid. And we are not spring chickens anymore. Know what I mean?"

His heart hammered so furiously that he felt light-headed for a moment. Was Dee going to fight him on this? After all the strings he'd pulled, the hurdles he'd overcome? Somehow he had not stopped to entertain this possibility.

Delores was looking at him, waiting for him to answer. "What would you like to do?" he said, hearing the tightness in his voice. "Have him be shunted from one foster home to another?"

Her head shot up and her eyes flashed with sudden anger. "Don't you dare lay this on me, David. It was your idea to go down this road. And as always, I went along, just to make you happy. In any case—"

"Wait, what? You did it to make *me* happy?" David felt his face flushing, felt a muscle work in his jaw. "You have some gall, Dee. I did this for you. For us. Because I thought—foolishly, as it turns out—that having a child in the house would—" He cut himself off, frightened by the look on Delores's face.

"Would do what, David?" Dee's voice was low. "Bring James back? Help me forget my only son? Erase the memory of my James in that coffin? What did you think would happen just because you brought a stranger into my house? And now you want me to do what? Kiss your ring in gratitude?"

He stared at her wordlessly. "This is how you feel? After all this time?" he finally whispered. And then, louder, "If this is how you felt, why the hell did you say yes? I never . . . I would've never done this thing if you'd objected."

She spat out a laugh. "Did I say yes, David? Did you even ask me if this is what I wanted? I mean *really* ask me? Or did you just assume what was best for us?"

He turned his back on her, afraid that he was going to cry. He picked up the small jewelry box on their dresser and set it back down absently, trying to gather himself. "I'm sorry," he said at last. "I—I had no idea. You must've resented me so much these past two years."

"David." Delores sighed. She patted the edge of the bed. "Come here. Come sit next to me." She rested her hand on his thigh. "Sweetheart. I know you meant well. I know that, okay? It's just that, you're like a hurricane and I . . . Everything that's in your path just gets swept along."

He shook his head. "I'm sorry," he said again. But he was wondering when he and Dee had drifted this far apart. Should they have gone for therapy, as she had wanted after James's death? He had refused, unable to bear the thought of talking to a stranger about his beloved son. And Dee had fallen so silent in those early months after the funeral. Often he would come home to find her sitting quietly in James's room, looking out the window. Something twisted in his gut then, but when he tried to ask her about her day and whether she'd left the house, she would smile that strange new smile and look away.

But that was years ago, David thought. Slowly, it seemed as if she had found her way back—volunteering again at the Rape Crisis Center, resuming her activities for the League of Women Voters, working alongside him in the yard. And yet it was true—he had lost the laughing, irreverent woman he'd fallen in love with. That Dee was gone, replaced by the woman who was sitting beside him, telling him that she wanted her life back. That he would have to relinquish Anton after all. David's stomach heaved at the thought.

He felt claustrophobic, their large bedroom closing in on him. He took her hand, kissed it lightly, and mumbled, "I need some fresh air. I think I'll go to the track and run a few laps. I shouldn't be long."

"You're not eating?"

"You go ahead," he said, not meeting her eye. "I'll grab something on my way back."

He forced himself not to notice the droop of her shoulders as she turned away from him. "As you wish," she said.

When David got home at nine, Anton and Delores were on the couch watching TV, Delores's arm flung casually around the boy. David shook his head imperceptibly, unable to reconcile Dee's resentful words earlier in the evening with the tableau of domesticity in front of him.

"Hey, David," Anton said, his eyes glued to the television set.

"Hey, buddy. How was your evening?"

"Fine."

Delores, he noticed, had not bothered to so much as acknowledge his presence. He stood around uselessly for another moment and then headed for the shower.

When he walked into their bedroom a half hour later, Delores was gathering her pillows. "What're you doing?" he asked.

"I'm sleeping in the guest room tonight," she said. "I want to watch some TV and don't want to keep you up."

"I don't mind. Tomorrow's Saturday—"

"—and you have the pancake-breakfast fund-raiser," she interrupted. "You have to be at St. Michael's by eight, remember?"

He moved toward her and put his hands on her shoulders, searching her face. "How do you do it, Dee? How—?"

"Do what?"

"Watch out for me even when you're mad at me?" He bowed his head. "I . . . You're the most important thing in my life, Dee. If you don't know that by now, I don't know what . . ." He felt the tears roll down his cheeks and brushed them away roughly.

"David. Calm down. It's okay. We'll figure something out. Okay? But please. Just for tonight I need a good night's sleep." She kissed him on the cheek. "I'll wake you in the morning. Now get some rest."

Alone in bed, he thought back on what had just happened, what he'd just said. It was true. Dee was the most important thing in his life. Between her and Anton, it wasn't even close.

But then something churned inside him. Why should he have to choose? Most men didn't have to decide between their children and their wives. But Anton was not his blood. And therein lay the rub.

He took several deep breaths, trying to calm his mind. Control yourself, he scolded himself. Nothing's been decided yet. Maybe Dee will come around. She cares about Anton. You know that. Now try and sleep.

But throughout the night, his hand kept feeling the empty place in the bed where Dee ought to have been.

★ ★ ★

Delores continued to sleep in the guest bedroom into the following week. Each night they waited until Anton went to his room and then said a perfunctory good night to each other. David knew he was being punished, but some instinct told him not to push Dee, to give her the time she needed to figure out whether she could imagine a permanent future with Anton. And yet, with each passing day, his anxiety and anger grew. Dee was holding not just him hostage but Anton, too.

And there was the other thing. If Dee refused to keep Anton and the boy was returned to the foster system, what would stop Juanita Vesper from changing her mind and claiming him? And if that were to happen, how long before she told her son or someone else about that strange nocturnal meeting with Anton's foster dad? Without meaning to, Dee was putting him in jeopardy. Hell, he could face criminal charges for what he'd done.

David rose from his armchair and went into the kitchen, where Delores was enjoying a cup of herbal tea. Anton was at a sleepover at Brad's, and the house felt uncharacteristically quiet for a Friday evening. "We need to talk," he said quietly, pulling up a chair across from her.

"I know."

"It's been a week—"

"I know." She stared into her cup for a moment, and when she looked up, her eyes were red. "What would you like to do, David? Do you want—I mean, should we seek permanent custody or something?"

He sat still, afraid to believe what he was hearing. "What do you want?" he asked carefully.

She smiled a smile that didn't reach her eyes. "I want you to stop moping around like I've just killed your pet hamster."

"Dee. You're the one who's been acting strange. You're the one who's been mad at me, and I don't even know what for."

She reached across the table and placed her hand on his. "David. Please don't. This is not about us anymore. We have a young boy we're responsible for."

When he spoke, he despised himself for the eagerness he heard in his voice. "That's what I've been trying to say. That we don't have a choice. We can't have Anton go from foster home to foster home."

"No, of course not. That would be cruel." She looked away for a moment, then nodded as if she'd resolved something. "Okay. I guess we're going through with this."

But he was suddenly panicked. This was not how he'd envisioned it, this grim, non-joyous acceptance of their new reality. "Dee," he said urgently, "I need to be sure. Are you going to be okay if this . . . if, you know, we get permanent custody?"

"I think so. I mean, nothing can replace . . . I mean, James was—James."

He shook his head vigorously. "Yes. No. Yes. Anton is not James. He never will be. And we should never do it for that reason." He tensed, waiting for her to say something, but she remained silent. Finally, at long last, she said, "How the hell are we going to break this news to poor Anton?"

His body went slack with relief. "Don't you worry," he said gruffly. "We'll figure out a way."

"Don't do it yet, David. Maybe the woman will still change her mind."

HE WAITED UNTIL Sunday afternoon to ask Anton if he wanted to run down to the hardware store with him. The boy, who was lying on the couch, looked up from his copy of *The Giver* and yawned. "Nah. I'm okay."

"Oh, come on," David said. "You're getting a little potbelly from lying around. You need the exercise."

Anton gave him that unbearable preteen look that David and Delores were beginning to despise. "How's riding in the car exercise?" he drawled.

The boy looked so smug that David laughed. He strode toward the couch and yanked the book out of Anton's hands and threw it on the coffee table. "Come on, sport," he said. "I need your help carrying the lumber home. And there's an Izzy's ice cream cone waiting for you somewhere."

"Izzy's," Anton squealed as he rolled off the couch. "Why didn't you say *that*?" He hurried off to the bedroom to put on his shoes.

David rolled his eyes at Delores. "He's the most easily corruptible kid in town. All you have to do is bribe him with ice cream."

She smiled, but he could see that she was worried. "You're not going to tell him today, are you?"

He shrugged. "I'll play it by ear. We don't have too much time to begin the paperwork."

"It all seems to be happening so fast."

He could hear Anton making his way down the hallway, and without warning, David's temper spiked. "We've waited a week already. Now, if you're having second thoughts, we need to talk."

"It's not that."

"Well?"

"Don't you think we should sit down with him together? Instead of on the way to the ice cream parlor?"

"Dee," he said, emphasizing each word, "I don't want to make this, like, some dire thing. So, go with us and we'll tell him together."

"But it *is* a dire thing. The kid's about to lose—" She broke off as Anton entered the living room. "Ready?" the boy asked.

David held up his finger. "In just a minute, Anton. You wanna go get in the car?" He turned toward his wife. "So? Come with us."

"No. Maybe you're right. It may be better to play this light."

He kissed her forehead. "Like I said, I'll only do it if the moment presents itself. Okay?"

"I guess."

THEY WERE HALFWAY to the hardware store when David decided to change course. "You know what?" he said. "Let's go get that ice cream first."

"Oh, wow," Anton said. "You're in a good mood today, David."

David smiled. "I am. And if I were you, I would watch the sarcasm. Because there's nothing like a sarcastic little shit to ruin my good mood."

They looked at each other and giggled. For the past six months they'd fallen into a routine in which, when out of Delores's earshot, David used mild swear words around Anton. It had brought them even closer, this ritual of male bonding. "Geez. I'm sorry," Anton said.

David smacked the boy's shoulder lightly. "It's okay. I know you're not trying to *act* like a little shit. It's just that you *are* . . .

". . . a little shit," they concluded together triumphantly.

It was a warm day, and they sat on a picnic bench at Izzy's, enjoying their ice cream cones, shooting the breeze. Apart from the difference in their skin tone, they looked like all the other father-and-son pairs around them, both of them dressed in polo shirts and jeans. The early-afternoon sun hit Anton's skin, turning it golden, and David felt a lump form in his throat at the sight.

David cleared his throat. "Hey," he began. "I've got some news for you. And it's not good news, I'm afraid." He saw with regret the shadow that crossed Anton's face. "Though it could be," he felt compelled to add. "It's all a matter of how you look at it."

The amber in Anton's eyes flashed, but he went completely still, as if afraid to breathe. The terse stillness of his posture tore at David's heart. It was easy sometimes to forget what this boy had gone through. "It's about your mom, Anton," he said, his voice low and gentle.

"She dead?"

"What? *No.* God, no."

The boy appeared to relax a fraction. He turned his head slightly to look at David, his mouth open. "What happened?"

David gulped. This was not going to be easy. "She's decided to give up custody of you, Anton," he said, wincing as he said those words. And after the boy didn't react, "You understand what that means, right?"

Anton shook his head. "Nope."

"It means she doesn't feel she can take care of you. So, she's telling the state"—no, that sounded too cold—"she's asking us, me and FM, if we'd take care of you."

Anton's lower lip quivered a bit, but he maintained eye contact with David. "For how long?"

"Well, for a long time. For . . . forever." David's eyes began to sting with tears, but Anton's were clear, even though the boy's nose was beginning to turn that telltale shade of red.

"Mam told you this?" The boy's voice was raw. "That she don't want to take care of me no more?"

How effortlessly Anton had slipped into his old way of speech at the mere mention of his mother, David marveled. But there was no time to reflect on this because the question burned like a house on fire between them. David reached out and held Anton's hand, sticky with the residue of ice cream. "Anton," he said, his voice husky, "you're a big boy now. Old enough to understand a few things. Right?" He waited until the boy emitted a faint response. "So you must accept something. Your mom is sick, Anton. She has a drug problem. A disease. You understand? She's not well. She can't take care of you, son. And so she asked FM and me to take care of you for her. It's her way of loving you." He looked around the patio, filled with laughing, seemingly carefree families, their faces shiny and unburdened, and for a moment he was filled with longing, remembering when his had been one of those families, smug and safe in their good fortune, and he couldn't have imagined, not in a million years, that he would be sitting across from an orphan—because let's face it, that's what he'd done, he'd orphaned Anton—letting his words splinter the light in his eyes. "Anton," he tried again desperately, "you know that FM and I love you. We will do our best for you, son. We will take care of you, I promise."

Anton looked up at him, a faint smile on his face. "I know," he said. "Thanks." Then he squinted. "But who will take care of Mam?"

David sighed. He knew this happened all the time in dysfunctional families, this odd role reversal—the more irresponsible the adults, the more hyper-responsible the kids. "Your mom's an adult," he said, almost by rote. "She can take care of herself. It's not your job, Anton." He stared at the boy, recognizing the skeptical look on his face, knowing that he had not convinced him. And then, in a moment of inspiration, he said, "God will. God will look after your mom."

The boy's face brightened. "That's what my mam says." His tone was matter-of-fact, as if he had spoken to his mother yesterday, as if the more than two years apart had not occurred.

"And she's right." Giving Anton's hand a final squeeze, David disengaged his hand from the boy's. "Well," he said, making a concerted effort to change the subject, "what do you think? Should we get another round of ice cream?"

Anton shook his head. "FM said she's making a big supper, David. We shouldn't ruin our appetites."

The boy's tone was so earnest and his words so perfectly echoed Delores's that David had to suppress a smile. He remembered the endless bowls of ice cream that Anton had wanted to consume when he'd first come to them. The self-control that the boy now exhibited—surely that was a sign of something. David felt his body quiver with pride. He didn't care what anyone believed, even Anton himself. This boy belonged with them. And he was destined for great things. He deserved a better life than his mother ever could have provided.

"Whatever you say, buddy," he said. He gazed at Anton's bowed head as the boy sat staring at the ground. "Do you have more questions for me?"

Anton was quiet for the longest time before he looked up. "Can I see her? To, you know, say hi?"

David knew from Anton's startled expression that the boy had caught the alarm that had flashed in his eyes. It was out of the question to arrange a meeting between Juanita and her son. She might let slip something that would implicate David. Or she might change her mind about signing away her parental rights. As for what the effect of such a meeting would have on Anton—David shook his head to snuff out that worrisome thought. "I'm afraid that's not a good idea, buddy," he said, hoping that the boy would not push.

Anton nodded and David wondered, not for the first time, how much the boy understood. "What else?" David said with a thin smile.

Anton shrugged. "Nothing, I guess." Without warning, his face crumbled. "David. How come Mam loves the drugs more than me?"

David felt the air rush out of his lungs. He looked at Anton helplessly, feeling as though he had never loved this small, lost, and vulnerable boy more than at this moment. "Don't say that, buddy. Because it's not true. Your mom—she loves you. She wants you to live with us because . . . she knows we can give you a life that she can't." He blinked back the tears forming in his eyes. "Anton. Aren't you even the least bit happy being with us?" he asked, hating the plaintive note in his voice, noticing the discomfort it produced in the child. You selfish bastard, he chided himself. Instead of consoling the kid, you're demanding that he console you. He forced a smile on his lips. "Aw, shit. You don't have to answer that, kiddo."

They sat for a moment, not looking at each other. Then David rose from the bench and fished out his car keys. "We should head on out to the hardware store," he said. "They close early on Sundays." He waited until Anton came around the picnic table and then put his arm around the boy's shoulder. "It will work out fine, son," he whispered as they walked. "You'll see. It's gonna be okay."

Anton nodded, the expression on his face inscrutable. They rode in silence, a million thoughts scuttling through David's head. He knew Delores would grill him about whether they'd talked and how the conversation had gone, but the truth was, he wasn't sure. Anton had maintained his composure, had not created a scene, but then, really, had David expected anything less from him? Maybe he would talk to Dee about whether Anton should see a therapist a few times. Although what could a therapist say? The fact was, Juanita had chosen to give up her rights to her son. And yes, David had played a role in nudging her toward that decision, but that was a secret he would take to his grave. And the only way to repay Juanita Vesper for her sacrifice was to be the best father that he knew to this boy riding next to him. David stroked the top of Anton's head, and the boy, who had been looking out the window, turned toward him inquiringly. "You okay?" David asked.

The boy shrugged. He looked out the window again, and David noticed the hunched shoulders, his face a profile of sadness.

I know you're sad, and I can't blame you, David thought. But you won't be for long. I promise. Because Delores and I—we are going to take such good care of you. You'll see.

CHAPTER TWELVE

Delores was babbling, not making sense on the phone. She was asking David whether Anton was with him, in his chambers. Why would Anton be with him on a workday? How would Anton get to the courthouse, for Christ's sake? Nothing that she was saying was making sense.

"Honey. Calm down. I can't understand. Why isn't he home? It's after five. He should've been home eons ago."

And now her words finally penetrated. "That's what I'm trying to tell you, David. He never went to school. He—"

"Then he should be home. Why isn't he—"

"He didn't catch the school bus. I spoke to Colin's mom, and Colin says he wasn't on the bus this morning."

David sat back in his chair, forcing back the panic and nausea that were threatening him. He had already lost one son. If something had happened to Anton . . . He couldn't finish the thought. I'm not this strong, he thought. Please, God. Don't test me. Not a second time. I will just lie down and never get out of bed again. Not a second time. If this is punishment for what I did to that woman, then punish me. Me. Not that sweet, innocent boy.

"David. Answer me. What should we do?"

"You've spoken to the school?"

"I told you. I've talked to the principal. He confirmed with the bus driver. Anton never caught the bus."

He felt sick at the image that came before his eyes. "Maybe . . . Do you think he got hit by a car?"

He could tell from Delores's voice that she'd had the same vision. "The bus stop's only a block away. Colin's mom says she's been home all day and didn't hear or see anything. We would've heard, David. If something happened in the neighborhood."

"The cops would know," he said dully, sick at the thought of uniformed officers in their house again. Again.

"I almost called them. But I wanted to check with you first. In case, you know, he showed up there."

"I doubt he even knows where I work, Delores," he said irritably. "He's never done that before. Why would he come here, for God's sakes?"

"Well, he hasn't been himself. Ever since you gave him the news. You know."

Out of the corner of his eye, he saw his secretary, Jane, peering into his chambers, her eyebrows raised in inquiry. He gave her an "It's okay" sign and then said into the phone, "Don't call the cops yet. I'm coming home."

HIS STOMACH DROPPED when he walked into the house a half hour later and saw Delores's distraught face. He felt his temper flare at an unknown God for inflicting this pain on her. "Dee," he said, gathering her close. "It's not what you think, honey. Now let's just—"

"How do you know? How do you know it's not what I think?"

His hands dropped to his sides and he gazed at her helplessly, a metronome of rage ticking within him at the sheer injustice of their situation and at his inability to protect her from a calamity that he knew he had visited upon her.

They were still staring at each other silently when the phone rang. David found himself paralyzed, unable to function. Not again. Sweet Jesus, not again. He dully registered that Delores had moved away from him and toward the phone. He heard her say, "Hello?" but it wasn't until she said, "Anton? Where are you?" that he could breathe once more.

He shut his eyes, unable to bear the visions that danced around him—Anton in a hospital bed, Anton in the back of a van, kidnapped by a stranger. "What? Oh, honey," he heard Delores say. "Are you in a safe place? Well, what's the building number? Okay, don't you move from there. We'll be there as soon as we can. We're leaving now, but it might take us a while to get there, okay? So don't panic. And Anton, don't talk to anyone, you hear?"

She hung up, relief lighting up her face. "Oh, David," she said, falling into his arms. "I can't bear this. I can't ever live through this again."

He put his arms around her, rocking her silently. "Where is he? He's safe, yes?"

"He's back there. At his old apartment. In the Roosevelt housing project. He went looking for his mom."

David felt his body grow cold. "He ran away from here? To go back there?"

Delores must have heard something in his voice because she pulled away from him and lifted her face toward him. "Yes, he did. And I can't blame him. He went to find his mom. Is that so hard for you to understand, David?"

He understood, he honestly did. And yet it was undeniable—the inexplicable shame that he felt, as if he'd just lost a secret contest that pitted him against a poor, uneducated black woman. Anton had chosen her. Of course he had. But Anton had run away to her—for what?

Comfort? To beg her to take him back? Well, who could blame him? As Pappy always used to say, blood seeks blood; blood is thicker than water.

"David? Are you going to just stand here? Anton's alone in that awful place. Shouldn't we go get him?"

"Yes," he said woodenly, grabbing his coat keys. All the while thinking that what he really wanted to do was climb into bed and pull the sheets over his eyes until he recovered from the insult Anton had levied at them. He turned toward Delores. "I'll go get him. You should start on dinner, yes?"

"I promised him I would go."

"Dee. I don't want you to go to that . . . place. It's not safe." He signaled her with his eyes, wanting her to understand. "I'll be back with him in a jiffy."

She looked like she was about to argue, but instead she ran her finger lightly across his cheek. "Don't say anything to him tonight, okay, David? We can talk to him tomorrow. Just . . . just bring the poor kid home."

"Of course," he said.

IN THE CAR, he pulled out a map to figure out the shortest way there. As he drove, he thought again of touring the Roosevelt projects with Pappy. Back in Kennedy's time, Pappy, then a newly minted senator, had been instrumental in the development of the project, the largest in the state and then considered state-of-the-art, with green spaces and redbrick buildings that spread over several city blocks. But by the early eighties, when David had accompanied his father on a tour, the buildings were blighted and crime-infested, and the middle-class businesses and homes that once dotted the surrounding area had long since moved away. David remembered the distaste he had felt as they'd climbed the dark stairwells with their burnt-out lightbulbs and the acidic smell of urine on each landing. He smiled grimly as he remembered what Pappy had said when they'd left: "If I'd known the shithole this place would become, I'd have begged them to name it after Nixon, not Roosevelt."

David had told Pappy two days ago, on the phone, the news about the possibility of their adopting Anton. To his surprise, Pappy had been pleased. "He's a great kid," he'd said. "I'm just glad the drugs have still left the woman with enough of a conscience to do the right thing. You know what they say—even a broken clock is right twice a day."

"Well, it took a little arm-twisting," David heard himself say.

"Whatever do you mean?"

"Nothing," he'd said, suddenly afraid of the senator's indignation if he ever learned the truth. Pappy, who had a reputation for scrupulous honesty, had served in the Senate with distinction. Residents in the state were still divided about his decision to resign his office in 1985, after Reagan's landslide victory, because he'd despised the direction in which the country was headed. David remembered Tip O'Neill himself visiting the senator at his home, asking him to reconsider.

No, Pappy would've found it unforgivable, what he'd done to Juanita Vesper, David thought. And the strange thing was, he didn't really care. He adored his father, admired him, but Pappy had never known what hell looked like, had never felt the lick of hellfire or stared into the void the way he and Delores had after James's death. The son became older than the father during that time, David thought. That first night when Delores and he had come home after visiting their son at the morgue and gone to bed in their street clothes—David shuddered at the memory. The way Delores had woken up in the middle of the night, sat cross-legged in the middle of their bed, and begun to wail. David knew that if he lived to be ninety, he would remember the ancient sorrow of that wailing; its terrible notes lived under his skin. Pappy had been devastated by the loss of his only grandson, and in some ways, he'd never recovered from the blow, same as them. But Pappy had never lived in the same house as James. Pappy had not made him pancakes for breakfast or taken him shoe shopping or—heavenly Father—shopping for his tuxedo. For the prom.

David wiped away the tears pouring down his cheeks. It was foolish, what he'd done, pinning all his hopes on Anton, a damaged boy from a damaged home. No wonder it had not occurred to the boy to leave them a note. The first chance he had gotten, he'd made his way home. Home, to that brutal, ugly place whose thumbprints they'd tried so hard to erase from his body. Home to the mother who had discarded him like an old pair of shoes. Anton had obviously believed that she was back there, living in that same apartment where he'd almost roasted to death. A feeling of despair gripped David. He had done everything that he could to win Anton over, and at the first mention of his mother, the boy had fled. How he had even figured out a way to get back to Roosevelt was a mystery. Well, he'd find out soon enough.

It took David almost forty-five minutes to get to the projects. He drove down the narrow streets slowly, careful not to hit the parked cars, not wanting to risk any kind of altercation in an unfamiliar neighborhood. Even with his windows rolled up, he could feel the reverberations of jarring music blasting from nearby cars. He took in the general disrepair of the roads and buildings and marveled that Anton had survived this blight as well as he had. He began to look for building 1301, knowing that Anton was waiting for him at a bus stop in front of it. Just then he saw the boy's forlorn shape, saw him sitting hunched on the bench of the covered bus stop, leaning his elbows on his knees. A stout, middle-aged woman was the only other person at the stop, although a cluster of young boys hung out not too far away. David saw Anton look up and recognize the car and give a little wave. All of his bitterness against the boy's thoughtlessness melted away at that wave. He pulled up in front and leaned over to unlock the passenger door. "Hi, Anton," he said.

"Get in." The boy smiled. He threw his backpack in the backseat and climbed in.

"And who would you be?" The woman was leaning into the car window from Anton's side, glaring at David.

David glanced at Anton, his right eyebrow raised in inquiry. "She says she's a friend of Mam's," the boy whispered to him, his irritation at the woman showing on his face.

"I asked who you were," the woman said again, louder this time. She looked at Anton. "Boy, you knows better than to get into a car with a strange man."

"He's not a strange man," Anton yelled. "I told you, he's my dad."

The honorific shot through David like a bolt of electricity. For a second the air between the man and the boy crackled. Then David turned toward the woman and smiled. "Thank you for watching out for my son," he said politely. "Good night." The look he gave the woman was so intense and imperial that she backed away from the car, muttering to herself.

They drove out of the housing division in silence. After they were on the main road, David put his arm around Anton and cradled him. "Hello," he whispered. "You all right, son?"

Anton nodded and began to cry. David let him. After a few moments the boy began to confess. How he'd gone to the school library and found an area map. How Pascal, the school janitor, had told him which two buses he had to catch to reach his old neighborhood. How he'd eaten his sandwich while riding the second bus and how scared he'd been because the only other passenger had alcohol on his breath and kept asking for money. How he now understood that his mam was still in jail and not at the old apartment, like he'd assumed. How he'd used his last quarter to call FM from the pay phone across from the bus stop. How, when the hairy man who now lived in their old apartment had opened the door, it had smelled weird, so unlike the nice scent of lavender that FM sprayed around their house. How tired he was and how glad he was to see David. How sorry he was for the trouble he'd caused David and FM.

David chewed on his lower lip, half-listening to the boy, busy as he was talking to God. Okay, he said. You've punished me today for what I did to that woman. Abuse of power, you could call it. And you reminded me of it by taking Anton away from me today. Made me stare into the void again. But there's no going back now, is there? There's only moving forward, so here's my promise—I will atone. I will more than make up for what I've done to Juanita Vesper. And I will do it by giving Anton every tool that I can to make him the best possible man he can be. But let me keep him. You took away James, and although I felt like clawing at the skin of the universe, I did nothing. Didn't I? Didn't I? When Pappy said to me after the funeral, "His will be done, son," I listened, didn't I? I let Thy Will Be Done. So this much you owe me. Let me keep the boy. Not even for my sake. But his. There are things only I can give him. Not even Delores. She's too afraid to push him to the heights I know he's capable of. And isn't that a kind of racism? To believe that a boy from Roosevelt has to be left unchallenged? But I know what this boy is made of, God. And I can help him. Let me help him.

Anton was still talking, the boy's voice soft and teary. But what David heard was the humming of his heart as he replayed again and again the sweet moment when the boy had scrambled into the car. The word "Dad" rang like a bell in his head and guided them home.

CHAPTER THIRTEEN

S o how'd it go? Did she accept the check?"

Connor flashed David a look as he sat down in the armchair beside him. "Of course. In the end. But man, she sure put up a fight."

David exhaled, the knot in his belly untying itself. "Whew. I'm glad that's over. Who did you end up sending to deliver it?"

"One of Smithie's clerks went, I think."

David looked up from the armchair to flash a smile to one of the club regulars as the man walked by. He waited until they were alone again and then turned his attention back to Connor. "I just wish we could've left Dee out of this completely."

Connor shook his head brusquely. "David. We've been over this ten times already. It's safer this way. I told you, Smithie was more than willing to cut Juanita a check himself. I mean, it's only five grand, right? But this way, it's cleaner. Out in the open—Delores, out of gratitude and concern for Anton's birth mother, writes her a check that hopefully will allow her to restart her life now that she's out of prison. It's beautiful, really."

He knew Connor was right, knew that his friend had looked at the situation from all angles and given him the best advice, but still David felt fretful. Juanita Vesper was apparently planning to move back to

Georgia, and as far as David was concerned, it couldn't happen soon enough. The money would cover a plane ticket and anything else she needed to get situated down south.

"Where is she staying right now?" he asked.

"With a friend," Connor said. "And before you ask, no, she's not at Roosevelt. So even if Anton were to try, he wouldn't be able to find her."

David took a sip of his sherry. "He's not going to try," he said, forcing a confidence into his voice that he wasn't sure was justified. "He—he's accepted what's happening." He looked at Connor's open, guileless face, and the lie was out of his mouth before he could stop himself. "Anton just told me last night how much he's looking forward to the adoption going through."

He tensed, waiting to see the skepticism on Connor's face, but his friend merely nodded. "Hopefully, he won't have to wait long."

David lifted his glass. "I'll drink to that. Cheers."

They clinked their half-empty glasses and sat back in the plush leather chairs. David felt a sudden urge for a cigarette. He pulled a pen out of his shirt pocket and tapped it with his index finger, as if tapping ash from a cigarette. Looking up, he caught Connor smiling at him.

"What?" David said.

"What is it?" Connor's voice was bemused. "What are you agitated about now?"

"Nothing." He looked around the room, with its Oriental rugs and wood-paneled walls. "It's just that . . . I don't know, Connor. I kind of wish we had made the check out to her. I mean, handing someone like her a check made out to cash? She's a junkie, for Christ's sake. She's liable to lose it, and God help us if it falls in someone else's hands . . ."

"David. Calm down." Connor snapped his fingers. "Look at me. We've got this taken care of, okay? Why did you think I insisted that you call that kid—what's his name?—Solemn, Solomon?"

"Ernest."

"Yeah, Ernest. Him. Why do you think I had you call him to say you wanted to help Juanita get settled in her new life?"

"Yeah, but he said it would be a mistake," David snapped. "And we ignored his advice."

Connor looked exasperated. "Yeah, but it gives us cover, right? She can't ever claim this was hush money, because look—" He flung out his arms dramatically. "We told the goddamn social worker we were doing this."

David ran his fingers through his hair. "I just want to put it all behind me." He leaned forward so that his knee was touching Connor's. "I don't want to have to look over my shoulder the rest of my life, worried that some guard or warden will someday spill the beans. About that night, I mean."

"David, look," Connor started, but David interrupted him: "No, you don't understand. Some party folks came to see me this week."

"Who?"

David made a dismissive sound. "Never mind who. The point is, Tufts has told them in confidence that if he wins again next year, he won't run for governor again. So his seat will be open in '98."

Connor let out a low whistle. "And they want you to run?"

"They're probably talking to a bunch of other guys, too." David shrugged. "Hell, 1998 is an eternity away. A lot could change between now and then."

"Sure," Connor agreed. "But the party obviously wants you to start considering this."

A waiter walked softly into the room and David signaled him for another round of drinks. They waited until the man left and then David said, "Maybe." He sat back in his chair. "Pappy will be disappointed, of course. He always thought I'd be senator someday." Something flared in him. "But I don't think I have the temperament to be a senator, Connor.

I'd be too damn bored. I think I'd be a much better . . ." He stopped as a club member he didn't recognize walked past.

"You'd make a great governor," Connor finished.

David smiled absently. "Thanks. But I could be happy continuing to do what I'm doing, too. I love the law."

The waiter set down their drinks, nodded, and disappeared. "In any case," David continued, "you can see why I'm concerned about the Vesper affair."

Connor locked eyes with David. "Nothing's ever gonna come out," he said. "And if, God forbid, something ever does, I'll take the heat for it. I'll fix it for you, I promise."

David cleared his throat. "You're something else, you know that?" he said.

Connor swung his arm and hit his friend. "Damn straight. And that's why you're buying the goddamn drinks tonight."

"You cheap bastard."

They grinned at each other. Connor raised his glass. "This news calls for a toast," he said.

"Connor, forget about it, will you? They were just floating a trial balloon, and like I said, I am perfectly happy in my current job."

"Bullshit. When the time comes, you will run. You know why?"

"Why?"

Connor grinned. "Because if you run, you'll win. Yes, you son of a bitch. You'll win."

CHAPTER FOURTEEN

He cried like a baby. Like a friggin' girl. Openly, unabashedly. In front of all of them. All of them—Connor, Jan, Dee, even Bob Campbell, who stared up at the ornate ceiling of the courthouse as if to escape David's mortifying display of emotion. David didn't care. He had eyes only for Anton. Anton and Dee. His new family. His newly constituted, newly minted family. Finally, finally, after all the waiting. He no longer had to feel defensive when he referred to Anton as his son, as if laying false claim to something that didn't belong to him. Now, with the adoption papers in his pocket, he could put his arm around the boy and pull him close, daring any of them to give him the look that made him feel like an imposter. This was the freedom that the adoption gave him—the freedom to love his son openly, freely, without apology or explanation. He had loved Anton almost from the moment he had laid eyes on him, and it was only now, three years gone, that he could declare that love. It was false, what everyone always said about tragedy. Tragedy wasn't *not* having someone to love. Tragedy was loving someone and not being able to express it.

He couldn't stop crying. Great heaving sobs right here in the courtroom, in front of all the people he loved most in the world. Dee was saying something, but he barely heard her. He sat on the wooden bench in the front row and sobbed while the rest of them milled around him. It was a private ceremony, Bob fitting them in at the end of his workday, probably impatient for David to get a goddamn grip on himself so they could all go home.

David reached for Anton, pulling the boy onto the bench next to him. He felt he had something important to say on this happy occasion, some solemn promise to make, but each time he tried to speak, more tears flowed, as if he were talking in a kind of strange Morse code: *Drip drip sob heave tear.* "I'm sorry," he mustered. "I . . . I . . . I . . ."

From behind him, he heard an echo. "I'm sorry," the voice said. "I . . . I . . . I . . ."

He and Anton turned their heads at the same moment. Brad sat three rows behind them, holding his sides, convulsed with laughter. "I'm sorry," he imitated David again. "I . . . I . . . I . . ."

Anton looked at David with a frown, unsure how to react to this mockery of his father. "Bradley," David heard Connor say. "Get over here. Right now."

Brad bit down on his lower lip and quieted his glee with considerable effort as he walked to where his dad stood. "I'm sorry, man," Connor was saying, taking a step toward David, when they heard a new sound, barely audible. It came from Anton. A giggle. Staring at his dad, trying his best to tamp down the giggles that escaped like squeaky springs out of him. Anton turned his head, made eye contact with Brad, and a loud bubbling sound escaped from his lips, and then both boys were in stitches.

David felt wounded for a moment, and then, watching the two boys so obviously teasing him, he felt the happiness of the occasion, like a sudden change in the weather. "You rascals," he said, grinning.

Bob Campbell cleared his throat. "Well, I guess we should all be making our way home."

They rose. "We're having a small celebration at home, Bob," David said to his colleague as they walked down the marble steps that led to the parking lot. "Will you join us?"

"Nah. Thanks, though," Campbell replied. "Sophia is waiting at home with supper."

"Maybe some other time."

"Yup." Campbell turned to leave.

"Bob," David said quietly. He stuck out his hand. "I just want to say—thank you. For. Everything."

The fierce, restless eyes softened. "You're fine," Campbell said, taking the proffered hand. "He's . . . he's a good kid. Congratulations to all of you."

David swallowed. "Thanks. I'll never forget your kindness."

He stood staring after the older man for a second, then said to Connor, "Hey. How about if you guys give Dee a ride with you? I need to have a quick talk with Anton."

"No problem."

"We'll see you back at the house."

Before marrying Dee, David had thought of marriage as a legal formality, a piece of paper that changed nothing. And so he was surprised to find out it did. There had been a new tenderness, a responsibility that he'd felt toward Dee that had not been there the day before. Now he felt that same tender responsibility, that sense of permanence, as Anton slipped into the passenger seat.

"How you doing, bud?" he asked quietly as he drove down the familiar streets.

"I'm fine, David."

He smiled ruefully to himself. "I have to ask you something. A favor." He glanced at the boy. "Any chance you could stop calling me David? And call me, y'know, Dad?"

Anton nodded. "I meant to. I even do, to myself. I practice it. But sometimes it just slips out as David."

David nodded. "I understand. I . . . just try. Okay?"

"Okay." Anton gave him a quick bashful look. "Why were you crying today, Dad?"

"Because I was happy."

Anton raised his eyebrow in the sly, teasing way that David loved. "So you cry when you're happy? Do you eat when you're thirsty? And stand when you're tired?"

David hit the boy playfully on his arm. "Wise guy." He was quiet for a moment and then said, "Have you never been so happy that it made you cry?"

Anton frowned. "I don't know."

"Maybe it's a grown-up thing."

"It must be," Anton said promptly. "That's why it makes no sense."

David grinned. "So I heard you and FM planned the menu for tonight's party. She let you pick all your favorite things?"

But Anton looked distracted. "David," he said after a second, "if I'm gonna call you Dad, I should call FM Mom."

David let the slip pass. "I guess so. You okay with that, buddy?"

It was so subtle, the iron that entered Anton's body and voice, that David thought he might have imagined it. "Yeah," Anton said. "It's okay with me."

They rode in silence for a few minutes, and then David had to say it, even though it sounded corny, even though he risked giving Anton the giggles again. "Hey, listen," he said. "You have a permanent home now, you hear? We love you. Nobody is going to hurt or harm you now. You understand? We're gonna protect you the rest of your life."

"I know." Anton's voice was soft, serious.

He'd had to say it. Even though Anton knew. Even though it was implied. Because it was like a wedding vow—something to be said out loud. Till death do us part.

TWO DAYS LATER, he broke his vow to protect Anton against all harm. Anton had a soccer match on Saturday afternoon, and David and Dee sat in the bleachers, along with the other parents and grandparents. Several people had drifted up to the Colemans before the match began, to offer their congratulations. "I can't believe how news spreads," David muttered to Delores. "It's like we still have a town crier." She squeezed his hand and nodded.

David was wiggling his fingers at a toddler in the row ahead of them when it happened. Even though he missed the sight of Anton running directly into the other player, he heard the sound, followed by the "Ooooh" of the crowd. By the time David's head snapped back to look, Anton was lying on the field, his legs splayed. Beside David, Delores screamed. But David was already up, running down the bleachers and onto the field. When he reached Anton, the blank look in the boy's eyes made him want to retch. "Call for an ambulance," he yelled at the coach. "Now."

They wouldn't let him ride with Anton in the back of the ambulance, so he rode in the front, next to the driver. Delores followed in their car. Every few minutes David would slide open the panel that allowed him a small window into the body of the ambulance, and he would talk to the silent boy, telling him that he was with him, reassuring him that he would be fine. He fought the urge to ask the young kid driving the ambulance to step on it, knowing that he was doing the best he could.

The news at the hospital was somber but not grim. Anton had a concussion as a result of the blow to his head. An MRI ruled out a brain bleed or a cracked skull. He would most likely be okay, the doctor said, but they'd keep him in the observation unit of the ER until the next day.

"I'm spending the night with him," David told Delores.

"You better ask," she whispered. "It's not like Anton has a private room. You don't want to get in their way."

He gritted his teeth. "I'm not asking them anything. I'm staying, even if I have to stand all night."

In the end, they gave him a chair next to Anton's bed. He lowered his lanky frame into it, caring about nothing but the fact that he would be there when Anton woke up. Already the boy had a shiner around his right eye.

He had just dozed off when he heard Anton yell in his sleep. David eyed the clock. Three A.M. He gazed at the boy, willing himself back to sleep, but Anton had his eyes open, staring wildly around him. "Hey, hey, buddy," David said, squeezing the boy's hand. "I'm here, okay? I'm right beside you."

For one awful moment, Anton looked as if he failed to recognize the man next to him. Then he said, "Is Mom here?"

"No, baby. She's home. But she'll come if you need her."

"No. That's okay. Do I have cancer?"

"No. *What?*"

"This is a hospital, right?"

"Yeah, but—"

"So I have cancer?"

"Anton. No. You have a concussion."

"Is that like cancer?"

David stared at his son. "No. You hit your head. You ran into another player during the soccer match today. Remember?"

Anton scrunched up his face, trying. "I don't. I can't remember." There was a film of sweat on his upper lip. "My head hurts," he said.

David pressed the nurse's button. "Okay. Just try and relax, okay, buddy? You just have a little bump on your head. Everything's fine. We're gonna give you something for the headache, okay?"

They were both quiet as they waited in the dark for the nurse to show. "Dad," Anton said, and David felt the word in his chest like a lit match. "I'm scared."

The tenderness in David's chest felt liquid, like milk, like honey, like something melting. He got up and carefully put his arm around the sleeping boy. "Don't be," he said gruffly. "There's no reason to be. Your daddy's here with you."

He felt Anton relax in his arms. He looked up, willing the nurse to come so he could ask her for pain meds, but also taking in this moment, this dark, this silence, this warm body relaxing into his strong arms. I could kill for this boy, he thought, I could wage wars, burn down villages, protect him with my dying breath. After James, he had never expected to feel this fierce a love again, this love that hissed and roiled and rattled in his chest.

The nurse gave Anton a children's Tylenol. After she left, David asked, "Do you know you have a black eye?"

Anton smiled, as David knew he would. "I do? Cool."

"Yeah, you look like a pirate."

"Oh boy. Can I see?"

"Tomorrow. When I can get you a mirror, okay?"

"What time are we going home?"

"I don't know, bud. Let's see what the doctor says." And then, compulsively, as if flicking his tongue over a sore tooth, "You don't remember *anything* about the game today?"

Anton blinked. "No."

"Okay." He ran his hand lightly over Anton's hair. "You try and sleep, buddy."

"Where are you gonna sleep?"

"Me? Right here. Beside you."

"But there's no bed."

"That's okay. Go on. Get some rest."

Anton closed his eyes and David sat in his chair, sleepy but alert, awaiting the dawn that he knew was surely around the corner.

BOOK TWO
September 2001

CHAPTER FIFTEEN

It was a movie. An epic disaster movie, like those 1970s chestnuts such as *The Towering Inferno* that his dad and mom sometimes watched on the old VCR. Plumes of smoke, burning buildings, the terrified people on the street running toward the camera, their eyes wide open with fear, covering their mouths from inhaling the smoke that already bore the hoofprint of death and the smell of flesh burning to a crisp. Even worse than the black plumes of smoke that rose like the wrath of God was the apocalyptic white snow-ash that fell on everything, portending a new world order. The white ash took every American metaphor—"pure as the driven snow,"—and turned it on its head, made it something sinister and ugly. A new world had arrived, delivered to their doorstep by CNN.

They were gathered around the television set at Eliot House at nine in the morning. Just a few years ago, they were still children, gathering around the campfire at night, trading ghost stories. But now they were grown, and what they were watching was the ghost story to end all ghost stories, written by a tall man in a cave, a man who was an engineer by profession, for crying out loud, but whose audacity, depravity, and creative imagination put professional screenwriters to shame.

None of them had ever seen a building tear open like fabric, with a giant hole in its center. None of them had ever seen a plane slice into a building. None of them had ever traced the slow drift of bodies falling from the tallest buildings in New York or experienced the sickness that they felt at the sight. Many of them had visited those iconic buildings on family trips to the city; not in a million years could they have imagined that the towers, which had felt so sturdy and strong under their feet, could collapse like a child's set of LEGOs.

It didn't occur to any of them to run off to class, because they understood in their bones that attending lectures and seminars was meaningless in a world gone mad. A day earlier they had been glowing because Professor Skip Gates had grinned at a smart observation they had made or worrying about the paper on Shakespearean sonnets that they'd written for Professor Helen Vendler. Now they took in the scene before them and saw the future go up in smoke. What did it matter if they went to law school or not? Who cared whether Derek slept with Carrie or Joan? How did it matter whether Karen was gay or just confused? As the towers collapsed, their individual lives, full of ambition and promise, collapsed, too. Individual destiny, they realized, mattered as much or as little as the rubble they were witnessing. Ashes to ashes. Dust to dust. Look where their trust funds, their titans of industry fathers, their Bryn Mawr mothers, their patrician grandparents, their fine sensibilities, their honed intelligence, their legacy admissions, had brought them—to helplessly watching their country's demise.

Now the first rumblings of outrage, the first stirrings of patriotic feeling, began. The TV anchors were already calling it terrorism, an unprecedented act of horror. Nobody knew how many were dead, but estimates were as high as ten thousand. When President Bush appeared on TV at nine-thirty, they cheered, even those who held the stolen election against him. A few minutes later they groaned as a third plane plowed into the Pentagon.

"This isn't terrorism," Bobby Falk kept saying. "This is war, man. I'm telling you, it's war."

Ahmed, an international student from Pakistan, spoke louder than anyone. "I hope they hunt down and kill the evil bastards who did this." They wanted to assure their friend, the only Muslim student present, but found their hearts weren't in it. They wouldn't rush to judgment, they wouldn't succumb to jingoism, they were Harvard men and women, liberal, fair-minded, they understood their country had its own sins, they knew about Pinochet and Chile and the 1953 CIA coup in Iran and Iran-Contra and all that, but enough was enough. This was their country, and it had been attacked. Someone would have to pay. By fuck, someone would have to pay.

It was just then, when the initial shock was leaving their systems and adrenaline was rushing in, that they heard a female voice from the back of the room.

"This is it," the voice said. "The chickens coming home to roost."

They all spun around, furious, Anton among them.

And he locked eyes with the blackest, funkiest, most beautiful woman he had ever seen.

CHAPTER SIXTEEN

Later, after he'd managed to get her the hell out of Eliot House and they'd walked across eerily deserted Harvard Yard and gone to Dunkin' Donuts for coffee, after they'd sat there for two hours arguing about American foreign policy, after she had said things so outrageous and downright unpatriotic that, offended, he had gotten up to leave, after she had made a rueful face and apologized for her bluntness and then, after he had sat back down half-appeased, asked him why, as a black man, he was so eager to defend the white military-industrial complex and he had laughed, shaking his head at her, after he had told her about his adoptive parents, one of whom was now the governor of a neighboring state, after he had noticed that her eyes had not sharpened with interest the way almost everybody else's did when they found out that he was the son of Governor David Coleman, after she'd told him that her doctor father was from Cameroon and her mother from Georgia, after he'd flirted briefly with the idea of telling her that his birth mom's folks had been from Georgia and then dismissed it, after he'd instead told her that the combo explained why she was the most beautiful woman at Harvard, after she'd arched an eyebrow and said, "At *Harvard*? That's not saying much," after they'd both laughed and she'd looked at Anton and mumbled, "You're pretty cute yourself," after he'd blushed and changed the topic and asked what she intended to do with a degree in political science and she'd told him, after she'd asked why he was wasting money on a degree in English and he'd admitted that his real ambition was to get in to law school and somehow combine the two, and asked, "Are you always this rude?" and she had nodded, after his stomach had rumbled and he had declared that he was hungry, after they'd gone to Hong Kong and gotten two take-out orders of lo mein and sat on a bench on Mass. Avenue under a blue sky that bore no trace of the fact that the world had ended earlier that day, after he'd given her one of his shrimp and stolen a piece of pork from her order, after they'd eaten sitting on the bench feeling young and happy and sad and desperate, the cotton of his shirt occasionally grazing her bare arm, after they had finished and he had thrown away their take-out containers and then extended his hand to help her up and she'd placed her hand in his and he never gave it back, after they'd walked hand in hand through a strangely quiet Harvard Square and the Yard, they went back to Eliot House and into his room and got into his bed, and stayed there the rest of the day and night.

CHAPTER SEVENTEEN

What kind of an engagement ring did one give a girl who hated the sight of gold and who saw in every diamond the blood of the wretched who had entered the bowels of the earth to mine it? And how did you propose to a girl when your anniversary fell on September 11 and common decency demanded that this was not a day of celebration or for planning your future?

Anton had been grappling with both these issues for several weeks, ever since he had been seized with the idea of the proposal, even though common sense told him that it was much too soon. He even made a list of the arguments against such a step:

1. He was pretty young and didn't want to get married until they'd both graduated from college.
2. After a year of dating her, he hadn't yet introduced Carine to his parents.
3. He hadn't met her parents, either.
4. He wasn't sure that she would accept.

On the pro side:

1. He loved her.
2. She was the coolest woman he had ever known.
3. Also, the hottest.

And so he had hunted in antique stores and used-jewelry shops until he had found an engraved silver band. He thought it was elegant and hoped that she would, too. What her politics were about silver, he hadn't a clue. He waited for a week to pass after the 9/11 anniversary. It felt wrong to be happy on that day, as if he were out of step with the mourning that engulfed the whole country. After a year, the trauma was still present—he still looked up nervously at the sky if a plane was flying at a low altitude—but the fact was, he was happy. He had been a happy fool from that first day with Carine, even though her political views and her outspokenness drove him crazy. At the beginning of their relationship, he was constantly trying to shush her in restaurants, on the street, where her loudly stated opinions were often met with hostile stares, even in progressive Cambridge. He often found himself looking around the room, smiling an appeasing smile, his skin tingling, his antennae up, prepared to get into a fight if need be to defend his opinionated girlfriend, but hoping to convey by his posture and body language his indulgent humoring of her, and that he was asking those around them for the same indulgence.

Until the day at the restaurant when she had fixed him a hard stare and said, "Whattsa matter, boy? I thought your name was Anton. Not Tom."

He had flushed, pushed away his half-drunk Coke, gotten up wordlessly from the table, thrown down a twenty-dollar bill, picked up his jacket, and left. All the way home, his eyes stinging with tears, he had called her names. Bloody bitch. Bloody crazy bitch. Who the hell does she think she is?

It had been a short-lived quarrel. She had knocked on his door two hours later, and when he opened the door, her eyes were red and her face small and pinched. She had apologized and he had accepted. But the impact of her words lingered like the reverberation of a bell. The next semester, he signed up for a literature class with Skip Gates and heard the term "the white gaze" for the first time. He had spent his boyhood and teenage years, he realized, mindful of that white gaze. What would it feel like, he wondered, to be free and direct the way Carine was? To not have to conduct yourself in a certain way at all times? To not have to constantly smile to prove that you were unthreatening, to continually demonstrate that you were intelligent, articulate, and not an affirmative action charity case? Carine seemed to have no such hang-ups. She often wore her hair in dreadlocks and had an eclectic wardrobe, so she could go from African queen to college student in no time at all. She laughed uproariously when something was funny and did not when someone made a sexist or homophobic joke. No, nobody would ever accuse Carine of being a Tom.

He began to grow out his hair. It wasn't an Afro, exactly, but it was longer than the close-cropped cut that he had worn ever since he had moved in with the Colemans. Carine went home to Georgia for a few days and returned with three collarless cotton shirts, all brightly colored, that her father had purchased in Kenya. Anton had balked at first—"I'm a T-shirt-and-jeans kinda guy," he'd protested—but now they were his favorite shirts. With his longer hair and new wardrobe, the transformation was startling. Just last week at a coffee shop in Watertown, the waitress had asked him, "Where are you from?" When he smiled and said, "America," she'd said, "Oh," and hurried away.

He was wearing his blue Kenyan shirt as he rushed to meet Carine on Friday. She was waiting for him outside the Au Bon Pain at the Square, as planned. It was an overcast day, and she wore an oversize army jacket over her black T-shirt and jeans. He fingered the ring in his pants pocket as he approached her. She hadn't spotted him yet, and he relished the few seconds of observing her. Even in repose, Carine's face was alert, and he felt giddy with pleasure at the sight of her. He had dated some in high school and during his first year at Harvard, sweet white girls from good families, but he had not been madly in love with any of them. He had been enchanted by them, had liked them well enough, but the partings had always been friendly and bloodless. What he felt with Carine wasn't so much love as a homecoming, and he honestly didn't think it was racial—though she was the first black girl he had ever dated—so much as chemical, protons and electrons coming together. I guess that's why they call it chemistry, he thought, but now she had spotted him, and he took the last few steps toward her and kissed her briefly on the lips.

"Your nose is cold," he said, touching it with his finger.

"Yeah. And whose damn idea was it to meet here on this bleak day?"

"Actually, it was yours."

"Oh. Well. In which case, what a great idea."

They smiled at each other. "Where do you want to go to dinner?" he said. He had a vague idea that he would give her the ring at the restaurant without making too big a deal about it. He had the feeling Carine wasn't the kind of girl who'd want a proposal on bended knee.

She scrunched up her nose. "You know what, baby? Do you mind if we just go back to your place and make some pasta or something? I feel like maybe I'm coming down with a cold."

"Oh, no." He nodded. "Pasta sounds perfect. You ready to go?"

He put his arm around her to protect her from the wind. She leaned in to him as they walked down Mass. Avenue toward his apartment. He took in the big gray clouds, the vivid green of the trees, and felt a trickle of happiness, pure and thick as honey, in his chest. This was the world, he thought, and he had a place in it. With this mad, crazy, impetuous woman by his side, he felt mighty, powerful, clear about his future. He realized now that he had never felt young until he met Carine. But he felt it now, and as they walked, he saw their future roll out before them like a plush red carpet.

She went into the kitchen as soon as they got home and picked out a knife to chop the garlic. He went up behind her and gently took it out of her hand. "I'll make supper," he said. "You go take a nap."

He poured himself a Coke and then got busy in the kitchen. He put on a pot of water to boil, chopped the garlic, added a few sprigs of basil, and quickly fried it in a pan of olive oil. He hunted in the fridge for the can of Parmesan cheese. "Dinner should be ready in about ten minutes," he yelled as he set the small table in the kitchen. All this time, while he was working, nervousness rattled like a large ice cube in his stomach. Should he give her the ring during dinner or immediately after? Should he slip it into the pasta, or was that gross? He wished he had consulted with his dad but also knew why he hadn't—David would have been appalled at the thought of Anton proposing to a girl whom he and Delores had not met. Anton would've had to sit through the you're-too-young-to-even-think-about-marriage lecture. He knew his parents loved each other, but his dad had recently confessed to him that he wished he had dated a bit more before settling down. Except he hadn't put it quite like that. He'd said something about wishing he had sowed some more wild oats, and Anton had cringed, put it down to the kind of yucky, cringe-making things parents said.

Carine had switched into sweatpants and one of Anton's shirts. "This looks yummy, baby," she said, dipping a finger into the olive oil sauce and licking it.

He pointed toward the tiny dining table. "Sit. I'll be there in a sec."

They were both hungry after a full day of classes and ate in relative silence. "So did your parents decide if they're going?" Anton asked with his mouth full.

"Yep." Carine swallowed before continuing. "To Mozambique. For two weeks this time."

Each year, ever since she had turned seven, Carine's parents ran a free medical clinic somewhere in the third world. It was like missionary work, she had explained to Anton, except her parents were not religious. It was simply her father's way of giving back, uncomfortable as he was with the affluence of his life in America.

"So you're going to be alone here over Thanksgiving?"

She gave him a quick glance. "Guess so. Though Veronica has already said that I could go home with her. But honestly, Anton, I have so much homework that it'll be easier just to stay around."

"How about going with me? To the Cape?"

She gave a short laugh. "I don't think that's a good idea."

"Why not?"

She shrugged. "I don't know. They just sound like . . . like not my kind of people."

He did his best to not show the hurt that he felt. "What does that mean?"

"Nothing. Just that . . . your dad's the governor, for chrissake. And I don't know, your family sounds so *white*."

"Veronica's family is white."

Carine covered his hand with hers. "Honey. I'm not trying to pick a fight with you. And I don't mean to be rude, either."

He shook his head, offended. "I don't understand what you're saying. Are you saying you're never going to meet my family?"

"Of course not. Just . . . not yet, okay? I mean, it's too soon, for one thing."

The silver ring in his pocket suddenly felt heavy, a ridiculous object that weighed him down. "After a year it's too soon to meet my family? That's insulting."

He saw the flame leap in her eyes. "Have you even told your white parents about me?" She looked at him for a second. "No, I didn't think so. I'll tell you what. That's insulting."

"They're not my *white* parents, Carine. They are my parents."

"Fine." She nodded her assent. "Agreed. But let me ask you this: How come you never talk to me about your birth mom?"

A hole opened up in his chest. She was going too far. He tried to control his temper, but when he spoke, his voice shook with anger. "Because there is nothing to say about her. I have told you everything that you need to know. You know that I was adopted."

They stared at each other stiffly, their bodies rigid, but suddenly, she capitulated, her face soft. "Aren't you curious about her, Anton?" she pleaded. "Don't you want to know where she is? Aren't you the least bit curious?"

She was clawing at a wound that had scabbed over for ten years. He looked down at his pasta bowl, trying to steady himself lest he say something that he would regret. "I don't want to talk about this," he said at last.

"But that's just it. Why not? She's your mother, for crying out loud. Don't you even care whether she's dead or alive?"

He turned toward her savagely. "No. I don't. She could be rotting in a crack house or rotting in her grave for all I care. That's the honest answer. And if you can't fucking deal with that, then, well, it's too bad, Carine. I don't have to explain myself to anybody. So you can take your judgmental tone and shove it."

He got up from the table, walked into the living room, paced around a few times, and then opened a window. It felt hot in his tiny apartment, and crowded, and he wished she would leave.

"Anton." She came up behind him and he tensed, hoping she would not touch him, not while his body was still pulsing with anger. She did not. "I'm sorry, I was totally out of line. I just wish you would talk to me about your past a little bit more. I just want to be let in, baby, don't you see?"

He looked down at her. "Don't ever call them my white parents.

They are my only parents. They were the ones who took me in when she wanted nothing to do with me. Because the drugs were more important than her only child. Everything that I have, everything that I am, is due to my mom and dad." Even through his anger, he was aware of the burning in his throat. Strange how raw, how close, the pain felt.

She opened her mouth to speak, but he raised his index finger to stop her. "And one more thing. Something that I've learned from my father. Life is about moving ahead, not looking back. That's the American way. And that's what I believe. I refuse to waste even ten minutes of my life looking back. So before you ask, no, I've never Googled my birth mom to find out her whereabouts. Because, frankly, I just don't care. And if that makes me a monster, well, you know where the front door is."

Carine looked at him, aghast, and Anton looked away first. "I'm sorry," he mumbled. "I didn't mean that."

"Do you want me to leave? To leave you alone?" She was openly crying now.

He gathered her in his arms. "No. Of course not."

"Good." She sobbed against his chest. "Because I really love you, Anton." She looked up at him and her eyes were worried, probing his face for something. "Please just know that if you ever want to talk to me about anything, I'll be there for you."

"I know. I will." But he was desperate to get off the subject.

Carine smiled ruefully. "You men," she said. "Always so tough."

He pulled her toward the couch and they sat down. He clicked the TV remote absently and then muted the sound. "Well, this was unfortunately a giant detour to a very simple proposal," he said. He enjoyed watching her eyes get wide with anticipation. He waited for a moment for maximum effect and then added, "Will you come to Pappy's house on the Cape with me for Thanksgiving?"

Her body seemed to fold upon itself, and when she looked up, her eyes held an emotion that he could not read. When she spoke, her voice was uncharacteristically low and uncertain. "Sure. If you think it's a good idea. If they'll have me."

He forced a heartiness into his voice that he did not feel. "Are you kidding me? They'll love having you there."

He stroked her hair absently as they settled in to watch a *Star Trek* rerun. After a few minutes he rose to make them a bowl of popcorn. Everything seemed fine and back to normal, but for the first time, he felt at a remove from Carine. He sat back down on the couch and put his arm around her, trying to get rid of this horrible new feeling. He thrust his right hand into his pants pocket, twirling the ring, feeling the cool inner softness of the metal. The future that had seemed so clear just a few hours ago now felt like an endless loop that went around and around and got nowhere.

CHAPTER EIGHTEEN

Anton and David had just finished hammering the shingles that had blown off Pappy's roof, and despite it being a windy day, they had worked up a sweat. Grabbing two beers from the cooler, they now sat on the two Adirondack chairs on the front lawn, overlooking the ocean.

"Pappy's looking old," Anton said.

"He *is* old."

Anton gave his father a sly grin. "So are you. But you look pretty good for an old man."

"Just you wait. It creeps up sooner than you think."

"Dad. Please. I'm only twenty."

David glanced at his son appreciatively. "So you are."

"Everything going okay in the statehouse?"

David rubbed his eyes tiredly. "You know. The same old shenanigans by the Republicans."

"Don't you ever just want to quit? I mean, Jesus, it takes forever to make anything happen."

David stared into the distance. The water today was the color of jade. "Like Pappy, you mean? How he up and quit?"

"I wasn't thinking of that. I just meant . . . I guess I don't have the temperament for politics. I'm too impatient, and I'd hate all the compromising."

David glanced at his son. Anton had changed. He seemed tougher, somehow, more brusque. It was the influence of the girl, he could see that. They had driven from Cambridge to the Cape yesterday, in time for dinner, and although it had been pleasant enough, she changed the electrical field when she was in the room. There was a sharpness to her that he wasn't sure yet if he liked. Also, none of the deference toward his elderly father that he himself felt and took for granted. She'd spoken to Pappy as if she were his equal. It had bothered David, even though he knew it ought not to. Young people today were different, he knew that. Also, the girl was from a different background. He'd tried talking to Delores about it in bed last night, but his wife had been tired and noncommittal.

"Dad? Where'd you go?"

"Sorry." David stretched his arms out and yawned. "It's so wonderful here, even on a cold day. Pappy had the right idea to retire here."

They sat in silence, sipping their beers, listening to the lapping of the ocean waves. Then David said, "So is it serious?"

Anton gave him a quick look. "I think so."

"I see." A pause. "Carine said you guys have been dating for over a year."

"Something like that."

"But you never mentioned her to us?"

"Dad—"

David shook his head. "I'm not mad. Honest. Just curious, as to— why not?"

"No reason. Really. I . . . I just . . . wanted her to myself, you know?"

He nodded as if he understood. But he didn't. He tried to remember if he had kept Delores a secret from his parents, but he couldn't. He doubted it—the senator had been such a large and looming presence in his life that he couldn't have kept any secrets even if he'd wanted to.

In fact, the first phone call he'd made when he found out Delores was pregnant was to his father.

But he and his dad hadn't been particularly close, had they? They certainly had not been friends the way he and Anton were. David had always told Anton that he could come with any problem and he would help, no questions asked. He was a baby boomer parent, after all. Drugs, sex, and rock and roll, the three biggies—he had counseled Anton on the first two and shared his passion for the third with his son.

"In any case," Anton was saying, "Carine and I, we're so happy to be here. Thanksgiving on the Cape—that's always special, right, Dad?"

"Somebody say my name?"

Both men turned around to see Carine come up behind them. She wore a white long-sleeved T-shirt and black jeans, and despite the cold, she was barefoot. The girl is beautiful, David thought appreciatively as Carine came around to Anton and leaned over to give him a quick kiss. David caught a flash of her cleavage and quickly looked away. "Hey, baby," Carine said. "Y'all done with the roof?"

"Yup."

"So now what?"

Anton pointed to the ocean with his beer bottle. "Just chillin'. Taking in the view."

"And sharing some quality father-son time." David regretted the words as soon as he said them, hearing the snippiness in his voice.

Carine's eyes widened slightly. "Sorry, Mr. C." She waited a beat and then continued, "But I'm on an errand from your wife. She needs one of you to run to the grocery store before it closes and buy us a bag of potatoes."

David felt himself flush. He turned to ask Anton if he'd want to run up to the Stop & Shop with him, but Anton was already getting up from the chair. "You wanna ride to the store with me?" he asked Carine, who nodded.

"I'll go get the car keys," she said, and left before David could respond.

Feeling foolish, David rose, too. "Well, this was nice," he said. He pointed to the roof. "Glad we got a chance to fix those shingles for Pappy."

"Yup." Anton was looking at him with an expression—bemusement? affection? apprehension?—that David couldn't quite place.

"Well." David rocked on his heels. "Guess I better go in and help your mom with dinner. You know how nervous she gets with holiday meals."

He turned to go, but Anton put out a hand and caught him by the wrist. "Dad."

David looked at him inquiringly. "Yeah?"

"Nothing. Just . . . I'm sorry I didn't tell you about Carine earlier. I just . . . I can't explain it. Anyway. I should have. In any case, I don't want it to spoil our weekend together, okay?"

David raised one eyebrow, puzzled. "Why should it?"

"No. That's not what I meant." Anton ran his fingers through his thick hair. "She means a lot to me, Dad. And I want you guys to like her. For y'all to be friends."

Y'all? Had his son ever said that word before? First the long hair, now the diction, David thought. "Of course we'll like her. We already do." He put his hand on his son's shoulder. "You need to relax. Okay?"

Anton nodded. "Okay. Thanks."

David passed Carine as he made his way toward the house. "Be back in a jiffy," she said, jingling the car keys.

"Drive carefully," he said automatically.

He watched as the two of them walked hand in hand toward the garage. Then he turned and went in the house to help his wife in the kitchen.

CHAPTER NINETEEN

I'm sorry it's just the five of us for dinner, my dear," Pappy said to Carine as he refilled her wineglass. "Our neighbors the Carmichaels usually join us, but they're in the Caribbean this year." He looked out the windows to where a steady rain was falling. "They may have had the right idea."

"That's okay," Carine said. She chewed on a piece of turkey and then asked, "Where in the Caribbean?"

The senator shrugged. "Damned if I know. Aruba, Belize, Antigua? All those places are the same, far as I can tell."

Anton, who was sitting to Carine's left, felt her stiffen. "Actually, they're really quite different," she said. "You should check out Jamaica Kincaid's *A Small Place*. You'd change your mind."

"No, not Jamaica," Pappy replied. "Pretty sure that's not where they are."

Anton squeezed Carine's hand before she could correct him. Just drop it, Carine, he silently willed her. "The Carmichaels are old friends," he said hurriedly, his voice a little too loud. "Marc Carmichael was a congressman for many years. He is my dad's godfather."

Carine raised her eyebrow. "Do you folks have any friends who are not politicians?"

Pappy laughed. "Touché, my dear." He turned to look at Anton. "You better keep an eye on this one here, son. She's a sizzler."

"Yeah, me and what army?" Anton said, and they all chuckled when Carine smacked his arm. Delores passed the platter of asparagus around. "Eat up, you kids," she said. "This has gotta be better than college food."

"No kidding," they said in unison. "Everything is delicious, Ms. C.," Carine added, forking more asparagus on her plate.

A look of satisfaction came over Delores's face as they helped themselves to seconds. "So what's the rush to get back? Can't you just stay until Sunday?"

There was a pleading in Delores's voice that Anton heard immediately. Mom is lonely, he thought. Being in the Governor's Mansion, away from her old friends, had clearly taken its toll on her. He knew how much it would mean to her if they extended their visit by a couple of days. He looked over at Carine. "What do you think, hon?"

"I can't." Carine's tone was regretful but resolute. "I'm sorry. I have a test on Monday that I have to get back to study for."

"Oh, come on." David's tone was teasing. "Anton tells us you're a straight-A student." He reached for more of the mashed potatoes.

Carine's smile was artificially bright. "Well, I got to be. You know what they say—folks who look like me, we gotta work twice as hard."

There was a stunned silence as they all absorbed the meaning of her words. "Ah, well, my dear," the senator said at last. "This isn't 1962, you know."

"Maybe not where you live, sir."

Pappy looked puzzled. He half-turned to look at Anton to ask for an explanation. "I . . . What does she mean?"

"What Carine means, Pappy, is that there's still a lot of racism out there," Anton offered weakly. He fought the urge to stomp on Carine's foot under the table.

"She's right," David said. "We have a case right now, working its way up the courts, asking the court to rule affirmative action illegal." He chewed slowly for a moment and then looked at Carine. "What do you think? Do you believe affirmative action has outlived its usefulness?"

They all turned to look at her. Anton made his eyes beg: Please don't make a scene. "Well, I don't know," she said thoughtfully. "It's a complicated issue."

Anton let out a sigh of relief. He racked his brain for a way to quickly change the subject.

But then Carine placed her right elbow on the table and turned sharply to look at him. "But let's ask Anton," she said. "After all, I'm not the only affirmative action baby at this table."

This time there was no mistaking her tone or attitude. Delores sat up in her chair. "Excuse me," she said pointedly. "I'm not sure what—"

"Honey," David said, cutting his wife off. "It's okay." He pushed his glasses up his nose and smiled pleasantly at Carine. "Actually, Anton is not an affirmative action case at all. He's a legacy admission. Because, you see, both his father and grandfather went to Harvard."

The senator thumped the table so hard, the wine leaped off his glass and spilled on the tablecloth. "Which, if you think about it, is just a different kind of affirmative action."

To Anton's great relief, Carine laughed. "Exactly."

"There you go." Pappy thumped the table again. Anton eyed his grandfather, suspecting that he was a little drunk. Pappy turned toward his son. "There's another legal challenge coming up, you say?" He shook his head. "It never ends. I remember when Johnson signed the affirmative action executive order for federal contractors. A lot of people were not happy back then, either."

"I'll bet," David said dryly, exchanging a look with Anton.

Carine rested her chin on her elbow as she spoke to the old man. "So who was the best president you worked with?" she asked, and Pappy was off, regaling them with stories about JFK's inauguration and the civil rights movement. "That Bobby Kennedy was a ripe bastard when his brother was president," he reminisced. "But I tell you, I never saw a man evolve as much as he did. He would've made a mighty fine president if we'd been so lucky." Pappy's eyes were wet. Anton discreetly moved the bottle of wine out of easy reach.

Though he had heard the stories a hundred times, Carine seemed enthralled. "Did you know Dr. King?" she asked.

The senator gave her a quick glance. "I only met him once," he said quietly. "He was a man of uncommon dignity." He looked around the table. "Do you know how old he was when he was shot?"

"Thirty-eight?" Carine said.

"Thirty-nine." The senator pulled out a white handkerchief and blew his nose. "Imagine that. He was just a young man. But he had the wisdom and grace of men twice his age. And because of this, he changed our country forever."

They were all silent for a moment, and when Carine spoke, her voice was deferential. "Do you really believe things have changed much, sir?"

The senator's eyes grew large and his face flushed red. "Young lady, did I hear Anton say earlier that your people are from Georgia? Yes? And you still dare to ask me that silly question?"

Carine wasn't chastised. "I know some things have changed for the better for sure," she began. "But I mean, income disparity has not changed. Housing segregation is still terrible. If you look at average wages for blacks versus—"

Pappy suddenly looked tired. He waved his hand as if to brush away her words. "My generation did what it could," he said. "We got the laws on the books. Now you young folks have to finish the job."

"Carine—" Anton began, but she ignored him. She stuck out her hand across the table toward the senator and said, "Agreed."

Startled, the old man took her hand and held it. "How'd you get your skin to be this smooth?" he said, stroking it with his other hand.

"Oh, Pappy." Delores was embarrassed. "Give the poor girl her hand back." She looked around the table. "Well? Shall we make a fire and have dessert in the living room?"

While Delores warmed the pies in the oven, Carine and Anton cleared the table. By the time they entered the living room, David had built a fire and he and Pappy were sipping on their sherry. Anton dimmed the lights and watched the glow of the fire on the faces of the four people he loved most in this world. Outside, flashes of lightning lit up the sky. For the longest time, the only sound was forks clicking against dessert plates. Anton felt relaxed for the first time since he had pulled up here yesterday with Carine. Despite a few bumps, dinner had gone well. Pappy seemed genuinely amused by Carine, and his old war stories had clearly won her over. As for Dad and Mom—he knew they were hurt by the fact that he hadn't disclosed his relationship to them, but he wasn't worried. Their unconditional love for him was his North Star, one of the few things he never had to doubt.

Maybe it was the wine at dinner, maybe it was the glow of the fire or simply the contentment he felt, but he was drowsy. A log sizzled and fell into the large fireplace, and just then he heard Carine say, as though continuing an earlier conversation, "Even if, as you say, things have improved here, they certainly haven't in foreign policy. Maybe now that we don't have Jim Crow here, we oppress people overseas."

She was at it again. Anton startled awake, prodded by a red-hot anger. What was wrong with this girl? Did she really not know how to be a guest in someone's home? "Huh?" he said. "That doesn't even make any sense."

"Really." It was Delores, seconding him, and in that moment, Anton knew the truth—his mom didn't like his girlfriend.

Carine chose to ignore Delores, focusing her attention on Anton. "What doesn't make sense? Or are you so high on your turkey and mashed potatoes that you can't put yourself in the shoes of those poor

Afghans who are being bombed back to the Stone Age? Or those wretched Iraqis who are about to be?"

They all spoke at once.

David: "There's no need to use that tone."

Pappy: "Just what are you talking about, my dear?"

Delores: "Anton? What is going on?"

Anton was rigid with embarrassment, unable to believe that she had humiliated him like this in front of his family. He remembered how he had come to her rescue on September 11, when she had provoked the crowd of students watching the horrific events on TV, how he had somehow diffused the situation by making light of her insensitive words. But he wouldn't—couldn't—bail her out this time. She had not wanted to come with him to the Cape, and this was her revenge, this unnecessary provocation, this acting out.

His father was speaking now, and Anton forced himself to listen. "I agree with you about the Iraq situation," David was saying. "And I hope to God our president isn't rash enough to take us into war. But I believe that in Afghanistan, we had no choice. We didn't attack them. They attacked us."

"But who attacked us? A ragtag army of crazies? That's reason enough to destroy an entire country? To kill civilians? And isn't it important to find out why they attacked us?"

"Because they are animals," Delores spat out. "Evil." Anton could barely believe that this was his polite, well-spoken mother.

"Oh, come on," Carine said. "That's so reductive, it doesn't deserve a response."

"Reductive?" Delores said in the same thick, ugly voice Anton had never heard before. "I'll tell you what's reductive. You and your—"

"Delores." David stepped in, a warning in his voice. "She's right. The reasons are more complicated than that."

"I'll tell you why they attacked us," Carine continued. "It's because they wanted us to get our military bases out of Saudi Arabia. That was Al Qaeda's one and only demand—"

"Young lady," David said firmly. "You're crossing a line here. I've been governor for many years now. I think I understand politics a little more than you do."

"Please don't patronize me, Mr. Coleman."

"That's Governor Coleman to you," Pappy roared, making Anton jump. "What you're saying—where I come from, we call it aiding and abetting the enemy. Treason. I won't have it in my house. I won't have a guest insulting the U.S. government by cavorting with the enemy."

"Pappy," Anton said desperately. "She didn't mean that. You don't know Carine, she just likes to—"

But she was having none of it. "That's funny," she said, addressing the senator directly. "In my house, we discuss everything. No subjects are off limits. My immigrant father encourages debate." She turned her head, looking at each one of them before she delivered the final insult. "That's what he thinks it means to be an American."

Nobody said a word. The crackle of the fire sounded deafening, as if it were enough to burn the whole house down. Then Delores stood up. "I can't take any more of this," she announced. "I'm going upstairs to bed." She looked at her husband. "You coming?"

David rose heavily to his feet. "Yup."

Delores crossed the room to where Anton was sitting and kissed his forehead. "Good night, sweetheart," she said in a flat, resigned voice. "You better get some rest. You have a long ride ahead of you tomorrow."

He was too embarrassed to respond.

David turned to his father. "Come on, Pappy," he said. "I'll walk you to your room."

After the three of them had left, Anton sat staring at the fire. Later, much later, he felt rather than heard Carine move. "Anton," she began, but he put up his hand as if to shield himself from her. "Don't," he said. "Don't say a word."

She sat mutely for a few seconds and then rose. "I'm going to bed, too. Good night." She looked at him uncertainly, as if she wanted to say more, but he remained still, staring ahead at the fire, and she left.

He sat up until the fire died, watching the last ember spark itself into oblivion. He tried his damnedest not to think that this was an apt metaphor for his life.

The senator stayed in bed the next morning and wouldn't come downstairs to see them off when they left. Delores had roused herself to make them turkey sandwiches for the trip and pack a couple of apples. Carine said an awkward goodbye and received a stiff "You be good" in return. After Carine was in the car, David put his hand on Anton's back and gently maneuvered him toward the garage for a brief talk.

"I'm really sorry for how last evening went, son," he said.

"Dad. It's not your fault. She was completely out of line."

David nodded. "I'm sure we're an overwhelming bunch to be around. But . . ." he hesitated, his eyes probing the young man's face. "I've never quite seen such a display before." He smiled weakly. "I thought the Black Panthers were defunct."

"She's not a Black Panther." Anton's defense of Carine was automatic.

"I know. But really, Anton . . ."

"I told you, Dad. I get it."

"Okay. Well. We'll talk soon, okay, sport?"

"Sure."

"And drive safe."

When they reached the car, Delores was leaning in and talking to Carine. Anton's heart swelled with love. He put his arm around his mom, turned her around, and kissed her on the cheek. "Bye, Mom. See you soon."

"Sweetheart. You take care, now."

He pulled out of the driveway and fidgeted with the radio, looking for a station that got good reception. He gave up after a few seconds and reached under the sun visor for his CDs. At this time in the morning, there were few cars on the road, and he scanned his CD collection before settling on Nirvana because he knew the music would drive Carine crazy. She had made her opinion of Kurt Cobain quite clear—according to her, he was a spoiled, whiny white boy who wrote songs for other rich, whiny white boys. But Anton loved Cobain, and as the music filled the car, he relaxed, thankful that he wouldn't have to talk to her.

They drove for a few miles before she turned the volume down and said, "So are you never going to talk to me again?" And when he didn't respond: "Can I ask you something? What did I say that was so offensive that you all turned on me?"

He took the bait. "Let's see. Maybe the part about Al Qaeda being justified in what they did?"

She tugged at her seat belt so that she could turn and look at him. "When did I say that, Anton? I just said that there was a reason—a political reason—why they attacked us. Not because they're savages or— What was the word your mom used? Animals. Is that so wrong?"

"Carine," he said as if talking to a child, "you were in the presence of a retired U.S. senator and a current governor. You were also my guest. Don't you think you should have modulated your opinions a little bit?"

"But that's just it. These are the people who make policy decisions that the rest of us have to live with, Anton. These are precisely the people whose views we need to change."

"But they are liberal Democrats," he cried. "Pappy was one of the first senators to come out against Vietnam, for chrissake. My father has been one of the most progressive governors in the country. So whom do you want to change?"

"And yet they got so bent out of shape because I was stating an easily documentable fact? Just think on that, Anton." Her voice was hoarse. "Don't you see what's going on? A year ago it was Afghanistan. Now it's Iraq. Doesn't it scare the shit out of you that we are getting ready to invade another country?"

"Of course I care. But my father doesn't get a vote in the U.S. Senate."

"But your mom said he's going to attend the governor's ball at the White House in December."

"So what should he do? Boycott it? You think that will change Bush's mind about Iraq?"

"Baby, listen," she said urgently. "You've never been to a third world country. I have. The way those people live, Anton. They already have so little. Such hard, miserable lives. And we're going to punish them some more? For what?"

He took his eyes off the road to look at her. "So who is disagreeing with you about Iraq? You're preaching to the choir, don't you get it? What I don't get is why you had to disrupt Thanksgiving dinner with your little diatribe. Isn't there a time and place for everything?"

She looked out the window for a moment, and he saw her brush away her tears. "So that's what matters more? We're on the verge of invading a sovereign nation, and you care about—table manners?"

He exhaled loudly. "You're impossible to talk to when you get like this. Forget it." He cranked the music up again. It was Brad who had introduced him to Nirvana. But by the time he had fallen in love with the group, Cobain was long dead.

A few hours later, he pulled in to Cambridge, his anger beginning to recede, replaced by a gnawing sense of loss. They had hardly talked on the way home, and although he had instigated the silence, he didn't know what that meant. Were they still a couple? Had they broken up? Did he want to be with her still? He stole a sideways glance at Carine, and the flip that his heart did was the answer. Chemistry. How the hell did one battle chemistry? Besides, he was beginning to wonder if she wasn't the only one who had behaved badly. Why had Mom sounded so shrill and hysterical? Why had Pappy been so dismissive when he spoke about the Caribbean? Dad had been okay, but he certainly hadn't defended Carine. Neither had Anton. In fact, the four of them had closed ranks against her. And then suddenly, swiftly, he knew—if Carine had been a white girlfriend arguing exactly the same points, they would've indulged her, cast a bemused eye toward her politics, maybe even admired her sensitivity toward the earth's poor. What're you, a Commie? his father would've teased. It was Carine's skin color, her blackness, that made her suspect, that made them feel there was an alien in their midst, a spy in their own country. Carine had posed the wrong question when she'd asked Pappy if he'd known King. The correct question would've been whether he'd known Malcolm. Anton would've been interested in that answer.

He opened his mouth and then shut it, unable or unwilling to share this revelation lest she think he was apologizing. In any case, they had reached her apartment building, and he double-parked near the front door. He left the engine running as he got out to get her bag from the trunk. He carried it to the stoop and set it there.

"Don't suppose you want to come in?"

"Probably not."

"Okay. See you around?"

"Definitely."

They looked at each other, and he kissed her chastely on the forehead, ignoring the incredulous look on her face. "Wow, that's cold," she said softly enough that he could pretend not to have heard her as he walked toward the car.

"Anton," she called, and he turned around, his left eyebrow raised in inquiry. "Yeah?"

She took a few steps to close the distance between them. "You know what confuses me?"

"What?"

"I can't decide if you're the blackest white man I've ever met or the whitest black man."

He sucked in his breath, the words crashing into him. He felt as if she had unmasked him, laid bare the central conundrum of his life. For the rest of his life, her words would haunt him. He knew this with an immediate and fierce surety.

She watched his face for a full moment and then moved away, as if putting her sword back in its sheath. "Bye, Anton," she said over her shoulder, and then ran up the four steps that led to her apartment.

He stood still, his chest heaving, as he stared at the closed door. He fought the urge to beat on that door with his fists, demand that she take back those malicious words. But after a few moments, his shoulders sagged and he made his way home, carrying an exquisite riddle that he would spend a lifetime trying to solve.

CHAPTER TWENTY

Anton stayed away from Carine for the rest of Thanksgiving break. On Monday night he returned to his apartment after a long day of classes to find a note of apology slipped under his door. He went to bed with a heavy heart that night, but the next morning, he called her while walking to school. When they finally got together for a quick lunch on Wednesday, it was as if they'd arrived at an unspoken agreement not to discuss the disastrous holiday. The same code governed his conversations with his parents, although during his first phone call to Pappy, the old man, true to form, boomed, "So how is that Trotskyite friend of yours?"

"She's fine, Pappy." He laughed. "She's not a Trotskyite."

"Could've fooled me." Pappy sighed. "Ah, the passion of youth. She'll settle down."

Anton wasn't so sure. The engagement ring rested at the bottom of his sock drawer. It seemed preposterous now, proposing marriage to Carine, when he was torn with so many doubts. Her passion, her indignation, which once seemed admirable to him, exotic, even, now felt tiresome. Sometimes he couldn't tell if she was self-righteous or mentally unstable. It would help if he could meet her parents, see her in the context of her family, but Carine seemed in no hurry for him to visit them. Besides, the thing she'd said to him on Thanksgiving night, the conundrum that she'd laid at his feet, continued to haunt him. Was it accurate, what she had said? Or did she just have an awful knack for getting under his skin?

A few weeks later, they were celebrating the end of classes at India Palace when Carine casually referred to a high school friend as an Oreo.

"Oreo? Wow, that's pretty racist," Anton said.

"How so? It's not a description of skin color, per se. It's describing an attitude—a brother who thinks he's white."

The flat casualness of her tone irked him, took him back to the night of her exquisite insult. "Do you know how often you do this, Carine, pigeonhole people? You do it all the time. Maybe there are some of us who are, like, you know, not obsessed with skin color. The world has changed, Carrie. It's not the sixties anymore. We are now in a post-racial age where we must—"

"Post-racial? I can't believe it. Did you really say that?" Carine's face battled multiple emotions—incredulity, disbelief, and vexation—until it settled upon murder. She shook her head. "Honestly, sometimes I don't even know how we got together, Anton. Do you ever hear yourself?"

"Do *you*?" he began, but she cut him off. "When you look in the mirror, Anton, what do you see?"

"I see myself. Just that. A guy who has his feet in two worlds. Who wants to act as a bridge between those two worlds."

She laughed humorlessly. "I'll tell you what. Just go with me to Georgia one time. Leave behind your Harvard sweatshirt and your checkbook and the fact that your daddy is governor. And what you will see on the faces of the white men on the streets of Augusta will tell you who you really are."

He rubbed his forehead in agitation. "Jesus Christ. It's like you're stuck in some time warp. Shit. My best friend is white. I don't think Bradley even notices my skin color when he sees me."

"You know why? Because you're so damn colorless, you're a ghost. Invisible. And if that's how you choose to go through this life, you shit-head, go right ahead. You go right ahead with your post-racial this and your Kumbaya that. I'll just call it what it is—an identity crisis."

He gripped his hand around his water glass to keep it from curling into a fist. So much for a pleasant celebratory meal. He had a sudden flash that it would always be like this with Carine—that she would challenge him, nudge him, provoke him. He saw a long string of tempestuous family gatherings, and suddenly, he wanted no part of it. His love for his parents was always reinforced by his gratitude—they had been a rich, successful couple, they could've adopted any kid, but they'd chosen to rescue him. He would not destroy his relationship with his family because of this headstrong, impetuous black girl who constantly seemed to want to battle the world. And him.

"Well? Black cat got your tongue?"

He laughed helplessly. "You see? You're incorrigible. Even your idioms are racialized."

"I didn't start it, baby. It started about three hundred years before I was born."

He shook his head in frustration. "You know, I've had a tough semester. I just finished my last exam, and we're supposed to be celebrating. Is it too much to ask that we have a nice, quiet meal?"

Carine put her hand on his thigh. "Is that what you want, baby?" she purred. "A nice, soft, pliant girlfriend?"

"I'm not sure," he said, bemused. "But hell, it'd be nice to find out what one looks like."

Her eyes flashed, but she kept up her new persona. "I see." She batted her eyes at him so coquettishly that he giggled. But then her hand moved higher up his thigh and he stopped giggling.

As if to teach him a lesson, she took him to her apartment after dinner and fucked his brains out. When they were done and his eyes were still misty, she leaned over his chest and whispered, "I hope you enjoyed your sweet Valley girl fuck."

CHAPTER TWENTY-ONE

The plan had been for Anton to return home immediately after finals. But as the time grew nearer, he found himself searching the Internet for a last-minute ticket to San Diego. Bradley and his friends from Stanford had rented a five-bedroom house on the beach for a week and had invited him. He had refused earlier, but now he was tempted. After the beach vacation, Brad planned on flying to South Korea and would not get home until the week after Christmas, and Anton didn't want to wait that long to see him. So Anton made a pact with himself—if he found a ticket for less than four hundred dollars, he would go.

The fare came to $463, but he booked it anyway. He needed to get away from Harvard and from home, needed to clear his head about Carine. Somehow they had lost their equilibrium, and things hadn't gotten back to where they were before the trip to the Cape. Now, try as he might, he could see her only through the eyes of his parents, and from that vantage point, he didn't much like what he saw. He could almost hear his parents say the words: Impetuous. Unstable. Not Our Kind.

Brad would not be so quick to judge. He had met Carine briefly and had seemed to like her well enough. If anyone could help Anton decide whether to break it off with her or not, it would be Brad.

Brad picked Anton up at the airport and drove him to the house they were sharing with three other guys, two of whom Anton knew. The third one, Jeff, was from Seattle and seemed nice enough, if a bit quiet. Anton never figured out who had bought the bottles of booze that lined the kitchen pantry—they were all underage and unable to buy alcohol legally—but the others had already started drinking, and there was nothing to do but join in.

He was a bit hungover when Brad shook him awake the next morning. "Come on," he said. "Throw on some sweats and let's go for a walk before the others wake up."

Anton was still groggy as they walked the nearly deserted beach. But it was nice to hear the sound of the waves, the cries of the gulls. Even in the morning fog, the Pacific looked so different from the Atlantic, with its promise of blue. Whatever his future brought, Anton hoped it included lots of travel. He would like to see all the oceans in the world before he turned forty.

Thoughts of the future made Carine bubble to the surface of his brain. This is your brain on Carine, he joked to himself, looking out at the fog, which seemed to have entered his head.

"So, this is great," Brad said, giving him a sidelong look. "I can't believe you're actually here."

"Me, neither. You're doing well?"

"Can't complain. Stanford's great. You?"

Anton sighed. "I'm okay. Actually, not so good." He slowed his pace. "It's Carine."

"What's wrong? Last time I was there, you couldn't keep your eyes off her. Or your hands."

"I still can't." He pointed to the wooden steps leading away from the beach. "Shall we sit?"

"So what's up?" Brad asked after they were settled, his face already red from the Southern California sun. "You just said you're still hot for her, right?"

Anton slipped off his sneakers and brushed the sand from his feet. "It's not that, Brad. It's just that she's, like, wild. Mouths off the weirdest stuff at the most inappropriate times."

"Like what?"

"Like . . ." And he told Brad the story of Carine's behavior at the Cape, noting Brad's shocked reaction with grim satisfaction.

"Wow," he said when Anton finished. "She said that to *Pappy*? Man, that's pretty rad."

"I know. And everything with her is about race. It drives me crazy." He stopped for a second, then took the plunge. "For instance, she said the only reason you don't . . . that you're not aware of my race is because I'm invisible. To you."

Brad frowned. "That's insulting." He looked at Anton, squinting in the sun. "Though I'm not sure which of us should be insulted. Both, I guess."

"Exactly. And when I said we didn't think along those lines, she mocked me." Anton stopped abruptly, feeling like a six-year-old tattle-tale, afraid that he was betraying Carine and painting her in a much harsher light than she deserved.

"Man, I tell you, these black chicks sure have a bug up their ass."

Anton turned his head sharply. Brad's tone was confiding, intimate, unself-conscious. He had said that thing about black women as if unaware that he was talking to a black man. Damn. Carine was right. Brad didn't even consider him black. But that was a good thing, wasn't it? I mean, Anton argued with himself, why would he? They'd known each other half their lives. They had double-dated together, had their first sexual experiences within two months of each other, gone to the same high school, been on the school's lacrosse team, vacationed together, gone rock-climbing together. Hell, he and Brad were like an old married couple. It would be downright odd if Bradley were suddenly aware of his blackness.

Damn Carine. She was messing with his head. If he had never met her, he never would have noticed what Brad had said, would've grinned and teased him about how many black chicks did he know and was his knowledge firsthand? This was what drove him crazy about Carine—how she took something beautiful and innocent, like his relationship with his best friend, and turned it into something sinister. Carine was a tortured person, that was it, and like most tortured people, she would drag down whomever was around her.

"Hey, dickhead," Bradley said. "You're not pissed by what I just said, are you?"

Anton stared at Brad; it was the first race-specific comment he had ever heard his friend make. He rubbed the rough stubble on his face, unsure how to answer.

"What I mean is, I wasn't making any specific comments about Carine's ass," Brad continued, a goofy grin on his face. "Although it's a monumentally great ass."

The sense of relief Anton felt was palpable. In response, he put Brad's head in a chokehold. "What's the matter, jerk?" he said. "Aren't you getting laid?"

Brad shook his way out of Anton's grasp. He dug his toes into the sand and then asked, "Seriously, though. What are you going to do? I mean, you still love her, yes?"

Anton looked out at the ocean, mulling over Brad's question. "I'm crazy about her," he said finally. "In many ways, I think she's the greatest person I've ever met. I mean, she's kind and loyal and funny and wicked smart. And she has a heart of gold."

"And the problem is?"

"The problem," Anton said slowly, "is that I don't know if I can live with her. It's exhausting. It's like . . . she wants me to be a better person than I really am." He looked at Brad, furrowing his brow. "You know me pretty well, Brad. You know I like my creature comforts. I'm . . . I'm basically a happy, easygoing guy, right?"

Bradley made a face. "If you were any more easygoing, you'd slide right into Hawaii."

"Well, there's nothing easy about Carine. She's too intense, man. It's like she wants to change the world *now*. Every fucking day."

Brad gave a single understanding nod. They sat in silence, listening to the ocean, and as the sun grew stronger, they removed their shirts, enjoying its warmth on their backs. "This is what we call," Brad finally said, imitating their eighth-grade social studies teacher, "a classic conundrum," they said in unison.

And that's exactly what it was. Anton felt young, inexperienced, and lost. He had come to California hoping Bradley would say something that would help him make up his mind, but here was the thing— Bradley was as young as he was. He wanted to talk to his father, but how could David possibly understand what he was feeling when he wasn't even sure what Brad really saw when he looked at him? What did Brad, what did all of them, see when they looked at him—the whitest black man in the world? Or the blackest white man? Which one was he? Whom did he want to be?

Without warning, Anton's mind went to his birth mom. Maybe she could've helped him solve the riddle. And then he scoffed at his own irrationality. If she had just been a mother to him, he wouldn't be in this situation in the first place. As it was, he had only two black male friends at Harvard. And if he posited this question to them, they would look at him with contempt or, worse, incomprehension.

He felt a sudden sharp pain in his side and yelped. Brad had poked him in the ribs and was laughing at the indignation on Anton's face. "Man, that chick's done a number on you. I've never seen you mope around like this."

"I'm not moping."

"Tell that to your face." Brad jumped to his feet, snapping Anton with his shirt as he did so. "Ah, enough of this shit. Come on, I'll race you to the house. We're having pancakes and bacon for breakfast."

A WEEK LATER, he and Brad shared a cab to the airport to catch their respective flights. The lines at security were thankfully short, and they decided to grab a quick bite before heading to their gates.

They flirted with their waitress, a dark-haired woman in her thirties who told them she was a surfer, and they left her a generous tip. Then they stood, grinning at each other.

"That was quite a week, huh?" Brad said.

"Great. I needed it. Thanks for letting me crash at the last minute."

"Any time. Well. See you back home in a couple of weeks. Dad said we're doing New Year's Eve at your place."

"Sounds great."

They hugged. Anton picked up his backpack, but Bradley lingered. "Hey," he said. "Don't make yourself crazy about the Carine thing. It will sort itself out."

Anton made a face. "Yeah, well, we'll see."

Brad's eyes searched his friend's face. "When it's time to break it off, *if* it's time, you'll know."

"How?"

"You'll just know."

Anton chuckled to himself as he walked toward his gate. This was what he'd spent almost five hundred dollars to come to California for—to hear Brad talk like Yoda. Well, one thing was clear. It wasn't time yet. The only thing he knew for certain after a week in California was that he was horny for Carine.

CHAPTER TWENTY-TWO

In the end, it was a white man who came between them and broke them apart. His name was Henry David Thoreau.

For each of the four years that Anton had been at Harvard, he had made an annual pilgrimage to Walden Pond. He had first discovered Thoreau's writing at sixteen, and it had opened up a world within him. He'd felt an immediate, almost mystical connection with a man with whom he shared little else—not race, or culture, not even a century. It was Thoreau who had introduced Anton to the idea that living a principled life was as much about what you didn't do as what you did. That what you rejected defined you as much as what you embraced. As a junior in high school, Anton had written an award-winning essay comparing Thoreau's "Resistance to Civil Government" to King's "Letter from a Birmingham Jail." It was Thoreau who'd made him want to become an English major; he had never mentioned to his dad or Pappy that Thoreau was the real reason he had chosen Harvard.

Anton had first visited Walden Pond at seventeen. He and David had driven there and spent the day walking through the nearby woods, sitting by the pond, reading Thoreau's writings out loud. They spoke but a few words to each other, but as they walked back to the car that evening, David had put his arm around his son's shoulders, and Anton had felt his chest expand with love and gratitude for his father.

His motives for inviting Carine to Walden in the spring of their final year at Harvard were unclear even to him. He had spent the past year tormented over what to do about their relationship. His reasons for being with Carine were elemental, primal, beyond articulation. His reasons for wanting to break up with her were intellectual. And every day, the tug-of-war between head and heart was tearing him down just a bit more.

It was a cold day in March with a big, dramatic sky. The woods crackled and complained as they stepped over twigs and dead leaves. Many of the tree branches were encrusted in frost. Carine had to stop every few minutes to blow her nose.

"So what do you do when you come here by yourself each year?"

He looked at her, surprised. "Just what we're doing."

"That's it? The same thing each year?"

"Yup."

She didn't say another word, but it was obvious that she didn't get it. He told himself it was okay, he didn't mind. But he did. Something pure and real had happened to him when he'd read *Walden* at sixteen. He remembered it well, that selfish moment of self-discovery, of finding something that belonged only to him. Up to that point, everything in his life had been borrowed. His bedroom was borrowed from a dead boy, as were his parents. His best friend was inherited, seeing as how Brad's dad and his dad were also the best of friends. The clothes on his back, the shoes on his feet, had been given to him. Whatever he was, whatever voice he might have developed, whatever pitch he may have learned to sing in, had been lost, muted, stolen from him. In broad daylight, in the middle of the day, he had been pulled out of his home, out of his old life, and transplanted into a new one. Without even knowing it, he constantly battled a film of inauthenticity that clung to him. Black boy in a white school. Black boy with light skin and golden eyes who looked vaguely foreign, exiled among people who liked the way he looked. Black boy who dressed so preppy that the occasional black person he encountered in his rich neighborhood—maid, janitor, gardener—looked at him with puzzled eyes, trying to solve the riddle of him. No, nothing in Anton's life had belonged to him until he got his own copy of *Walden*. And then it seemed to him that the book had given him a new lineage, a saintly, courageous, self-reliant man who needed only himself and nature for company and validation. A man who occupied his own skin comfortably and thoroughly, a man who never had to ask himself the deadly, unknowable question, "Who am I?"

It was private, this obsession with Thoreau, so private that he had never shared it with Carine or anyone other than his dad. So why should he mind if she didn't realize that he had given her a gift, his very soul, when he'd invited her along? Why should he mind her chatter, on the way back to Cambridge, about how Thoreau had influenced Gandhi in India and King right here at home—inane facts that every schoolboy knew, but ones that she was reading from some pamphlet that she'd picked up in downtown Concord?

They had eaten hamburgers in the car on the way home but decided to get a cup of coffee at Dunkin' Donuts after returning to Cambridge. He placed her cup of latte before her, and she took a few sips before saying, "This was a wonderful day. Thank you."

Her words moved him, precisely because they were unexpected. In that moment he felt closer to her than he had in several months. He looked at her with the gratitude that the giver feels when his gift has been appreciated. "Really? You had a good time?"

She looked puzzled. "Of course. It just feels so good to get out of town once in a while. I'm so sick of being in Cambridge all the time." She smiled. "And it was wonderful spending time with you."

He smiled back, but his heart sank. This is what the day had been to her—an excursion. They could've gone to the Boston Aquarium, for all the difference it made. To her, the trip had been a picnic, not a pilgrimage.

He had felt many emotions around Carine—anger, frustration, ecstasy, contentment—but he'd never been lonely before. He felt lonely now because he'd offered her the truest, purest part of himself, and she had not known it.

He was arguing with himself about the unfairness of his thinking when she said, "Guess how much time Thoreau spent in prison for his civil disobedience?"

He shrugged irritably. "I don't know. A couple of weeks?"

She looked at him, a glint in her eyes. "A night. A single night."

"Okay."

"Guess how much time King spent in prison for *his* civil disobedience."

Too late, he saw the trap. When he spoke, his voice was cold. "I don't know. And I don't really care."

"Eight days in Birmingham jail, alone. And many, many more times before and after."

"So what's your point, Carine?"

She shrugged. "Nothing. Just that he's part of a trend, right? In a country where one third of black men are serving time, why would King have been different?"

"I thought we were talking about Thoreau."

She rested her arms on the table and leaned in. "Thoreau's theory, baby. Martin is practice."

"I see." And he did, saw it clearly, saw before him endless years of argument and miscommunication. He felt a sudden sense of liberation, as if the last thread binding her to him had snapped.

"That's all you got to say? 'I see'?"

He drained the last of his coffee and pulled himself up to his full height. "Yes," he said. "That's all." He faked a yawn. "You ready to go? I have a long day tomorrow."

Neither of them said much as he walked her home to her apartment. Anton felt enveloped in a cold white silence. But inside that silence, impenetrable by Carine's voice or the sound of car horns or the desultory laughter of passersby, his thoughts were as sharp and lethal as ice. He glanced down at her as they walked and, for the first time, didn't find her beautiful. The beauty that had dazzled and blinded him fell away, as if he had drunk a potion in a fairy tale, and he found himself walking beside an ordinary black girl, one who hid her insecurities behind a facade of bravado and radicalism. Her radicalism is phony, he thought, because it keeps her from seeing the world, blinds her to its mysteries and charms. Even her intellectualism is suspect because it's not open-minded and skeptical and probing but, rather, circular, chasing its own tail. To chastise Thoreau for having spent only a single night in jail was to miss the forest for the trees.

"You coming in?" she asked when they reached the front door.

He hesitated. Would it be easier to say what he had to say in her living room? But then he felt her gaze on him and saw the uncertainty in her eyes and he knew that Carine suspected something. Brad's words came back to him, except now they didn't sound like something inside a Chinese fortune cookie. Now they sounded like the wisdom of the ages. *When it's time, you'll know.*

"Carine," he said, and the word must've carried more than he realized —a sweet regret, an embarrassed gentleness—because already her eyes were filling up with tears and she was beginning to turn away. Still, he forced himself to go on. "I'm sorry. This isn't working for me."

"I know." She brushed away her tears with such force that he wanted to take her hand in his to make her stop.

The wind swiveled the dead leaves at their feet, and he shivered a bit against the chill of the night, against the deadly cold entering his body.

It would be hard to give up this impetuous, lost, blundering girl with her loud mouth and her lofty opinions and her bruised heart. At that moment, he loved her more than he ever had.

But then he thought back to Walden Pond and the solitude that he'd felt the first time he'd been there on his own. *When it's time, you'll know.* He knew. Now was the time, two months before graduation, *now*, before they made decisions driven by sentimentality or inertia that would tie their futures together, *now*, before they wasted the next decade of their lives trying to mix oil with water.

Carine looked up at him and he closed his eyes, bracing himself for a verbal assault of recriminations and insults. So he was startled to feel her fingers brushing his right cheek. "Bye, Anton," he heard her murmur. "I hope you find what you're looking for."

He kept his eyes closed. The world looked safer that way, in the dark. When he finally opened them, the front door had shut and she was gone.

CHAPTER TWENTY-THREE

Anton returned home the day after graduation, away from the possibility of running into Carine or any of her friends. He knew he would be back in the fall to attend Harvard Law School, but she would be gone by then, back to Georgia, and he wouldn't have to tense each time he entered the Coop or the Harvard Book Store or any of their other haunts.

She had sent him a long email the week before graduation, telling him her future plans—she was going to take some time off and then go to grad school in international relations somewhere in the South—and asking him to stay in touch. She had included the phone number to her parents' home, something she'd never shared with him. She also wrote that her parents were going to be in town for graduation, and would he like to have breakfast with them? He found this curious and then, upon reflection, mildly offensive, since she'd made no previous attempt to invite him to meet them. But the part of the email that made him guffaw was the postscript. It read: "Please say hi to your folks from me. I really enjoyed my time with them."

Was it really possible that two people could see the world in such different ways? Were they all like those blind men, each one describing a different part of the elephant? He traced the disintegration of their relationship to that disastrous Thanksgiving weekend at the Cape. Was it possible that Carine really had seen it differently? Dimly, he recalled something she'd said about how political debates and arguments had been part of her family life. At that time, he had heard the statement as a challenge and a taunt. But what if she hadn't meant it that way at all? What if Carine, the daughter of an African father, saw debate as a way of claiming her Americanism?

Dammit. This was precisely the reason he had broken it off, this twisted logic, this maddening way she had of messing with his head. He had not imagined her rudeness that day, nor his parents' relief when he'd told them last week that he and Carine were no longer an item. His mom, who seldom had an ill word to say about anyone, had gone so far as to say, "Well, there was just a degree of hostility there that was . . . unnecessary."

He spent half a day composing a response to her email in his head. And then it came to him. The whole beauty of being broken up with someone was that you didn't have to reply.

Still, it wasn't until he was on the plane at Logan airport with his parents the day after graduation that he relaxed. He would never see Carine again. And instead of nicking him like a blunt razor, the thought soothed him.

He looked out the plane window. Boston looked blue and sunny and distant, sort of like the future that awaited him. Law school would be a challenge, but he was up for it. His parents had been ecstatic when he'd gotten in, David more so, because his son would be following in his footsteps yet again. And like David decades earlier, Anton had graduated summa cum laude from Harvard College.

Anton reclined in his plane seat and yawned. He had no plans for the summer except hanging out with Brad and their friends, going fishing, swimming in the lake, and playing soccer. At some point he would run up to the Cape for a few days to visit alone with Pappy. Or Pappy might come down to see them—Uncle Connor was apparently engineering a political event with three generations of Colemans in attendance.

"Happy to be going home?" Delores asked from across the aisle.

Anton beamed. "More than I can say."

BOOK THREE
November 2012

CHAPTER TWENTY-FOUR

Anton Coleman stood before the microphone, blinded by the flash of the cameras. A trickle of sweat ran down his face. It was hot under the klieg lights. Out of the corner of his eye, he could see his parents standing in the wings, the wattage of David's smile even brighter than the stage lights. He tried to think, but it was impossible, his thoughts scrambled by the raucous crowd chanting his last name over and over again. Anton smiled his toothy grin, and their cheers grew even louder. He ran his fingers through his hair in a nervous gesture and flashed an imploring look at Uncle Connor, who was standing at the bottom of the stage, part of the cheering crowd. For the next thirty seconds, the sound of their celebration mixed with the sound of the floor monitors pleading for quiet.

"Thank you," Anton said. "Thank you. Thanks. Please." He made a gesture with his hand, at once placating and commanding, asking them to take their seats. "Wow," he said as the crowd fell silent. "What a night. Friends, we have made history tonight." And with that, they were back on their feet, stomping, cheering, hooting in the Hilton ballroom.

Anton turned slightly to his right, to where his father was standing just out of the line of vision. David was pumping both fists in the air, looking happier than he had on any previous election night that Anton could remember. Anton laughed spontaneously, different from the slightly strained smiles and grins with which he had greeted his supporters as he'd strode through the room a few minutes earlier. It had been David's idea that Anton personally thank and greet all the campaign workers from the floor before making his acceptance speech, and although Anton had agreed at once, these interactions never came easily to him. Unlike his father, who had grown to genuinely love the glad-handing with voters, Anton was a wonk, focused on what he wanted to accomplish once he got into the attorney general's office. The election was simply the means to an end. Throughout the campaign, Anton had been acutely aware of a slightly ironic internal critic who mocked him as he tried to play the role of politician. He had, after all, grown up in the age of Barack Obama's cool and Jon Stewart's puncturing wit, and the internal critic seemed to be lodged permanently in his body.

What he had no doubt about, however, was his vow to clean up the AG's office.

He pulled his carefully prepared speech out of his pocket and cleared his throat. He had practiced the victory speech enough times to have it memorized. He would begin by thanking his parents and repeating that their state had made history tonight by electing the first father-son team as governor and attorney general. Then he'd get into the laundry list of challenges that lay ahead of them.

They were finally quiet, waiting for him. He opened his mouth to speak and found that he couldn't. All at once, the momentousness of the occasion hit him—he had graduated from law school just a few years ago, had worked briefly as a trial lawyer and then served as a federal prosecutor. And now here he was, the youngest ever AG in the state. His eyes filled with tears and he chewed on his lower lip, trying to regain his composure. He looked around the crowded room, his eyes searching for the one person he knew wouldn't be there—Pappy. What a triumph this night would've been for him. But Pappy had died nine months ago, felled by a massive stroke.

Anton looked into the crowd and started again. "There is one person absent tonight who should've been here," he said. "And that's my granddad, Senator Harold Coleman." He glanced up at the ceiling, as if expecting to find the old man there, and pumped his fist in the air. "Pappy, this night is for you."

The crowd roared. Connor gave him an approving thumbs-up, as if this had been part of the prepared remarks. Anton looked away, a trifle annoyed. That was the thing with politicians and their handlers—everything was fair game, everything was fodder, and nothing was left to chance or spontaneity. But then he remembered how he had been lagging in the polls just before Pappy passed away. Their own polling had shown that voters thought he was too young and inexperienced, that they suspected him of riding into office on his father's coattails. The day after Pappy's funeral, Connor had released to the press a picture of Anton by his grandfather's gravesite. His face was grief-stricken, pensive, and the way the afternoon sun hit his hair from behind gave him an ethereal look. His girlfriend Jenny's gloved hand lay lightly on his shoulder as she consoled him. It was a private, intensely intimate moment, and somehow, the fact that the picture was all over the Internet didn't lessen the intimacy. Anton had been furious at Connor for releasing it, David had been philosophical, and Connor himself had remained silent in the face of Anton's protestations. But a poll released the following week showed Anton in the lead for the first time, a lead that he never lost. Connor had taught him the oldest axiom in politics—you take your weakest card and play it. Not only had Connor played on the public's misgivings about political dynasties, he had doubled down on it. He had not tried to hide Anton's family background—rather, he had flaunted it, reminded everyone of the senator's long years of service to the state. And then he had asked that they give an opportunity to his grandson—Connor had long since banned the word "adopted" from descriptions of Anton's family relationships—to continue that tradition of service.

So it was understandable that Uncle Connor thought the reference to Pappy was canned. So be it. Anton glanced at his notes and said, "We all know why you're really here. The governor will address you in just a few moments." He waited for the applause to subside and then turned toward Delores and David, waiting in the wings. "Mom and Dad, I love you." His words echoed through the cavernous room. He paused for a second and then pulled out the crowd-pleasing line of the night: "And Jenny, thank you for putting up with me this past year, as I've traveled from one end of this mighty state to the other. I couldn't have done it without you." As he expected, the crowd of campaign workers went wild. Chants of "We want Jenny, we want Jenny" rang out, and from her perch in the first row, Jenny leaped to her feet, turned around, and waved to the crowd. She blew Anton a little kiss and he grinned.

By the time he was winding down his victory speech, his shirt was soaked with sweat, but he didn't mind, swept up in the enthusiasm of the crowd cheering at every wonky proposal as if he had scored a touchdown. The usual kernel of loneliness lodged deep within whenever he was in a crowd had not surfaced tonight and he was grateful, wanting to enjoy the moment. "So let's give it up for the governor of our great state, David H. Coleman," he yelled, and the din in the room grew to an ear-splitting level.

David strode onto the stage, grinning from ear to ear, enveloping Anton in a bear hug that almost knocked the younger man off his feet. "Whoa, Dad," Anton whispered, but the microphone picked it up and the crowd loved it. After a long moment of simply gazing at his son with pride—a moment when Anton had goose bumps all over his body—David finally took the microphone. "Friends," he boomed, flinging his arms wide open, "thank you for being here to celebrate the happiest and proudest day of my life."

Anton looked over to see Delores wiping the tears from her eyes. She caught him looking at her and winked. He smiled, looked away, and out of the blue, as happened every time he accomplished something— when he'd been named captain of the school lacrosse team, when he'd walked down the stage clutching his high school diploma, after he had finished law school—he thought of *her*. Where was she now? If she still lived in the state, she would've heard of him winning tonight, right? Right? Even if she lived on the streets, in the gutters, surely she would hear about her son, the fourth most powerful man in the state. But who was he kidding? She was most likely dead, or so out of her mind, or had so many other kids, that she probably had forgotten she ever had a son named Anton.

Some of the disgust and loathing he felt must've shown on his face, because David threw him a quizzical look. Anton recovered immediately, patted his father's back, and then went over to sit on a stool that someone had thoughtfully placed on the side of the stage while David gave a variation on his stump speech, which Anton knew so well that he sometimes would recite it to himself as a way of lulling himself to sleep after a long day on the campaign trail. So he struck his listening pose— thumb pushing up his lower lip a bit, slight frown on his face, head nodding in agreement every few seconds—and let his mind wander. Did she read the newspaper? Watch TV? Was she so far gone that she might not connect the dots to realize Attorney General Anton Coleman was the son she had discarded? If she was alive and well enough to know what she had thrown away, he wished her a lifetime of regret.

"Aaaanton, I love you," a female supporter screamed, interrupting David's speech and Anton's reverie, and before they could react, a male voice responded, "Jenny, I love you," and the crowd began to laugh appreciatively when another female voice cried, "Jenny, I love you, too," and David, quick-witted as ever, leaned in to the microphone and boomed, "Well, folks, I guess we just proved we ain't Alabama," and the room erupted in whistles and whoops. Everybody got the governor's reference to having signed the bill legalizing gay marriage in the state. Playing to the gallery, David half-turned to look at his son, his tall, lithe frame shaking silently with laughter, and Anton felt compelled to stand up and wave to the crowd. Thoughts of his mother had soured his mood slightly so that his smile was a bit strained. Only those who knew him well—Jenny, for instance—knew how uncomfortable he was made by the doting of strangers. He was not a natural politician with an insatiable need to be adored by millions. Still, he felt obliged to please the crowd by landing a long kiss on Jenny's lips when she, along with Delores, finally joined their men on the stage. He and Jenny had been dating only about eleven months, and already the first fissures had begun to appear in their relationship, but this crowd of young campaign workers and supporters didn't need to know that. No matter how much he wanted to focus on law and policy, there was a showbiz aspect to politics in the twenty-first century, and the story of how he had administered first aid to Jenny after a skiing accident in New Hampshire had even made the papers. Somebody on the ski slopes had apparently recognized him, shot a video of him making a tourniquet for her, and posted it on YouTube. That Jenny was a statuesque blonde who ran one of the IT start-ups in the state and he was the scion of a political dynasty made for a good story. It was almost inevitable that he would ask her out on a date; it was almost inevitable that, within weeks, she began to appear at his side at important political events, Uncle Connor beaming every time.

Anton followed his parents off the stage, bounding down the six steps that led to the floor of the ballroom, the knowing voice in his head working overtime—*There he goes, the young, dynamic new AG, descending the steps without so much as using the handrail*—and was immediately mobbed by supporters. Each one, it seemed, wanted something. Some of them shook his hand, some posed for pictures, some thumped his back, some told him exactly what he should do the day he assumed office. He smiled, he nodded, he winked, he shook hands, he hugged, he kissed. Mostly, he kept his eyes on his father's back, looking to follow the path that David was carving out of the long room and out the door.

THREE HOURS LATER, it was just the two of them in the small sitting room David had off his bedroom in the Governor's Mansion. Delores had gone to bed; Bradley had offered to drop Jenny and Uncle Connor home. And really, they should be headed to sleep also, but they couldn't stop grinning at each other, couldn't stop reminiscing about the campaign. David had been reelected with sixty-five percent of the vote. And despite a few early scares, it had been a relatively easy campaign for Anton, his path smoothed by Uncle Connor's extensive contacts, David's impassioned endorsement, the outpouring of sympathy and goodwill that resulted from Pappy's death, and his fortuitous rescue of Jenny. Anton had to ruefully admit that in spite of his best efforts to make the campaign about the issues, it had been about everything but the issues. It hadn't hurt that in September, *The Monthly*, the largest magazine in the state, had put him on the cover and named him "The Most Eligible Bachelor in the State." Bradley and his other married friends had a field day with the headline and teased him mercilessly. David and Connor had chortled and immediately come up with a strategy to target female voters on Election Day. Only Delores seemed to have a different reaction—she had phoned Anton and asked what he was waiting for when he'd found a wonderful girl like Jenny, reminding him that he was not getting any younger.

"So," David said, pulling out a cigar and handing one to his son. "How does it feel to be an elected representative of the people at long last?"

Anton pretended to shudder. He leaned forward as his father lit a cigar and handed it to him. "Well. Being AG is not exactly like being in the swamp of politics." He grinned. "It's more—lofty."

David took a long drag, eyeing his son. "We'll see, my boy, we'll see."

They laughed and then fell quiet, both of them exhausted by the day. David rocked in his chair, eyes closed, a small smile on his lips. The cigar burned in his left hand.

"Dad," Anton said.

David opened his eyes. "Yeah?"

"I just wanted to say . . . thank you."

"Quite the contrary, my dear Anton. It's not often that a man has the pleasure of experiencing a historic day like today. You've made me very happy."

"Dad. One more thing." Anton hesitated, then started again. "I think we should agree not to discuss the cases before me outside of work. That is, I don't want to treat you any differently than I would any other governor I'd have as a boss."

David stared expressionlessly at Anton for a moment. Then he smiled. "I agree. And I expected nothing different from you."

Anton knew the relief showed on his face. "Good deal." He stared at the floor for a second and then looked up. "I want to give the voters exactly what I promised—the cleanest, most ethical AG's office ever." He shushed the voice in his head that sang, *Corny, that's just corny.*

David nodded. "Absolutely." He rolled his eyes. "After what we've just been through, it's the least they can expect." He was referring to the corruption scandal that had embroiled Peter Duke, the former AG. Peter, who had held the office for over twenty years, had decided not to seek reelection, thereby paving the way for Anton to run.

They sat for another moment, and then David stifled a yawn. "Got to get to bed," he muttered. "Tomorrow's going to be a long day." But he made no move to get up. Instead he asked, "How come Jenny didn't stay the night?"

Anton shrugged. "She didn't want to."

"Everything okay between you two?"

He shrugged again. "I dunno. I guess so."

"I see." David waited a moment, and when he spoke, his voice was gentle. "You're going to have a lot on your plate in just a few weeks. If you think the relationship is over, it'd be best to let her know now. Don't you think?"

Anton let out his breath slowly. "Mom likes her," he said absently. Then, "I'm afraid it's gonna look like I just used her for the election. You saw the crowd tonight—they love her."

David nodded. He looked out the window into the dark and then at Anton. "If I were advising you only as a fellow politician, I'd agree with you. To some people, it *will* look like you used her. But I'm talking to you as your father. One thing I've learned about politics—you've got to carve out a little space that's all your own. A place where you don't let in any of the outside chatter. If you don't, you're finished. Know what I mean?"

"Not really."

"What I'm saying is, you can't let everything be about politics. If you do, you end up soulless, not knowing who you are. Some things have to belong only to you. Take me, for instance. When I—when Delores and I—first took you in, Pappy hoped I'd enter politics someday. And he was nervous, you know, how it would come across in this lily-white state, us fostering a boy who looked like you. He told me on the phone that he was opposed to it, that it was political suicide. He said my future opponents would have a field day with it." His voice cracked. "And they did. By golly, the bastards did."

"Dad—"

"No, it's okay. Let me finish. So after we'd had you for a few months, I invited Pappy to come visit. He came and stayed for a week. I don't know if you remember. He and I didn't discuss his apprehensions again. He just watched us going about our daily life. I took him to see you play soccer one evening, I remember that. And then, during the drive to the airport, I asked him if he still thought having you was a bad idea. If he believed that my being governor or senator someday would make me happier than fostering you." David fell silent, a muscle in his jaw moving compulsively. "And he didn't say a word. But when he got out of the car, he leaned in and said that I was a better man than he'd ever be. And that's how I knew that he approved."

Anton didn't know what he found more shocking—that Pappy once was opposed to him, or that his father could be so affected by the memory. This was unlike Dad, to be so sentimental. He looked at his father closely and noticed how tired David looked, took in the thinning hair, the sudden stoop of the shoulders, and the unhealthy paleness of his skin. Dad's getting old, he thought, and it frightened him to think that the man who had always seemed invincible to him, supremely capable, the most self-assured man in the room, could show the first signs of mortality.

Anton reached over and put his hand on David's shoulder. "It's late, Dad," he said. "You're tired. Let's go to bed."

But David shrugged his hand away. "What I'm trying to tell you is—what I'm trying to *teach* you—is you gotta be guided by your own lights. If you love Jenny, marry her. If you don't, then let her go. But for chrissake, don't use her. She's a woman, not a political mascot." He took a breath, then turned toward Anton. "The most important decision you'll ever make in your life, son, is whom you marry. I pray that you find someone who makes you as happy as Dee has made me."

Without warning, a picture of Carine making blueberry pancakes for him on a Sunday morning flashed in Anton's head. He had mentioned

Delores's famous pancakes to Carine during a stroll at a Saturday farmers' market, and she had risen early the next day to make him breakfast. He shook the memory out of his head. "There's no woman as good as Mom," he said. "She's the best."

David smiled. "No argument there."

Anton rose to his feet and stretched. He faked a mighty yawn. "Lord, I'm tired," he said.

As he could've predicted, David rose to his feet immediately. "Let's get you to bed. We can't have the new AG facing the world sleep-deprived."

CHAPTER TWENTY-FIVE

They were in the nation's capital, Anton and Katherine. It felt good to be out of the state with her, away from the scrutiny that usually followed him. Earlier this afternoon, he had delivered a well-received keynote address at the national convention of federal prosecutors. It was an honor to be asked, but what was even better was getting together with his former colleagues in the Department of Justice. Even among the smart, ambitious men and women who made up the government's lawyers, Anton had distinguished himself for the systematic way in which he had targeted white-collar crime in his state. In fact, during the 2012 campaign he had played up his successful crackdown on the money-laundering scheme involving local casinos—an achievement that Eric Holder, the nation's AG, had mentioned in his introduction earlier today.

But now he was off the clock, and he and Katherine were looking forward to dinner at Tamarind, the new Indian restaurant on Capitol Hill that they'd heard so much about. They had been dating only a few months, but he was plenty smitten by her. He had met Katherine Banks at a fund-raiser for the human rights organization where she worked, and drawn to her good looks, he had gotten her phone number before he left that evening. What made him ask her out on a second date, and then a third, was the fact that unlike many of the women he came in contact with, Katherine seemed not the least bit impressed by his position or his family history. That and the fact that she teased him mercilessly, deflating his self-importance and ego every chance she got. The only girl in an Irish family of four boys, Katherine had learned to stand up to her brothers' teasing from an early age and had, as a result, grown sharp elbows. Anton thought she was the most intriguing combination of femininity and an almost masculine briskness that he'd ever known.

It was a beautiful night in May, and they decided to walk to the restaurant. Katherine looked ravishing in her black shirt and tight blue jeans, but Anton eyed her high-heeled sandals dubiously. "It's at least a seven-block walk," he said. "You think you can walk in those things?"

"Watch me."

He laughed, took her hand, and smiled at the doorman as they exited the hotel. It was a warm night, and the District was brimming with young, dynamic couples much like themselves, out on the town, celebrating their good looks and golden careers. They were the next generation of movers and shakers, and they knew it. Some of them, like him, were thoroughbreds, groomed for success. Others were strivers, those who fled the mill towns of Cleveland and Detroit and the farmlands of Iowa and Nebraska, trading on personal smarts and searing ambition. It didn't matter how they'd gotten here, really, just that they had. They all worked like Roman slaves during the day at their jobs at the White House or on the Hill or in the lobbying firms that formed a kind of parallel government in the District. But the nights belonged to them, and they poured out of their tiny but well-appointed apartments eager for entertainment. Fueled by their expensive wines and the latest microbrews, munching on grass-fed beef and organic chicken, they traded the latest gossip, the news from the Hill, insider information on sex scandals that had yet to be reported and indictments that would soon be front-page news. They thought they were happy, that these were the best days of their lives and that they were smart enough to recognize them as such. If, when they returned home to Cleveland or Omaha for the holidays and were asked by a machinist uncle or a farmer cousin, "But what exactly do you *do* down there?" and were at a loss for an answer, they assumed the fault was with the relative and not with them. Or they might try and explain that the age of *doing* was over, that cars and toys and machinery could all be manufactured *over there* at a fraction of the cost, that it was all about information now, and that they were the vanguard of this new age. If the relative still looked puzzled, they would look away with some irritation and, at the first available chance, text a friend back in the District, "Counting the days until I'm back home."

Anton was enjoying the anonymity of being in the city with his girl, and he felt a looseness in his limbs, in his gait, that he seldom experienced back home. They had made love just before getting ready for dinner, and he could smell the damp scent of sex in her hair as they walked. A warm wind blew, and he was glad that he'd made reservations on the restaurant's outdoor patio. Tomorrow they would check out a few of the Smithsonians before meeting Andrea, a friend from Harvard who now worked at the National Portrait Gallery, and her husband for dinner. He had been desperately busy the past few weeks—the Right to Life folks had descended on the state in droves after a federal appeals court had ruled in favor of a hospital that wanted to pull the plug on an indigent man who had been in a coma for six years—and Anton needed this time away. Also, he was really enjoying getting to know Katherine. Things were passionate and romantic between them, and back home it was impossible to spend an entire weekend away from the office.

They were seated right away when they got to the restaurant, the perfume from a nearby honeysuckle bush wafting toward them. They ordered drinks and then relaxed in the comfortable patio chairs. Even though they had debated whether to risk ordering martinis at an ethnic restaurant, they were not disappointed.

They were smiling at each other across the table when a woman in her early twenties approached their table. "Excuse me," she said, and Anton looked up at her. A few tables away, he could see a few of her friends giggling at her boldness.

"Yeah?"

"Aren't you Anton Coleman?" she asked.

He flung a quick, apologetic look at Katherine before saying, "Yes."

The young woman smiled. "I thought so." She looked over her shoulder at her friends. "Actually, we—my friends and I—we have a bet. One of them says you were named the Sexiest Man Alive by *People* magazine last year."

He was used to such occurrences, but it didn't make them less embarrassing. "I wish," he said lightly. "I'm afraid your friend is wrong."

"Oh." The woman stared at him, unsure how to keep the conversation going. She blushed. "Well, I think they should've," she said in a rush.

He heard Katherine gasp, a light sound that perhaps only he heard. He rose to his feet and stuck his hand out. "Well, thanks for stopping by. Enjoy your dinner."

"Oh. Okay. Thanks." He stood watching as she walked back to her table, guarding against any further intrusions. He rolled his eyes as he sat down. "They're all a little drunk."

Katherine gave him a bemused look. "Apparently, women get that way in your presence."

He tried laughing it off. "Aw, come on. You can't blame this on me."

"No, of course not. I just don't know whether to be flattered or insulted when these little episodes happen whenever I'm out with you in public."

He reached out for her hand. "Baby, forget it. She's just some silly college girl. Now, where were we?"

"We were complimenting each other on our good judgment in ordering these fabulous martinis." She looked down at her glass, which was almost empty, and Anton immediately signaled the waiter for another round.

They began their meal by ordering Tamarind's signature appetizer, a combo of crispy spinach and yogurt, and devoured it within minutes. "Wow," Katherine said. "Guess we were both hungry."

He looked at her knowingly. "Certain activities always give me a good appetite."

Katherine laughed. "Yup. Nothing wrong with your appetites. I can vouch for that."

He leaned over and kissed her. Her mouth tasted faintly of cumin. "Wanna get another one of these?" he said, pointing to the empty dish.

"Sure."

They went through the second appetizer and then ordered their main dishes. As they waited, Katherine asked his opinion about a human rights violation case in Rwanda that she was currently working on. She knew more about human rights law than he ever would but Anton still appreciated her occasionally asking for his counsel. Her auburn hair fell across her face as they talked, and he resisted the urge to smooth it back.

The chicken sizzled on its platter as it was served to them, and they tackled it in silence. This was another thing Anton appreciated about Katherine. Unlike so many women he had dated, she ate as heartily as a man and didn't pretend to hide her appetite out of some misguided sense of femininity. After they were done, they felt compelled to look at the dessert menu, even as they swore they couldn't eat another bite. But the desserts looked fabulous, and they decided to split a mango kulfi. They were waiting on it when Anton's phone rang. It was Brad. Anton turned the ringer off. "It's okay." He smiled. "I'll call him back tomorrow."

"You can answer. I don't mind."

"Nah. He probably wants to hear how the talk went today." Anton grinned wolfishly. "Besides, I have some other plans for tonight, which involve you."

She began to laugh. Other than his father, Katherine was the only person he knew who laughed silently. Anton thought it was the most charming thing in the world.

His phone buzzed again. Good God. It was Uncle Connor. He checked his watch. It was after ten-thirty. What the heck? Had they all forgotten that he was out of town? He decided to ignore the call. "Sorry," he said. "I'm gonna turn this sucker off for the night."

"You don't have to."

"Yes, I do." He reached for the phone when it rang again. Uncle Connor. Anton felt a sense of unease. They sure were being persistent. Something was going on, and it probably had to do with the Right to Life case. He mouthed a "sorry" to Katherine and answered the phone. "Hi."

"Anton? Where are you? We've been trying to get ahold of you."

"I'm at a restaurant in D.C. Did you forget I'm here?"

"No, of course not. Anton. Listen. I have some bad news, I'm afraid."

"What'd they do? Firebomb the hospital?"

"What? Who?"

"The Right to Lifers. This is about them, right?"

"What? No. No, forget them. This is . . ." Connor's voice cracked. "Anton. You need to come home. David's had a heart attack. It's not looking good."

Anton's heart fluttered so dramatically that for a moment he thought he was having a sympathy attack. His mind went blank, like a movie screen after the projector had snapped. Katherine was making inquiring gestures, and asking him something, but he couldn't hear because of the whistling sound of his fear.

"Anton? You okay, son? I'm sorry to—"

"I . . ." He tried collecting his thoughts and found that he couldn't. "Where's Mom? How is Mom?"

"She's okay. She's with him. You need to calm down, son. Take a few deep breaths and . . ."

At last, the fearful thought that was welling inside him like a bubble burst to the surface and he asked, "Is Dad alive? Tell me the truth, Uncle Connor. I can handle the truth." His eyes welled with tears and he looked down at the table, but not before seeing Katherine's stricken face. "Please don't lie to me."

"Anton. Listen to me. He's alive. They're trying to stabilize him so they can do a heart cath to see the extent of the damage to the heart muscle. Okay? It's serious, but you know your father. He's tough. He's hanging in there."

Perhaps it was the relief he felt that tore away the blankness, but his mind was his own again, sharp, focused. He signaled to the waiter for the check, pantomiming that he needed it urgently. Katherine was already rifling through her purse for her credit card, and he let her pay. He heard her ask the waiter to call for a cab right away, and he nodded approvingly. "Where is he now?" he said into the phone.

"He's at Metro-General. So you know he's in good hands."

Anton wanted to ask a thousand more questions, but he was wasting time. They had to get to the airport, fast. But then he looked at his watch and realized it was close to eleven P.M. Would there be a flight out so late? "Uncle Connor," he said urgently. "Can you have someone check about the last flight out? We can leave for the airport directly from here." He stood up as Katherine hurriedly signed the credit card receipt. "Would National or Dulles be a better bet?"

"There are no flights from D.C. at this hour. I already checked. Now, listen to me. We have a private plane waiting for you. One of Bradley's friends has offered it. You need to make your way to the private airport where it will be waiting. Grab a piece of paper and write down the address."

SIX MINUTES LATER, they were in a cab tearing through the city. Katherine was on the phone with the hotel, explaining the situation, asking the person to store their luggage until they figured out what to do. Anton was on hold as the hospital staff tried to reach Delores, who was in the ICU with her husband.

"Hi, honey," Delores said, and the emptiness in her voice sent a chill down Anton's spine. He fought back the tears that flooded his eyes. "Hey, Mom," he said softly. "How you holding up?"

"I'm okay, baby," she replied, but he was listening to her tone, not her words.

"Listen, I'm on my way home," he said. "Everything is going to be fine, okay? Mom? I promise you. He's going to be fine."

In the brief silence, he could hear people's voices in the background. When she spoke, she lowered her voice. "The doctor said it was a massive heart attack. He says it's a good thing your father had the attack at the office. The paramedics were there within minutes, you know. They had to shock him three times."

Anton looked out of the cab window, struggling to control his fear. "So . . . did they say what the prognosis is?"

"They won't know anything until they do the heart cath. But for that, they need him to be stable."

Anton nodded. "Okay. Okay." Breathe, he said to himself. Breathe. But then his throat constricted as he thought of his father gasping for breath, and he couldn't bear the thought of being this obscenely healthy while his father lay struggling for his life. "Mom," he said. "When you go back into the ICU, I want you to tell Dad that I'll be there in a few hours. Okay? Tell him that." He paused. "And tell him I need his advice on a legal case before me. So he has to be well enough in a few days to help me with it. Can you do that?"

"He can't be thinking of work, Anton. He's not even conscious."

"Mom. I just want him to know that . . . we're not giving up on him, okay? So can you please do this? Just trust me, right?"

"Whatever you say. You be safe, honey." Delores sounded wooden, numb. It's because she has looked across the river and seen death again on the opposite bank, Anton thought.

Was it his imagination, or did they have the slowest driver in D.C.? And were they hitting every friggin' red light in town? Anton fought the urge to kick the seat in frustration. He pulled a twenty-dollar bill out of his pocket. "As we said, this is an emergency," he said, leaning forward so that the driver could hear him. "Here's a little something extra for stepping on the gas."

The driver turned his head a bit. "Speeding ticket costing over two hundred dollars, mister," he said. "Cop stop me, you going to get even more late." That didn't prevent him from accepting the cash, although as far as Anton could tell, it made no appreciable difference in his driving.

The phone rang again. It was Bradley to say he'd just arrived at the hospital and not to worry, he'd be with Delores until Anton arrived. Uncle Connor was already at the hospital, Brad informed him. "Thanks, man," Anton said, thinking there hadn't been an occasion in his life, sad or celebratory, that he hadn't shared with Brad. Though what he'd give not to have to share this.

He turned toward Katherine, and she shifted in her seat and snuggled against him. "I'm so sorry, sweetheart," she whispered, and he was glad that she was with him. He couldn't imagine being alone in this dreadful taxi, with the incense burning on the dashboard and the slowest driver in the world at the wheel. He kissed the top of Katherine's head absently as he looked past her into the now-deserted Washington streets and thought, May eighteenth, 2014. I will remember this night for as long as I live. This is the most awful thing that has happened to me in my life so far. Because the person I love most in this world is sick and I am not by his side.

It was a small private plane but it came stocked with a mini-fridge, and the pilot, who was apparently aware of the situation, told Anton to help himself to something strong. He smiled and declined. He and Katherine had shared a bottle of wine during dinner, and that, along with the two martinis, was enough drink. He knew it was going to be a long night at the hospital, and he wanted to keep his wits about him.

The shaking started as soon as they were buckled in and the plane began to taxi. It was as though now that there was nothing to do but sit and wait, the iron control with which he had commanded his body thus far began to slip. Please don't let Dad die, he prayed. Please. Please don't let him. I need him. Katherine took his hand and held it in her lap, held it until his trembling subsided, and he felt a profound gratitude. He wanted to tell her this but found that he couldn't, couldn't talk without totally losing it, so he merely squeezed her hand and turned his head to look out the window. Washington looked beautiful at night, lit up like a carnival, but he knew that he would never again visit it without remembering this terrifying night. Pappy had been dead for almost two years, and he still missed him so much. But Pappy had lived away all of his life, an influential but ultimately distant figure. His father had loomed larger in his life than any other person. Every happy memory he had of his boyhood and teenage years featured him. As if in a fairy tale, his dad had taken him out of the projects and turned him into a prince. It was he who had opened up his home, his alma mater, his entire way of life, to Anton; who had given him his last name, which came along with two hundred years of family history; it was he who frowned if anyone ever referred to Anton as his adopted son. He's my son, period, he'd correct them. And if he ever asked for anything back, it was that Anton marry a woman who would make him happy, that he find a fulfilling career, that he attend a college that was challenging and worthy of his intellect. In fact, in all their years together, his father had made only one personal request: On the way home from the courthouse after signing the adoption papers, David had asked to be called Dad.

It had been a simple enough request, and once they'd adopted him, Anton had been so grateful to be able to jump-start his life that it was easy to acquiesce. He'd started calling Delores Mom around the same time. And he saw the pleasure it brought them as a couple, this simple thing on his part, and that alone made him realize the magnitude of their love for him. He was theirs. Permanently. No red-faced cop, no kindly social worker, was ever going to take him away from them. He knew, of course, about James; someone (although he couldn't remember who) had told him about the car wreck on prom night, and it made Anton feel good, so good, to take the sadness out of their lives. He couldn't tell which felt better, needing them or being needed by them, but by then he knew the phrase "win-win situation," and by God, that's what it was.

He picked up the cell phone and dialed Brad's number. "Hey," he said when Brad answered. "We should be landing soon, I think. How is he?"

"He seems stable at the moment, Anton. Try not to worry too much. The State Patrol guys will meet you at the airport. They have orders to bring you straight to the hospital."

"Thanks." Anton's hand was beginning to cramp, and he retrieved it from Katherine's lap. "So what happened?"

"Nobody seems to know. He'd just gotten out of a meeting with a state delegation. He escorted them out of his office and told Ashley to go home. Said he planned on working for another hour or so and then packing it up for the night. Thank God Ashley hadn't left yet, because five minutes later, she heard this loud crash and found him on the floor."

"So he fell? Is he hurt elsewhere?"

"His right hand's pretty bruised. He must've hit his desk on his way down. But they don't seem to think there's a brain bleed or anything like that, thank God."

"Thank God," Anton repeated. The pilot's voice came on. "We're about to land," Anton said. "I'll call you from the car."

"Right-o."

"Take care of Mom until I get there."

Bradley gave a low chuckle. "Your mom is already taking care of the relatives of the other ICU patients here. She's unstoppable, that woman."

Anton smiled. "That sounds like her."

"Oh, Anton? Before you hang up. Word's gotten out to the media. There are already a few reporters in the lobby and more on their way, probably. I've told the Patrol guys to escort you right up to the hospital entrance, but you may want to just make a dash for it once you're in the building."

"Okay. Thanks for the heads-up. See you soon."

"Not if I see you first."

Brad said it automatically, their old childhood sign-off. It cheered Anton, this familiar, ritualized response, on this night when everything else felt uncertain and uncharted.

CHAPTER TWENTY-SIX

ICU.

But what do you see, really? The shell of a man, unshaven, suddenly old, uncharacteristically gaunt and dull-eyed. And the fear in those eyes, a fear masquerading as sleepiness, so that one moment the eyes flicker on and the next they shut. The indecipherable, drug-induced mutterings, at once desultory and insistent.

The heart was designed to be broken, yes, but broken by others—by girlfriends and spouses, even children. What to make of this self-betrayal? This bright red organ, so elegantly efficient in its simple task of pumping blood, suddenly dribbles blood instead, its electric circuitry gone haywire. Ventricular fibrillation. The heart quivers, and just like that, you go from being the most powerful man in the state to an elderly man being kept alive by machines.

One good thing about being in the ICU—it took away Anton's fear. And replaced it with a clean, oxygenated anger. Get up, he wanted to shout at his father. Is that stubble on your cheek? Drool on your chin? You want people to see you like this, lying butt-naked beneath that stupid hospital robe with these tubes attached to your chest? Dad. *Dad*. Remember when we hiked the Appalachian Trail for two weeks for my twenty-third birthday? When you took me parasailing in Florida?

When the storm blew in from the Atlantic that evening on Pappy's boat and you sang old Irish folksongs as you fearlessly steered us home? Or the night in Madrid when all our money was in your wallet and we got held up? You didn't panic even then, just calmly figured out the way back to the hotel. That's the father I know and respect. That's how high you've set the bar. So don't expect sympathy from me as you loll around playing dead in this hospital bed. Come on. Get up. Get *up*. Don't you pull a Pappy on me. Don't you die on me, Dad, I'll be so pissed, I swear I'll haunt you in your grave.

Now that Anton was with his mom, now that he'd held her close to him longer than he perhaps ever had, he was angry with her, too. Look how easily she appeared to have accepted the situation, sitting in the waiting room with the relatives of the other patients, some of them knitting sweaters, for cryin' out loud, as if this goddamn hospital was their damn living room. He watched Delores get up to fetch an elderly man two sugar cookies and the coffee that the hospital provided; saw her put a consoling hand on another relative's shoulder. He stood as she introduced him to the young cardiology resident, noticed the breathless quality in her voice as she spoke. He hated how resigned she seemed, how docile her demeanor was, how she nodded acceptingly when the resident explained the risks involved in the heart catheterization, how willingly she signed the forms that they put before her. The resident seemed singularly unimpressed with the fact that his patient happened to be Governor David Coleman, the man to whom Anton owed everything. If the doctor had been obsequious, Anton would've hated him for that, but he was also irked by this matter-of-fact normalcy.

He was being absurd. He knew this. Everybody was behaving wonderfully well. Mom was her usual thoughtful self, and he could see the wonder and appreciation on the faces of the other people in the waiting room. The doctors were professional, keeping the family in the loop every step of the way. The nurses were competent, cheerful, with the right combination of sympathy and efficiency. No, the only person he had a beef with was the man lying in that hospital bed who would most likely need bypass surgery and may not come out of it. Someone who, the doctors said, probably had destroyed over sixty-five percent of his heart muscle wall. Someone who was getting ready to break Anton's heart. This he could not forgive.

They were all staring at him; they were asking him to sit down, for God's sake, he was driving them all crazy with his constant pacing. The nurses were beginning to get that "God, what a dickhead" look each time he walked past their station. Bradley had tried putting a hand on his shoulder; he had shaken it off. Katherine had tried to console him; he had told her that it was late and she should go home and he'd call her if there was any news. He ignored the hurt look on her face, and if he was gratified by the fact that she disregarded his advice, he wouldn't know it. Nothing registered except the purity of his anger. It was his saving grace, this anger, because without it, he would've lost it. Would've sat down like the rest of the dazed and confused sheep in this waiting room, or howled in sorrow. But until his father got up from that hospital bed instead of lying there with his eyes closed like some goddamn Christian martyr, he would not sit down.

David groaned as if he'd read his thoughts, and Anton felt knocked down to his knees. Dear God, was his father in pain? He looked around the room for a nurse, but David had fallen back into his shallow breathing, and there was nothing to do but watch, transfixed, as the machines did their work.

Anton loosened his collar, feeling hot and faint, even with the air conditioner on. Why weren't there any windows in this room? He leaned on the mattress with his fingertips to steady himself. He felt trapped, unwilling to stay in the oppressive room for another second, but dreading the crowded waiting room, too. A wave of nausea hit him—the martinis and wine, the heavy food, the sudden plane ride—and he felt a sense of déjà vu. And then it came upon him, an image that he couldn't have called up in his conscious mind even if he'd tried: the helpless, trapped feeling of trying to open the sealed window in that small, hot apartment and being unable to do so. The sheer animal desperation that had made him swing that chair.

"Anton," somebody whispered behind him. It was Uncle Connor. The older man's face looked lined, and his eyes were tired. "Let's go sit someplace quiet, you and I. I just received a call from Johnny. We need to talk."

Anton knew immediately what Connor meant. Of course. It was a sign of how he was not thinking correctly, that the issue of succession had not occurred to him. Johnny was John Newman, the lieutenant governor. If Dad had to undergo a procedure, Newman would take over as governor. Anton swallowed. "So Newman becomes acting governor until Dad recovers."

The two men stared at each other. Connor's eyes grew teary. "When we pushed the general assembly to clarify the succession laws last year, did I ever think we'd be using it to replace David? Not in a million years." Connor's voice was hoarse, his expression bewildered. "I just don't get it. He's in such great shape. The guy can do a five-mile run without breaking a sweat. He beats men half his age at tennis." Connor pointed with his thumb. "So how the heck did he end up here?"

Anton pulled the older man toward him. Uncle Connor had given up his own legal career to become Dad's right-hand man from the time he decided to run for governor. David had said a thousand times that it was Connor who'd gotten him elected and Connor who had made him a successful governor. "It's just temporary," Anton said. "You know how tough Dad is. He'll be out of here in no time."

Connor nodded. "I just wish we had changed the laws so that it was the attorney general who could succeed an ailing governor."

Anton raised his eyebrow. "Yeah, right. As if the charges of nepotism that dogged me throughout my campaign weren't enough."

They lingered beside David's bedside for another second, and then Connor put his arm around the younger man and together they walked out of the room. "There's a small chapel in the hospital," Connor said softly. "I'm going to phone Johnny and ask him to meet us here within the hour. You can administer the oath of office to him in there."

Anton gave a short, sharp laugh. "Uncle Connor. Do you ever stop thinking about politics?"

Connor shrugged. "The optics will be wonderful. Voters will love the fact that it's the governor's son administering the oath. Besides, there are probably a dozen reporters and photographers out there. Why let such an opportunity go to waste?"

Anton shook his head. "No wonder Dad calls you his secret weapon."

Connor's lips trembled. "You know there's nothing I would not do for your father. Nothing." He fell silent and then said, "I used to say that the day he was elected governor was the happiest day of my life. Not anymore. Now it will be the day he resumes his office. In the meantime, Johnny can keep his seat warm."

CHAPTER TWENTY-SEVEN

People asked Anton how he did it, and he said he didn't know. But for over two weeks now he had worked all day, then come to the hospital to spend the night with his dad. Delores left soon after he arrived, and when she returned the next morning he would rush home for a quick shower and then go to work. Connor had lectured him on the phone this afternoon, forbidding him to visit, urging him to go home and catch up on sleep instead, but here he was again, watching his father take a short walk down the hallway, a hefty attendant holding him up from the thick safety belt they had attached to David's waist. Watching his timid, unsteady gait, Anton felt a pang of fear at the enormity of what lay ahead for them. "Come on, my man," the attendant said in a thick accent, "just a few more steps. You can do it," he added in the tone of a parent encouraging a toddler. Here, in this hospital, nobody cared that his father was governor, a man with the power to withhold or double their state funding. Here he was simply a patient who had to be constantly reminded to press the heart-shaped red pillow to his chest when he rose from a chair and coaxed to take a few more bites of the reduced-sodium diet. In some ways, Anton was glad that his father was so out of it; he would've found unbearable the realization of how far he had fallen.

"Okay, let's take a few seconds to catch our breath," the attendant said. The man helped David sit on the hallway couch next to Anton, who patted his father's knee. "You're doing great, Dad," he said with insincere enthusiasm, feeling like a hypocrite. But apparently, David was more aware of his surroundings than Anton had realized, because he shot him a wan look. "Don't you bullshit me," the look said, and Anton felt suitably reprimanded.

"Where're you from?" he asked the male attendant.

The man shook his head. "A little place you never heard of. Antigua."

"Are you kidding me? I know Antigua. Former British colony in the Caribbean. Beautiful place."

The man smiled back broadly. "Most folks never heard of it. You been?"

"No. But I've read about it. In a book by Jamaica Kincaid. Can't remember its name. Have you read it?"

"Nah. Never heard of him. But then I'm not much of a reader."

"She's a woman. She's from there. Originally, I mean."

The man laughed. "That's Antigua for you. Everybody's from there originally. But now they live someplace else." He stuck out his hand. "I'm William Tell."

Anton looked at him suspiciously, not knowing whether his leg was being pulled.

"No, really. That's my name."

Anton whistled. "Well. Somebody in your family likes books, even if it's not you."

"That's a good one, Mr. Coleman."

While they were chatting, David was sitting back on the couch, his head resting against the wall, his eyes shut. William touched him gently on the wrist. "Sir. Let's get in one more round and then I'll take you back to your room. Now, remember, grab that ole cushion and press it to your chest as you get up."

David gave Anton a look that he couldn't quite comprehend, though his distress was palpable. Anton leaped to his feet. "I'll walk with you guys," he said, and down the hallway the three of them went.

After they got back to his room, David had to use the bathroom. William accompanied him in and then shut the door lightly. "Remember, pull the cord if you need me," he called out.

"You gotta watch for the depression," William said to Anton as they waited. "Very common side effect after open-heart surgery."

"He'll be okay. Once we get him home, he'll be fine."

William gave him a long look. "Don't kid yourself. It's a tough recovery. I just want you to be prepared."

"Speaking of prepared, we're looking to hire someone to help him at home after his discharge. Do you know of any home health aides you could recommend?"

"When are they discharging him?"

"I think they said day after tomorrow?"

William thought for a moment. "I don't know if this will work, but I'm on vacation for two weeks starting Monday. If you like, I can help you out."

"Don't you have plans for your vacation?"

William shrugged. "Not really." He pulled a piece of paper from the pocket of his scrubs and wrote on it. "Here's my number. Call me if you can't find anyone else."

"No, no, no. I'd be thrilled if you'd help us. I just didn't want you to work on your vacation, man."

"Don't you worry about that. I love to stay busy."

Anton offered his hand. "Well, that's a huge load off my mind. How much do you charge?"

They heard David flush, and William hurried toward the bathroom. "Going rate's fifteen an hour. But you can pay me what you like," he said over his shoulder.

"How does seventeen an hour sound?"

"Sounds beautiful, baby."

Anton grinned. He listened as William helped his dad in the bathroom, heard the sound of running water in the sink. The relief he felt at the thought of entrusting David's care to someone as obviously competent as William was enormous. And as his father recovered, he would hit it off with William, Anton was sure. It would be good for Mom, too, to have a strong, capable man help with the bathing and other stuff.

After William had finished tucking David into bed, Anton bent down to kiss his forehead. The older man whispered something he couldn't catch, and he leaned in, putting his ear to David's mouth. "What'd you say, Dad?"

"*A Small Place*," David whispered faintly.

Anton's eyes shone. So Dad had been listening to his earlier conversation with William. "That's right," he exclaimed. "How on earth did you remember that?"

A look of pride flashed across David's exhausted face. He smiled, a slight stretch of the lips that perhaps only Anton could recognize as a smile. "That silly girl," he rasped. "She argued with Pappy."

Carine. He hadn't thought about her in so long. She'd obviously made an impression on Dad, negative as it may have been. "I remember." He laughed. "Boy, the look on Pappy's face when she argued with him. She *was* a silly girl."

Without warning, David's face turned teary. "She was right about the war, though," he said, gasping. "It was a dreadful mistake. I was so wrong. And we were all so angry with her for—"

"Dad. Dad. Calm down. That was a long time ago. If you were wrong, so was half the country. In any case, it's all water under the bridge."

David nodded, but his eyes were wet as he turned his face away to stare out the large window. Anton kissed his cheek. "Get some rest, Dad," he said. "You're going home soon. Focus on that."

Turning off the lights, Anton motioned William to leave the room with him. "What was all that?" William asked the minute they were in the hallway.

"It's a long story," he said. He stood rocking on his heels for a moment and then felt compelled to ask, "Do you . . . you do know that my dad's the governor, right?"

William looked incredulous. "No, man, I didn't know, because I live in a cave in Timbuktu. The fact that I have to pass by a gaggle of reporters to come into work every day, must've slipped my mind." He laughed a loud, crackling laugh, scrunching up his shoulders.

Embarrassed, Anton said, "Hey, look, you never know. There are people in this state who don't know who the president is, okay?"

William put his large hand on Anton's shoulder. "Listen, Mr. Attorney General, when I said I don't *read*, I meant I don't read novels and stuff. But we Antiguans—we are literate folks. Chalk one up for the Brits, to give the devil his due. I read the dailies every single day, thank you. And I vote." He looked at Anton in mock insult. "So yes, indeed, I know who my governor is."

Anton laughed. "Okay. You made your point. I'm sorry I asked."

But William was on a roll. "You think I'd bring in my sorry black ass to work an extra job if I wasn't going to be spending it in the executive mansion?"

"William. Don't you have any other patients to go razz?"

"Tell you what. I'll stop picking on you if you promise to go down to the cafeteria and fix yourself a good dinner. I'll call you if your dad needs anything."

"It's a deal." Anton waited until William had walked away a few paces and then called, "Hey, William. You married?"

The man turned around. "Nope."

Anton nodded. "I can see why not."

William grinned appreciatively. "Bet you're good at talking trash on the basketball court, Mr. AG."

"Soccer's my game. But you bet."

They smiled at each other, and then Anton took the elevator down to the cafeteria, replaying the earlier conversation with his father. The fact that David had recalled the name of the book was the sign of a mind that was functioning well. But it had unnerved him to hear David saying that Carine had been right, and the manner in which he'd said it, as if he were apologizing to her across the years. It made Anton feel as if he had wronged her, too.

He sighed. It was ancient history, so long ago that it might as well have happened to someone else, for all the difference it now made. He couldn't worry about the past, not when there was so much to worry about in the present. He made his way to the hospital cafeteria, picked up a prepackaged box of sushi, paid for it, and dialed Katherine's number on his way back to the room.

CHAPTER TWENTY-EIGHT

Anton frowned. The *Rolling Stone* interview was not going as well as he had hoped. Uncle Connor had assured him that it would be a laudatory piece and had personally attested for the reporter, John Crow, as someone he liked and trusted. But as he faced the gray-haired man sitting across his desk, Anton questioned Connor's judgment. The questions so far had been tough. Maybe Crow was miffed because Anton had postponed the interview twice, but good God, surely the man understood that his father recently had a heart attack and that Anton was trying to run a statewide office.

But the questions kept coming, and as the minutes ticked by, Anton found himself wishing, not for the first time, that he could handle reporters with the same ease as David, who was always quick with a quip or a compliment that seemed to disarm even his toughest media critics. Anton was too cerebral, too flinty, and knowing this about himself was not enough to make him change. Bradley had often joked with him that with his lack of tolerance of fools, he had better never aspire to higher political office. "You would've done better in the business world, like me," Bradley teased. "There, you don't have to kowtow to reporters and pretend they're the guardians of democracy. Instead, you can see them for what they are: self-serving, self-righteous bastards."

But John Crow was neither a fool nor a prick. He was simply dogged in his refusal to allow Anton to change the subject. They had spent the last ten minutes sparring over whether, as AG, Anton should've insisted that John Newman take over as acting governor as soon as he found out that David was in the hospital. Instead, over six hours had passed before Johnny was sworn in—a fact that the local media had had a field day reporting for the past couple of weeks.

Crow pushed his reading glasses up his nose, sat back in his chair, and peered out at Anton. "There's also a rumor that the delay was because you and Connor Stevens were trying to figure out a way for you to step in as governor," he said. "Care to comment on that?"

Anton let his disdain show. "Do I care to comment on that? No. The accusation is so ridiculous that I will not dignify it with a response."

"That may come across as an admission of guilt to some."

"Listen. As you may recall, I was in Washington when my father collapsed. I rushed back to be by his bedside. We didn't know if he would survive the night, okay?" Without warning, he felt himself choking up. "Hatching some Machiavellian plot was the last thing on my mind. Or do these anonymous critics also think that my father faked his heart attack?"

Crow ran his fingers through his thick gray hair. "This is obviously an emotional issue for you," he murmured.

"You bet."

"Yes. Well. Just one more question and then we'll move on. I've read that the minority leader is asking for an investigation of the private plane that brought you home from Washington."

Anton sighed. "Jack. I'll tell you exactly what I told my local newspaper. My office is calculating how much the ride would cost any citizen of the state. And we will reimburse the owner of the plane to the full extent. That has been our intention all along."

"With all due respect, why hasn't that been done already?"

"Because I've been a little tied up." Anton did not bother hiding his irritation.

Crow smiled faintly. "Touché. Let's move on to more pleasant topics. How goes it with the lovely Miss Katherine Banks?"

Anton bit down the urge to say, "None of your business." Instead, he smiled back and said, "It goes well."

"So is this it? Is the most eligible bachelor in the state spoken for, at long last?"

He laughed. "We'll see."

Crow nodded. "Do you care to speculate on why you've avoided marriage for so long?"

"Oh geez. Give me a break." Anton fixed his gaze on the older man. "Are you married, John?"

"Divorced, actually."

"There you go. That's a vast improvement over never having married, right?"

Crow gave him an appreciative look. "Fair enough," he said at last. He peered at his notebook and then looked up. "During the campaign, you made it an issue how your biracial background would help you bridge the racial divide. Yet polls show that many of the minority citizens of your state don't even see you as one of them. And the charge is you have done precious little to help them."

I can't decide whether you're the whitest black man or the blackest white man I've ever met. Carine's words, spoken a lifetime ago, came rushing back at him with their full, shameful velocity. The memory made Anton grimace. "Wait a minute. The charge against me? Can I ask who is leading this charge? Or are these just more anonymous accusers?"

For the first time during the interview, Crow appeared to be on the defensive. "Well, every black woman I have interviewed for this story has commented on the fact that all your girlfriends have been white. That's just for starters."

"I see. So this is no longer a political issue. Now we are talking about my personal life?"

"Well, you know what they say, Mr. Coleman. In politics, perception is reality. And it's undeniable that you have only been seen in the company of white women."

Anton stared at the spot on the wall behind Crow's head as he struggled to control his temper. "It may be undeniable to you, John, but I'm going to deny it anyway." His voice was cold, dripping with hostility.

John Crow gave a start of surprise. "Mr. Attorney General. Are you telling me you've dated a black woman?"

"For three years in college," Anton said. And realized, with satisfaction, that he had thrown Crow off his stride, albeit momentarily.

"Really. What was her name?"

Anton smiled and wagged his finger. "You'll just have to take me at my word. The last thing I want to do is have the poor woman see her name in *Rolling Stone*." He looked at his watch pointedly. "As you know, I have another appointment at three-thirty. Are we almost done here?"

Crow smiled. "Almost."

THE INTERVIEW RAN three weeks later, and it was not the hatchet job he'd feared. He was mentally composing a thank-you note to Crow when he turned to the jump and his heart stopped momentarily as his eyes fell on Carine's name. Fuck. Damn that John Crow. How the hell had he managed to track her down? Stomach muscles clenching, Anton read the paragraphs dealing with his relationship with the "enigmatic, charismatic Carine Biya," as the article described her. John had done his homework—there was Colin George, Anton's doubles partner at Harvard, recalling, "They were inseparable. And very much in love."

And then there was a quote from Carine herself. Jack had managed to find her in a suburb of Atlanta, where she now lived. Anton closed his eyes for a second, bracing himself for the worst. And was flooded with gratitude when he read what she'd said: "He was the most even-tempered guy I'd ever met and not the least bit pretentious. I mean, I think we'd dated for months before I even found out who his daddy was." She went on to tell some funny anecdote about an old red flannel shirt with holes in the elbows that Anton refused to throw away despite her cajoling. He hadn't the slightest idea whether the story was real—he could recall no such shirt—but he read the anecdote with an appreciative politician's eye: It was the kind of story about frugality and regular-guy behavior that voters loved.

He almost immediately signed on to his personal email account. His in-box was already flooded with friends offering their congratulations; apparently more of them read *Rolling Stone* than he'd been aware of. He began to compose a thank-you message to John Crow, then stopped. Instead, he picked up the phone and dialed the reporter's cell number.

John answered on the third ring. "Yup?"

"John? It's Anton Coleman. Good piece. I just wanted to call and thank you."

"Great. Glad to know it worked out."

"Though I do wish you'd left that poor woman alone." He said it friendly, with just the slightest reproach in his voice.

"Carine? Oh, she was fine. She was more than happy to talk to me about you."

"Yeah?"

"Yeah."

Anton hesitated a second before asking, "So, do you have an email for her or something? I'd—I'd like to thank her, you know, for her gracious remarks."

He heard John's low chuckle, knew that the reporter had picked up on his awkwardness. "No problem, Mr. AG. Give me a second to find it." He heard Jack rummaging around. "Here it is. You ready?"

After they hung up, Anton stared at the piece of paper where he'd written Carine's email address. Would Katherine be mad if she found out he'd written to Carine? Well, there was no reason for her to be jealous. Carine was someone from his distant past, and all he was going to do was send her a note thanking her for her kind words. Why, it was virtually part of his job description.

His tone in the email was friendly but polite, and he was careful to avoid any personal reminiscence. In other words, it was Katherine-proof. He reread the email and was about to hit send when he added, "P.S. Let me know what's new in your life?"

Even though he hated himself for it, he found himself checking his in-box during the day, but Carine had not written back. As had become his custom, he drove to see his father directly after work and agreed to stay for supper when he caught the look of loneliness in his mother's eyes. He sent a quick text to Katherine explaining the situation. William, who had taken a leave of absence from the hospital to be full-time in his father's employ, cut David's chicken for him as they ate.

"So did you see the article, Dad?" he asked, and David nodded.

"I read it to him this morning, honey," Delores said. "He wouldn't even go for his bath until I had."

His father was saying something in the low, raspy voice that he'd acquired after his bypass, and Anton leaned in to catch what he was saying. "That girl—Carine—she said nice things."

"Why wouldn't she?" Delores's voice was tight with remembered insult. "We were nothing but good to her."

Anton grinned. "Mom. Relax. Everything's fine."

Delores nodded. "Where's Katherine tonight?"

"At home." Anton kept his tone light. "Why?"

"No reason. I like Katherine. She's more—your type."

William was looking at them quizzically and Anton sighed. "I know, Mom. I know."

After he got home, he and Katherine stayed up to watch *The Daily Show* and then went to bed with their personal iPads. Both insomniacs, they would listen to music or watch a movie until they dozed off. He was almost asleep when he heard the ping announcing the arrival of a new email, and his stomach lurched when he saw it was from Carine. He glanced over at Katherine, lying inches away from him, and with a spasm of guilt, he realized that he wished he was alone. He rolled out of bed, ignoring Katherine's half-asleep "Where're you going?," and went into the kitchen, taking his iPad with him. He pulled a carton of milk out of the fridge, slamming the refrigerator door loud enough for Katherine to hear it, and opened the email. He was gratified to see that it was several paragraphs long.

She had received his email earlier today but wanted to wait until she'd put the kids to bed. Yes, she had kids, twins, five-year-old boys. Could he believe it, that she was a mom? Some days she could hardly believe it herself. And boy, did they keep her busy. There was no mention of a husband, a fact that Anton noticed immediately. It didn't surprise him, the possibility that she was a single parent. She was brave enough to do something like that.

She had kept tabs on his career, of course. She confessed that she had a Google alert that informed her of his accomplishments. The night he'd won his AG election, she'd toasted him with some friends. She was so proud of him, she wrote, but not the least bit surprised that the boy that she had known and loved in college had made his way in the world. Anton's gaze lingered over that word—*loved*—and suddenly, something opened up within him, a large, hollow spot, and he was crying. He knew he was being ridiculous, knew that Katherine could walk in on him at any moment and that he'd have a hard time explaining away his tears, but he couldn't stop. Carine had been his first real love, and he was grateful that he had chosen someone as decent and kind and substantial as she. He had not always been so lucky or discriminating, had dated some real doozies. He had seldom argued with those women the way he had with Carine, but, it occurred to him now, it was only because he had cared less.

But Katherine's not one of those women, he now reminded himself. Katherine is smart and funny and compassionate and sensitive. You love her. And she would be mortified if she knew that you were coming undone because of an email from a woman you loved when you were a boy. Katherine is the present and possibly the future. Carine is the past. A woman whose life, by her own admission, is deadly dull and boring. Whereas Katherine had dinner with Bill and Melinda Gates a week ago. In Rio. And that's not even it. The point is, it is Katherine, not Carine, who is in the bedroom, waiting for you to crawl under the covers with her.

He poured the glass of milk into the sink, rinsed it, and turned off his iPad. Then he switched off the kitchen light and slipped back into the bedroom.

CHAPTER TWENTY-NINE

Uncle Connor was glowering at the man who sat across from him when Anton walked into the conference room. The only other person present was Annie Bunter, John Newman's press secretary. "Hey, guys," Anton said as he pulled up a chair next to Connor. "What's so urgent that it couldn't wait till after the ceremony?"

Before either one of Newman's staff members could speak, Connor pushed a sheaf of papers toward Anton. "Get a load of this," he growled. "This is what Newman plans to say in his acceptance speech. In less than half an hour." Connor bared his teeth at Bill Schroder, Newman's speechwriter, who scowled back. "Over my dead body," Connor added.

Anton glanced at the highlighted section:

> Our previous governor came into office nearly two decades ago promising to clean up corruption. Instead, we have seen one scandal after another during his time in power. After our last attorney general resigned in disgrace there was a real chance to clean house, to bring fresh blood into that office. But what did Governor Coleman do instead? He threw his support behind his own son, despite the thinness of his résumé. The people of this state are sick of nepotism.

While we are grateful to Governor Coleman for his years of service, the time has come to turn the page. From this day forth . . .

The paragraph rolled on, but Anton looked up, sickened by Newman's treachery. "You bastards," he swore, looking straight at Bill. "This is how you repay my father for putting Johnny on the ticket? By kicking him while he's down?"

"For chrissake, Anton," Bill said. "We've been more than patient, I'd say. Any other politician would've demanded that your dad resign months ago, given his prognosis. The state's been left in limbo for five months now."

"That's what this is about? Johnny's pissed because he didn't permanently get his grubby hands on the levers of power fast enough?"

"Aw, come on, man," Bill protested, shifting in his seat. "You guys are taking this far too seriously. It's one lousy paragraph. He praises David elsewhere in the speech. Look, it's politics. We have the freakin' Tea Party breathing down our necks. It's nothing personal."

Anton's hand, which was resting on the pile of paper, curled into a fist. "You're calling my father corrupt, you jerk," he said. "So you bet your ass it's personal."

Bill shook his head. "Anton. Be reasonable." He turned to look at Annie for support, but she stared straight ahead. "I don't believe this," he said. "I've never seen such thin-skinned people."

Anton stood up and pulled a pen out of his shirt pocket. He picked up the paper and drew a large X over the offending passage. "You take this back to your boss, you New York flack," he said, his eyes flashing. "You tell him to delete any insults to my dad. Or else he's going to have a primary challenge for 2016."

Out of the corner of his eye, Anton saw Connor's head jerk up. Annie, too, was staring hard at Anton, her eyes searching his face. But he focused his attention on Bill, who seemed unsure what to do next. "You're full of shit," Bill said finally, but his voice lacked conviction. "You'd just be throwing the election to the Republicans. You know that."

Anton smiled a slow, predatory smile. "And that is precisely why you will change your goddamn speech." He nodded to Connor. "Come on, Uncle Connor. Let's give Billy here some time to rework his pretty little speech."

Anton could feel Annie's gaze on him as he crossed the room. He and Annie had always liked each other, and he had a hunch that she was rooting for him on this one. His body vibrated a little as he walked out of the room, adrenaline surging through him. He crossed the hallway, heading toward the ballroom in the Governor's Mansion. Connor hurried to keep up with him, saying something laudatory, but Anton wasn't really listening. He was amazed by the purity of his anger, that rush of aggression, something he had always abhorred. But now that he'd had a taste of it, he knew he wanted to taste it again. He understood now why his father had clung to his office until today, five months after his heart attack, hoping against hope that he'd recover enough to run the state again. Power was a drug, a high, an addiction. Truth be told, he felt a little high himself, his body reverberating, his small but brutal victory over Bill compensating in some tiny way for the sad, empty feeling he was about to feel, watching his father hand over the governorship to a man they all knew could never fill the shoes of a giant named David Coleman.

CONNOR AND ANTON slipped into a small room to the side of the state ballroom, where supporters and state officials had begun to gather. David was in his wheelchair facing Delores, who sat across from him, their heads bowed together. With a start of surprise, Anton realized that they were praying. He felt embarrassed, as if he were an interloper, but David looked up, smiled, and opened his arms toward Anton in a gesture that was so loving and unguarded, it brought a lump to the younger man's throat. "Hey, Dad," he said, his eyes tearing. "How you doing?"

David shrugged. "It's a sad day," he said simply.

Connor walked up to his old friend, a broad smile on his face. "Don't worry," he said. "There's gonna be a Coleman in this office again, you mark my words." He pointed at Anton. "You should've seen him in there, taking on Bill Schroder. I'd been going round and round with the jerk for an hour. Anton walks in and demolishes him in two seconds flat. Told him his boss could expect a primary challenge if he didn't remove his bullshit remarks."

David laughed his silent laugh, and for a second he looked like his old self. "Did you really?"

Anton looked at his dad shyly. "Aw, you know. I was just messing with him, Dad."

"From your mouth to God's ear," Delores said unexpectedly, raising the water glass she'd been holding. "Here's to another Coleman in the Governor's Mansion."

"Amen."

"Okay, people. I already have a job, remember?"

Connor had opened his mouth as if to argue when Brad walked in. "You guys ready?" he said. "They're waiting for us."

They all froze in place, David's eyes resting on each of them for a second. "Thank you," he whispered. "It's been a great ride. And I couldn't have done it without each one of you."

Anton stared at the ground, unwilling to let his father see the tears filling his eyes. Then he stepped behind David's wheelchair. "Let's get it over with, Dad," he said.

ANTON SAT IN the front row, flanked by his mother and Katherine, and watched as his father said a few words, formally resigning from his post and wishing Newman well in the task ahead. He listened to Newman's speech, ready to bristle at the slightest hint of a slam against his father, but the few times Newman did mention David, he was complimentary. After the ceremony, Anton glowed with pride as several officials gathered around David's wheelchair, shaking his hand and thanking him for his years of service. He thought back to election night, when he and his father had shared the victory stage as the first father-and-son team to win two statewide offices together. Who could have predicted this abrupt, ignoble end to David's career?

Annie Bunter walked up to Anton. "That was quite a performance in there," she said dryly, her eyes brimming with laughter, her manner flirtatious.

"Thanks."

She touched his arm lightly. "What you said in there. About a primary challenge. Were you serious?"

"Annie," he said, looking deeply into her face. "If I were, you'd be the last person I'd confide in."

She searched his face for a long moment and then laughed. "Yup. That's what I figured." She walked away, her high heels clicking on the tile floor, and then she stopped and looked back. "It'd be fun. Having you as an opponent, I mean."

He stood staring at her back, trying to parse what she'd said. Was she encouraging him to run? If he could capture the aggression that he'd displayed in the conference room, trap that feeling of power, like lightning in a bottle, he would win. If he ran, there could be a Coleman in the Governor's Mansion again. And there was nothing, he knew, no gift he could give his father, that would mean more to him than that.

BOOK FOUR
August 2016

CHAPTER THIRTY

The news kept getting better and better.

Any misgivings Anton had had about challenging the incumbent governor had been laid to rest by the twelve-point blowout in the April primary. And even though Uncle Connor would bite off the head of anyone who said it out loud, internal polling showed that Anton would beat Joe Irving, his Republican opponent, by an even wider margin, an almost unheard-of rout in this political climate.

Indeed, it was obvious that the Coleman name was still golden within the state. On the campaign trail, as Anton worked the ropes, person after person would stop him with a fond recollection about his dad or about Pappy, and despite his exhaustion, Anton left these encounters more certain than ever why he was running. He enjoyed these interactions with the older residents of the state much more than he did the screaming and adulation that now greeted him when he was surrounded by girls too young to vote and women old enough to know better, but as Brad always said, this was the state of retail politics now, and he'd best shut up and learn to enjoy it.

In fact, he was enjoying the campaign. Even if the June issue of *People* magazine had featured a picture of him with the headline "The Stud Muffin Governor?" He had been mortified, but Brad, who had taken a leave of absence from his business to run the campaign, was thrilled. Anton tried to argue that such fluff pieces undermined the rationale of his campaign, which claimed that he had reluctantly chosen to throw his hat into the ring only because John Newman had governed from the center right and had moved away from the progressive legacy he had inherited. "If we wanted a Republican governor, heck, we'd elect a Republican governor," Anton had said at the news conference announcing his candidacy. The press had loved that line. But when Anton reminded his campaign manager of the reasons for running, Brad was having none of it. "Listen, idiot," he'd growled. "I worked for months to get you that *People* piece. This is national exposure, baby."

"I know," Anton had said ruefully. "It's the exposure part I'm worried about."

The truth was, he had opened up an even wider lead against Irving since the article appeared. Barring some unexpected calamity, it was hard to imagine how Irving could close the gap. Each time he challenged Irving's extremist positions, Anton went up a couple of points in the polls. He was not taking anything for granted—and Brad was skulking around all day, warning the campaign staff not to get cocky—but it seemed as if a Coleman would once again be occupying the Governor's Mansion.

Being attorney general had made Anton much more aware of what was at stake, how quickly a progressive political legacy could be allowed to unravel, how the decisions that political leaders made had real-life consequences. What happened in the corridors of power could make the difference between an elderly man going to bed hungry or not, or whether a child would find his local community center open or shuttered closed, or whether a woman would be forced to carry a child she didn't want. His first three months in the AG's office, he'd felt battered by the sheer number of decisions he had to make on any given day, and he'd had to react to so many competitive agendas coming at him from all sides that it had been impossible to work on any long-term strategy. David had made it clear that he was always available for counsel, but Anton's pride and his determination to keep his personal and professional worlds as far apart as possible hadn't allowed him to ask for help. So he had turned to Brad, who had come in for a week, sitting in on meetings, taking notes, observing where Anton spent his time. Anton still consulted the seventeen-page memo that came out of those sessions and got a chuckle every time he read the title: "How to Be Street-Smart and Not Just Another Putz with a Harvard Law Degree."

One of Bradley's suggestions was that Anton actually read the letters and emails his constituents wrote to him, rather than turning them over to his assistant. And that he write back to a few each week. It was a recommendation Anton immediately adopted. Even though the number of letters had increased dramatically since he had announced for governor, reading them relaxed him. He would come home after a long day at the office or on the campaign trail and go through the correspondence, because it connected him in the most unfiltered, honest way to the public. People poured out the raw contours of their lives on these pages, spoke of their dreams and aspirations in ways that sometimes made Anton cry. The biracial gay teenager who asked if Anton could pass a law banning bullying at school. The seventy-five-year-old widow looking after her ninety-seven-year-old mother who wrote to ask why assisted suicide was not legal in the state. The successful real estate broker who begged him to reopen her local library if he became governor because that was where she'd studied to get her GED and she couldn't bear the thought of other children not having the same opportunities that she had.

Anton got up from his desk and made his way to his liquor cabinet to refresh his Scotch. He glanced at the clock. It was past ten o'clock, and after days filled with juggling the duties of his office and the obligations of campaigning, his entire body felt sore. His throat hurt from talking to hundreds of people; his palms were raw from the hand shaking and excessive hand washing. He was sleep-deprived, and as lovely as it was to share a bed with Katherine, some nights he simply wanted to sprawl out on his king-size bed and sleep unencumbered by the rhythms and patterns of another human being, even if that human being had a sensational body and a kind, generous heart. Tonight, he was thankful that she was away on an overnight trip.

He splashed soda water into his Scotch and padded his way back to his desk. The pile of letters would take at least another two hours to read, and there was no way he'd last that long. He flipped through the envelopes, hoping to find a letter written by a kid, because even though they could be the most heartbreaking ones in the lot, occasionally, they were just plain funny, and Lord, he could use some levity tonight.

He struck out. Instead, he picked up a letter that caught his eye because it was addressed to him in pencil. Who the hell writes a letter in pencil? he thought. He turned the envelope over, and the return address read Georgia, which was not unusual—since the *People* article, he'd been getting fan mail from across the country. Intrigued, he cut it open with the ivory letter opener that he had inherited from Pappy. The letter itself was written in block letters, also in pencil. There was no date.

Dear Baby Boy:

I swear, I never thought I'd see your sweet face again. And then yesterday I went to the dentist because I needed the root canal. My tooth was hurting something wicked and I was so scared that I thought I was gonna pass out in the waiting room but just then a little angel came into my life because I see you looking at me. From the inside of a magazine. It says you gonna be the next Governor. Lord, Anton, you could of just blown me down. I was so excited, even that root canal didn't hurt, I swear.

I am so proud of you, Anton. With your smarts, I always

knew you would be a big success some day. And you always were a beautiful boy and now you this big, handsome man. You've changed, but I would recognize you anywhere. How can a mother forget what she made? I don't know if you ever think of your old Mam but not one day passes without me thinking of you. You did the right thing by choosing that white family over me, Anton. In those days, I had nothing and that's what I would of given you—nothing.

I prayed for you every day, Anton, that you grow up to be strong and smart and happy. Looks like the Good Lord has answered all my prayers. You always were the answer to my prayers. And now I'm gonna double up and pray for you to become Governor.

I love you, yesterday, today, and tomorrow.

Your old Mam,

Juanita Vesper

P.S. Please forgive me for the hurt I caused you.

He sat back in his chair, the letter fluttering in his shaking hand, knowing he needed to take a big gulp of the Scotch in order to calm the thudding in his chest, but being unable to reach for it. His eyes roamed over the letter again, his lawyer's brain trying to pick it apart, to figure out if it was a fake, for any evidence that would allow him to dismiss it, to defuse the bomb that had just gone off in his life. What was that phrase she'd used? "Blown me down." Yeah, that's what he felt like. Blown down.

Where to begin? There was the fact that the entire letter was written in block letters. In pencil. In poor grammar. The ridiculous declarations of eternal love. The excessive use of "always." The reminder of his infantile name for her, Mam. The absurd declarations of prescience, as if it were a fait accompli that he would grow up to be the man he'd become were it not for his parents. The claims she was still making on him. The calling him by that old childhood nickname, the one he'd forgotten about: Baby Boy. How dare she call him that, and how patronizing it sounded, how it reduced him to being nine again, trapped in that shabby little apartment. With her. Without her.

But then he located the locus of his anger, and the rest of it fell away. He reread the sentence: "You done the right thing by choosing that white family over me, Anton." *You* did the right thing? *He* chose the white family? He was a child, for Pete's sake, with no agency. For the almost three years that he lived with the Colemans before his adoption, he had held some part of himself aloof. It hadn't been easy—David and Delores had been attentive, loving, kind, thoughtful, caring. Never once had he felt unsafe with them, never once had they disappeared for a week and left him to fend for himself. There were so many times when he almost slipped and called David Dad, so many times he saw the hopeful light leap up in David's eyes only to be snuffed out a second later. Anton had been ashamed of himself then, had known he was being unkind, but he had never wavered. He had been saving himself for his reunion with her. His mom. Whom, in those wild days when his life was turned upside down, only he seemed to understand and love. When the police, the social workers, even David seemed to judge her, he did not. All he could think in those days was his mam had made a mistake, just like he made spelling and grammar mistakes. Together, they would correct those mistakes. Of this he had no doubt.

Until the day a grim-faced David had sat him down and told him what had transpired. How she had decided to give him up. Because she believed he would be happier with his new family. Because she was weak, and needed to get strong, and couldn't take care of a twelve-year-old boy while she got healthy again.

What he had felt then, he couldn't bear to remember now. Anton shoved the feeling down, much as he had all those years ago, the sob in his throat that he had tried to swallow because it was choking him, the scream that rose from his very toes and almost escaped before he clamped down on it, the feeling of utter abandonment, so much more powerful than anything he'd felt in that hot apartment where he'd waited for his mother to return.

Anton rested his forehead on his desk. For a second, he weighed the price that young boy had paid for the loneliness that he had spent a lifetime running away from. But then he dismissed it. There was no room for sentimentality now. This was a time for action. This woman—he could no longer think of her as his mother, he had a new mother now, thank you very much—was a threat, a cancer that had resurfaced, that had to be irradiated. This woman with her false accusations, her insinuation that he had chosen David's wealth, his white privilege, over her poverty and blackness, had to be stopped from spouting her falsehoods. Because next thing you knew, this story was going to hit the press.

Anton rose swiftly from his desk, crossed the hallway into the bedroom, and slipped on his sneakers. He folded the letter, shoved it into the pocket of his pants, and grabbed his car keys.

Ten minutes later, he was knocking on Bradley's door, and when Brad answered, he entered without being invited in.

CHAPTER THIRTY-ONE

The two men stared wordlessly at each other for a minute before Brad exhaled. "I gotta tell you, man. I don't see it," he said.

"Don't see what?"

Brad frowned. "What you're seeing. There's no threat here. No blackmail. Just a mom trying to reconnect . . ."

Anton looked incredulous. "I don't believe it. Don't you see? How she's trying to frame the issue? That I chose to abandon her rather than the other way around?"

"Dude. People believe what they want to believe. Okay? Maybe this is the story she needs to believe."

"Yeah. Because otherwise she has to live with the truth—that she sold out her only child so she could get high." Anton's voice was savage, and he knew his eyes were bloodshot.

There was another silence, and when Anton looked up, Brad was staring at him, a new understanding in his eyes. "I'm sorry," he said softly. "I can't imagine how you feel."

Anton didn't want pity. He didn't want sympathy. He wanted blood. "No, you can't," he said curtly. He sprang to his feet and began to pace the room, picking up a silver candleholder and setting it down, lifting a photograph frame and turning it unseeingly in his hands.

"Anton. Sit the fuck down. You're making me dizzy," Brad said after a few moments.

He couldn't sit, but he stopped pacing, standing a few feet away from his friend. "Listen," Brad continued. "We have a goddamn election coming up in a few months. You need to put this behind you. After you're governor, we can . . . do something. Maybe fly her out here or something. But for now you need to ignore this. I'm telling you, there's no threat here."

Anton sat back down on the couch with a thud, tapping his left foot on the hardwood floor. "I can't. I know myself. I won't be able to focus." His head shot up as the thought hit him. "I'll go see her. See what she wants. Explain to her that we can't have this—any of this drama—before the election." As he spoke, the feeling of agitation that had gripped him since he'd slit open the letter receded a bit.

Brad looked aghast. "And how do you propose to leave town without the entire press corps knowing? Have you lost your mind, Anton?"

He caught himself shaking his leg and stopped. "Get me a private plane," he said quietly. "I'll pay out of pocket. I'll be back in town before anyone will notice. If anyone asks, you can tell them I'm felled by a cold. Anything." He pulled out his phone to check his calendar. "I can take Friday off. And I should be back the same night. Or Saturday at the latest. Depending on how it goes with her."

Brad shook his head. "Anton. You know better. It's too risky. Lying to the press? If they catch on, they'll think you're doing a Mark Sanford."

Anton focused on Brad. "I'm asking you to help me, Brad. Don't fucking make me beg."

Brad jutted out his lower lip. "I can't. As your campaign manager, I can't let you do this. Your dad will kill me if he finds out the unnecessary risk to the campaign. Hell, *my* dad will kill me. You know how much this election means to both of them." Brad scowled suddenly. "And for what? All you have to do is pretend you never read the letter. After November eighth, you can do whatever you want. But not now."

"And what if my hunch is right? What if the letter is something more than a guilt-stricken woman writing to her long-lost son? What if she's after something? Blackmail, maybe?"

"Then I'll handle it. I'll go." Brad looked at him wryly. "Though I think you've been watching too many episodes of *House of Cards*."

"Bradley." Anton rose to his feet and pulled himself to full height. "I'm going. With or without your help. So the question is whether you will get me a plane or whether"—and here he played his card, knowing Brad would never let him take so heedless a risk—"I call one of our donors and ask for a political favor."

As he'd guessed, Brad took the bait. "You're being reckless," he said, wrinkling his nose as if he'd smelled something foul. "You keep this up and Joe Irving will be the next governor of this state." But his voice was mild, and he pulled on his lower lip, a sure sign that he was already plotting how to make Anton's getaway possible. "What're you gonna tell your dad? And Katherine? That you're just skipping town?"

"I'll tell Kat," Anton said. "She'll understand. But I'm not saying a word to Dad." He grinned suddenly. "Actually, we're gonna tell Dad and Uncle Connor that you and I are going out of town for some R and R."

"Oh yeah? And what about when—"

"They won't see you around town during the weekend, Bradley, because you're going to stay in your beautiful house all day Friday and maybe Saturday, too. Just make sure you have enough groceries."

"You son of a bitch."

"Yup."

"You arrogant son of a bitch."

"Yup."

"It means that much to you to go see her? That you'd jeopardize . . ."

"Yup."

Bradley sighed heavily, searching his friend's face. "Okay, then. Let me make a few calls. And now get your ass out of my house and get some sleep. Okay?"

"Okay. And Bradley?"

"Yeah?"

"Thank you."

"Get out of here, you fucker."

"I'm going."

"You crazy, obsessive, maniacal son of a bitch."

Anton nodded. "Yup. I love you, too."

"Go get some rest. I'll call you tomorrow."

"Good night."

CHAPTER THIRTY-TWO

Georgia was beautiful. Wildflowers everywhere. Bloodred earth, which felt as familiar as his bones, even though he had no recollection of having seen it before. Big white clouds in a flawlessly blue sky. Every few minutes Anton felt his heart soaring as the sheer beauty around him blew away thoughts of why he was here. And then he would remember, and something in his chest would tighten. And so he drove, his heart soaring and pinching, forgetting and remembering his reasons for being on this road, in this borrowed car, making his way from the private airport in Augusta where he had landed to 322 Cherry Lane in Ronan, Georgia.

As he drove, he rehearsed what he would say to his mother—but he wouldn't call her that, wouldn't even think of her in that way, because that was a trap. Then what *would* he call her? What demeanor would he present? He thought it through, how he would conduct himself, and finally arrived at matter-of-fact. Not threatening but stern. Firm. To the point. He had to convince her that there was nothing to be gained from going to the press with her falsehoods. That nobody would believe her. And that running for governor or not, he wasn't the kind of man who could be blackmailed by a junkie who had sold her only child down the river. Convince her of this and then get the hell out of Dodge.

But here, his determination broke. The truth was, it was hard to know, really, what he'd do when he saw her face-to-face. What sort of condition he would find her in. Fallen down drunk or spaced out? Or had she gotten her shit together? Married or living alone? Other kids? Good God, half brothers or sisters? And his grandma. Where was she? Dead or alive? Well, he would know the answers to all these questions in just a while longer. Without meaning to, he stepped on the gas.

To his great chagrin, Katherine had sided with Brad. "I don't know why this can't wait until after the election," she'd argued. "In any case, there's nothing in this letter that sounds like blackmail. It—she—actually sounds sweet." He had been unable to meet her eye. "I have to," he'd mumbled, and then he'd hated the way she'd cocked her head and given him that quizzical look, as if she could see right through him, as if she knew some truth that eluded him.

"If you want to go see your mom, honey, that's totally legit. But for God's sake, just say so," Katherine had said, and he'd felt the blood rush to his face as he looked from her to Brad, who sat staring at a point over Anton's shoulder.

"She's not my mom," he replied, aware that he was stammering, angry with Katherine for causing it. "And in any case, that has nothing to do with it."

He'd sneaked out of his home and into Brad's car early this morning, and they had arrived at the airport hangar while it was still dark. And now here he was, in the state where he'd been born but didn't remember, less than a half hour away from the woman who had abandoned him.

If she was even home, that is. If not, he'd have to ask around, which could blow his cover. The *People* article had put him on the map in unexpected ways. Folks recognized him in faraway places. Maybe he should've allowed his oldest friend to come along; Brad was much better at strong-arm tactics. But he hadn't, couldn't, let him. No, this first meeting, however it went, was between him and her. For a moment the tears blurred the road ahead of him, and he took his foot off the gas pedal. Damn. After all this time, it still hurt like a son of a bitch, what she'd done. No wonder he never, ever thought about those days. But here she was, popping back into his life at the least opportune time. Things were going well with Katherine, the campaign was finally humming along, he was already meeting with aides to plan the first month's agenda should he become governor, and now he had to sneak out of town to deal with this unsavory matter. Apart from the mental distraction, there was the risk. If the media got hold of the news, there would be a lot of explaining to do. At the very least, it would remind white voters that despite the Coleman name, he was adopted, the illegitimate son of a junkie. It was the weirdest thing—despite his complexion, his kinky hair, poll after poll showed that voters in his state didn't think of him as black, per se. They *knew* he was biracial, of course—but it was as if Pappy and Dad cast a shadow so deep, it hid his blackness.

So far.

Anton let out an exasperated growl. Stop getting ahead of yourself, he thought. Why should he get caught? He had used Google Earth to look up her house, and it showed that she lived out in the country, with not too many other houses around. He would find her, look her in the eye, say what he had to say to convince her that talking to the media would be a bad idea, and then leave. If things went well, he could be making his way back to the airport later tonight. Or, if he was too tired, he'd check in to a small motel—a baseball cap, a pair of dark glasses, and paying in cash should do the trick—and fly back the next morning. Brad had rented the plane from Beau Branson, one of his millionaire buddies who had business interests in Georgia and who had even provided the Lexus he was driving. So really, things had gone as well as he could have hoped for.

He got off the freeway, and the sign said it was twenty-two miles to Ronan. He drove down a four-lane street with the usual big-box stores and fast-food restaurants, a road that looked depressingly similar to any other in the country. But after a few miles, the road narrowed to two lanes, and then he was driving through a series of small towns with brick buildings and mom-and-pop restaurants and ice cream parlors. Despite the summer heat, he lowered the car windows to savor the full experience. He wished he could stop for an order of grits or a bowl of mac and cheese; although his stomach let out a low growl at the thought, he pushed on. The sooner he could finish what he'd come here to do and leave, the better. He searched through his duffel bag and pulled out a small packet of peanuts to nibble on instead.

But letting the Georgia air into his car might have been a mistake, because as he drove out of town and through the countryside again, something within him began to slow down. For a moment he thought that he was drowsy—he had awakened early this morning, after all— but it wasn't that. It was as if he had let the South into his car and it was acting upon his senses, cradling him, lulling him, and dulling the urgency of the task before him. He heard the whooshing of those elegant magnolias, he felt dizzy at the sight of the vividly red earth, his eyes widened at the sight of a peach tree orchard. He passed a tiny church, its steeple white as Jesus against the deep blue sky. The houses were now few and far between, and already he could guess who lived in which houses—white people in the big, opulent homes with the wraparound porches and blacks in the smaller, modest homes or, worse, in the shacks near the plowed fields. Occasionally, he would see a lone black man, old but straight-backed, sitting on a porch swing, and inevitably, the man would wave at the passing car. Anton felt a choked sensation in his throat the first time it happened, something primitive and familiar pounding in his blood. *I am home*, he thought, and then, aghast, drove the ridiculous thought out of his mind. He was being romantic. Melodramatic. Sentimental. Idiotic. Georgia was no more his home than Rome was. *But this is where your ancestors are from*, the voice rose again,

and again he snuffed it out. What're you going to do next? Chew to-
bacco? Eat watermelon? This was the Deep South, a red state with terrible politics, and he was no more from it than Pappy was.

It was in this laconic-agitated state that he went over the railroad
tracks and almost missed the small road sign for his mother's street. He
braked hard and turned sharply onto the gravel road. She really did live
in the middle of nowhere. He hadn't even passed another house for the
last five minutes or so. He drove down the bumpy road, a flat, heavy
feeling in his chest, bracing himself for squalor, dirt, dysfunction, a
falling-down shack, maybe, like several others he had passed.

And so he wasn't ready for the sweet light yellow bungalow that bore
her address. Nor for the neat front yard with a vegetable garden on one
side and a flower bed on the other. He checked the address on his phone
against the one on the mailbox, and it was right. Knocked off course,
knowing he needed to recalibrate, he kept driving down the gravel
road past her house, taking in deep breaths, gathering his nerve, asking
himself what this new information meant. Finally, unable to decide, he
turned around and headed back. There was a gravel driveway to the left
where he parked behind an old-looking red Civic. He sat in his car for
a moment, ran his fingers through his short hair, looked at himself in
the rearview mirror, and then pushed open his door. He waited for a
dog to bark and come rushing toward the vehicle, but nothing stirred.
The place was so quiet he could hear the buzzing of the afternoon air.
He walked to the front of the house and stood looking at it. Now that
he was up close, he noticed the areas where the paint was peeling, the
fact that the third step leading up to the front porch had a large crack
running through it. It was a modest house, to be sure, but it looked neat
and well-maintained.

He shook his head. What the hell was he doing, standing in the middle of her yard, worrying about peeling paint? If she sensed the slightest
wavering in him, even a hint of weakness, she would take advantage of

it. He would not allow himself to feel sorry for her. He would not. He would be polite but curt. Businesslike. He had come too far, risked too much, to fail. He was scowling as he knocked on the front door. The muscle in his jaw worked compulsively when he heard her unlocking it. But the face that appeared at the door was so guileless and alert, the eyes so clear and kind, her recognition of him so immediate, the smile that flooded her face so wondrous, that he felt an immediate reciprocal warmth. He stood there, staring back, his mouth slightly agape, so that when she moved toward him and touched his cheek with her thin brown hand and said, "That you, Baby Boy?," he had no choice but to become nine years old again and respond, "Yes, Mam. It's me. It's Anton."

CHAPTER THIRTY-THREE

Anton. Anton. Anton.
Anton. Anton. Oh Lord, Lord, Lord.
Praise be Jesus.
Anton.

Juanita said his name over and over again, chanting it like a prayer, yelling it out loud in disbelief and excitement, wiping her tears away, and then saying it some more. He laughed the first few times she did it, caught up in her giddiness, flattered by being the object of her obvious joy, but when she didn't stop, he fell quiet, embarrassed by the flagrant display of maternal devotion, then puzzled by it, then distrusting. He looked away from her and around the room, relieved at how tidy and clean it was, far more neat, truth be told, than his own apartment. Katherine was forever straightening up for him when she visited. Katherine. Damn. He should've called her again before he went in.

"Anton," Juanita said. "Baby. Here, sit. My goodness, you so tall. Sit in this rocker. It's the most comfortable. How tall are you, anyways?"

He laughed self-consciously. "Just a little past six feet. Not that tall, actually."

She nodded. "Your daddy was—" She caught herself and stopped midsentence, and he allowed himself not to notice.

He lowered himself onto the chair, and before he could sit back, she said, "You want something to eat, son? I make you a PB and J?" She smiled. "Every time I make them at Sal's, I think of you. How you used to love them."

"Sal's?"

"The diner. Where I work. In town. I work in the kitchen."

He must've driven right past it on his way to see her. How strange. Half an hour ago, he had not known that his birth mom held a job, lived in a modest but decent home, far removed from the squalor and dissolution he had imagined for her. And this small brown face, framed by a schoolgirl's pigtail on either side, the big brown eyes, alert, trusting, with not a hint of the sloth and meanness he had been bracing himself for. They were his eyes, he realized with a start, a different color but the same shape, and yes, even the same warmth and guilelessness that people always commented upon.

She was staring at him, an uncertain smile hovering on her lips, and he realized she was awaiting an answer. He shook his head. "No, thanks," he said. "Nothing to eat." He saw her disappointment, realized that hers was the kind of face unable to hide its emotions, and despite his intentions, he understood that he couldn't bear to see her hurt. "But I will take something to drink," he added politely. "Do you have some pop?"

She cocked her head. "Pop?" Her face brightened. "You mean Coke." She laughed. "You're a real Yankee now, boy." She rose, chuckling to herself as she went toward the kitchen. "Pop, he says."

He heard her opening the fridge and took the chance to look around the room. The couch was worn but had three cheerful-looking embroidered cushions on it. Had she embroidered them? Did she know how to back when they . . . he . . . in the old days? He tried to remember but couldn't. The room was painted a light green, and one wall was covered with several framed pictures. He rose to his feet and walked over. There were a few pictures of her, looking improbably young, with an older woman he assumed was her mom. His grandmother. His childhood name for her came to him suddenly. Nana. And then he was staring at several baby pictures of himself. The hazel eyes were an immediate give-away, and Lord, did he have a wild mop of hair. She was holding him in one of those pictures, her slender face staring straight at the camera with not a trace of a smile. But there was something so protective and maternal in her stance, as if she were carrying a child she would risk her life to hold on to. Something stirred in Anton's chest as he gazed at that picture, and he knew that if he allowed it to, the feeling would swallow him whole. He turned abruptly away from the photograph and briefly studied one of him at probably six years old. It had been shot at a photo studio, and he was wearing suspenders and a cap and grinning as if he didn't have a care in the world. Anton looked closely at the picture, trying to detect something in that boy's eyes—fear, wariness, distrust—but found only brightness. This was not the look of an abused or neglected boy.

He heard her footsteps and returned quickly to the rocker but rose to help her when he saw she was carrying a small tray. There was his Coke, and she had made him a PB&J sandwich anyway. He opened his mouth to protest, but she shushed him. "Try it," she said. "It's your mama's sandwich. No one will make it for you like me."

She said it defiantly, but he heard the dip in her voice, saw the trepidation in her eyes, as if she were awaiting his judgment. He sighed. She was not making this easy. He had prepared himself for so many scenarios, but a mother who missed her son was not one of them. He picked up the sandwich and took a bite. And closed his eyes to the flood of memories that assaulted him.

He spoke with his mouth full. "I came to see you," he said, while chewing, "to talk—"

"Yes, you did. Praise the Lord. When I sent that letter, I never—"

"—to you about . . ." He swallowed. "Yes, the letter."

"A miracle, that's what it is. A million times I pray—"

"Mam." His voice was loud, harsh, shattering the quiet of the afternoon. But he had her attention. She looked at him with those big eyes, her face tilted upward, a penitent awaiting his judgment. He felt a moment's unease at how easily she had submitted to him but ignored the feeling and plowed ahead. "I came to see you because, as you know, I'm running for governor. And we can't—we don't—we can't afford any media attention about . . . this . . . about what happened. In the past." He knew he was stuttering, losing his thread and perhaps his authority over her, and found himself desperately wishing that Brad were here with him.

She opened her mouth, but he held up a hand to stop her. "I'm trying to say." He reached into his pocket and pulled out her letter, aware that his right hand was shaking, hoping she didn't notice. He leaned forward as if to share the letter with her. "This part here, where you say I chose . . . I decided to live with my . . . new family." He willed himself to look up and stare her directly in the eyes. "Why would you say that? I mean, why the lie, when everyone knows you gave me up? I mean, if you think you can intimidate me with this lie." He stopped abruptly, noticing the stricken look on her sallow face, the tears glittering in her eyes. Oh, shit. This was going to be easier and harder than he'd imagined. He had braced himself for a confrontation with a drug addict. He was unprepared to deal with a woman who looked as if he were ripping her apart with each word he spoke. Maybe Katherine had been right. Maybe, just maybe, he had misread both the letter and her intentions?

"That's what you think? That I gave you up?" Her voice was sharp, raw as glass. "You think . . ."

He looked at her incredulously. "Well, of course you did. I think that's beyond dispute."

Her lip curled. "That's what you think of me? All this time. That your mama is the kind of woman who would give up her only child? To white folk? What's the matter with you, boy?"

He felt the balance of power in the room shift away from him and toward her. It was the way she had called him "boy." Powerful-like. Stern. Like a mother. "Look, I didn't come here to argue," he tried. "All I'm saying is, there's nothing to be gained from renegotiating the past. Or—"

Her voice was flat, her face affectless. "You're a lawyer, right, son?" She nodded. "You act like one. Like those white lawyers in town."

"What is that supposed to mean?"

She leaned forward in her chair and looked him in the eyes. "You know exactly what it means, boy," she said softly, and kept watching him as he flushed. She looked away for a moment and then pinned him with her eyes again. "Why did you come here, Anton? What do you want?"

It was hard to answer that question honestly, but he did. "To get your word—your assurance—that you're not going to the media with your story."

She spat out a laugh. "And what story would that be, boy?"

"Don't call me that."

"Don't call you 'boy'? Then why do you act like one? You find your mama after however many years, and all you think is that I want something from you? And you had to come before I go tell my 'story' to the papers?"

He slammed his hand on the side table. "Look. You're the one who gave me away," he said. "You're the one who made a deal with the devil. What kind of woman locks a kid up for seven days in an apartment? What kind of mother—" His face contorted, and he wiped his nose with the back of his hand.

"A bad mother." Her voice shook, but it carried across the room. "The worst kind. A monster. Okay?" Her face crumbled. "But Anton. I was tryin'. All the time I was in prison, I was tryin'. I was clean. Did it cold turkey. You know how hard that is, son? But I did it. For you. But you couldn't wait for me. You were angry at me. I get that. I'm not blaming you. You were just a kid. I know. And those rich white folk, they had so much to offer you. All those skiing trips and all. I had nothing in those days. I . . . I couldn't . . . compete."

His head was pounding. "What do you mean, I couldn't wait? Wait for what? How?" All at once he felt sleepy, the activity of the day catching up with him, and he closed his eyes briefly. But then he was wide awake, his attention caught by something she'd just said. "The skiing trips. How would you know about those?"

She shrugged. "He told me. How else?"

"Who?"

"Who? Mr. Coleman. The man who wanted to be your daddy. When he came to see me."

The world stopped; in that pause Anton heard the ticking of the clock, heard the song of an unknown bird in the yard. He sat still, his mouth dry. When he could speak, he said, "When?"

"I don't remember the exact date. When you're in prison, you know, the days just roll into one big mess of nothing."

"He came to the prison? To see you?"

She looked as puzzled as he felt. "But you knew this, baby. You just forgot. You were so young." She looked at a spot beyond Anton's head for a minute and then collected herself. "No, not to the prison. They brought me to some, I dunno, office building, I think it was. At night, when there was nobody there but him and one other gentleman."

This woman was more conniving than he'd ever imagined. To think that he'd almost fallen for her act a moment ago. Anton felt something akin to relief—she was just an ordinary con artist with a ridiculous cock-and-bull story. Let her go to the media with it; they would simply laugh her out of town. He felt triumphant, giddy, and also strangely let down. He fought down an urge to laugh. "My dad brought you to an empty office building?" he said mockingly. "Really? At night?"

She sat very erect in her chair and looked at him intently, the earlier girlishness having disappeared from her demeanor. He willed himself to stare back, not bothering to hide his disdain, his contempt, and, now that he was willing to acknowledge it, his fury. Hadn't she mangled his life enough, all those years ago? Did she really have to appear in his life again, with her preposterous tales?

He stood up and took a step toward her. "Enough," he said. "You've done enough damage. Don't you dream of maligning my dad's name ever again. You hear me? Ever." He stood towering over her, idly noticing the single strand of white hair on the top of her head.

She raised her head slowly to meet his eyes. "You think I'm lying to you, Anton?" she said at last.

"You bet," he said. "You bet I think you're lying, you . . ."

She lifted her left eyebrow. "That's how they teach you to talk to your elders up north?" she said.

He snorted. "Please. Let's not go into the old parental routine . . ."

She got up quickly from her chair. "Wait here," she said, and disappeared into what he assumed was the bedroom. He shuffled from foot to foot, anxious to get out of there. He stood in the middle of the room, his fists clenching and unclenching by his sides, debating whether to slip out into the yard and call Brad. He would know what to do, how to convince this woman that she'd better quit while she was ahead.

But before he could move, Juanita strode back into the room, clutching a manila folder in her hand. "Anton," she said in an authoritative voice that made him bristle, "sit down."

To his surprise, he lowered his body onto the rocker. She sat across from him, the folder in her lap. A sheet of paper flew out and onto the floor, and as he bent to pick it up, he saw that it was a cutout of the *People* magazine story from a few months ago. He handed it to her wordlessly, and she made a sheepish face. "I tore it out of the magazine at the dentist's office," she confessed. "I . . . I was so excited . . . It felt like a miracle when I saw your face." She stared at the article, and when she looked up again, her eyes were red.

"All this time, I believed what he told me. Mr. Coleman. Your . . . the man you call your daddy. That you choose him and his wife over me. And so I think you're pleased with me, Anton, for respecting your decision. That's the only way I survived all these years. Thinking I gave you what you wanted." Her face collapsed. "But now I see you've been mad at me. All these long years. For letting you go. Now I see I truly am what the world says I am—an ignorant black woman. Who got fooled by the white man with the oldest trick in the world. It's slavery, what he done to me, Anton. Slavery."

The tears rolled down her cheeks, and despite his confusion and a gathering sense of terror, Anton felt the urge to comfort her. He fought it down, unwilling to weaken, trying to figure out what game she was playing. After a few moments she stopped crying, rubbed her eyes on her sleeves, and continued rifling through the folder. She found what she wanted and held out a photograph to him. "Here," she said simply. "He gave me this. To show me how happy you were with them."

Anton recognized the picture immediately. The family trip to Vail. Him, posing at the top of the hill in his brand-new parka and skis, his hands on his hips, looking for all the world like a young prince. "How did you get this?" he started, and then caught himself. "Did they—did my parents—mail it to you? In prison?"

She shook her head impatiently. "No. I told you. He told me I could keep it. I wanted to keep all the pictures he showed me of you. One of them was you on a sailboat, I remember. I had to choose between that one or this, quick. Before they took me back to the facility."

He listened dumbly as she kept talking, telling him about the mysterious ride to the deserted office building and the tall, distinguished-looking man she met there. The stories David had told her about her baby boy, how well he was doing in school, how happy he was with his new life. And then the proof, the pictures of her own Anton, a little older now, the baby fat burned away, the clothes stylish and tailored to fit him, not the hand-me-downs she used to get at the Goodwill store. Her Anton, already a stranger, on ski slopes and on a sailboat and playing a sport whose name she didn't know. What mother worth her salt would deny her only child such a life? She waited for him to answer, but he stared mutely at her, not wanting to believe her, believing her. "Why would he?" he said at last, his voice hoarse. "Why would he come to you? And how could he have gotten you out of prison?" Even as he asked the question, he knew the answer. And so he closed his eyes and sat back in the rocker, savoring that last minute of an intact world, his last brush with innocence, before he asked the next question. "The judge who sentenced you . . . who locked you away, do you remember his name?" As he asked, he was ashamed of the fact that he had never bothered to find out for himself. He had truly acted as if he had been hatched into the Coleman family as pristine as a chick from an eggshell, with no past and no curiosity about that past.

Juanita gave the barest of smiles. "I sure do. Judge Bob Campbell. I know that name sure as I do the devil's own. He gave me three times the sentence we plea-bargained for. My court-appointed lawyer said I got railroaded." She was quiet for a moment and then she laughed. "I like Georgia," she said. "Down here, you know exactly where you stand. White man is king here, yesterday, today, and tomorrow. But up north, they talk sweet to your face. And then cut your throat when you ain't looking."

He wished she would shut up so he could think. Find the flaw in the yarn she was spinning. But she kept on talking, and now she was pulling out something else, a piece of paper, no, a check, and pushing it at him. He took hold of it reluctantly, holding it between his thumb and index finger. He stared at the familiar address—their old Arborville address—and then at Delores Coleman's signature. He saw the date, saw that it said "Cash" on the payee line, and saw that it was made out for the sum of five thousand dollars.

"He sent me this," she was saying. "After I was released. The man who delivered it said it was for me to start a new life. Your mam—his wife—sent a real nice note with it, thanking me for giving you up. She promised to provide a good life for you. And she hoped that I stay clean and have a great life. That's what she said—'I hope you have a great life.'"

He stood up. "Excuse me," he said. "The bathroom?"

He bent over the toilet and retched a few times, though since he had not eaten anything but a few peanuts and a bite of the sandwich, there was nothing much to bring up. He stood up and splashed cold water on his face and then leaned against the door, trying to steady his breathing, wrestling with the weakness in his limbs, the queasiness in his gut. He forced himself to remember that day when David had taken him for ice cream and told him gravely that his birth mom wanted to surrender custody to David and Delores. "Try to understand, son," David had said. "It's not her fault. She's just really sick and can't care for you the way she knows we can." Anton remembered again what he had felt in that moment, that orphaned, cut-off feeling, knowing that he had permanently lost not just his mom but his old apartment, his neighborhood, his old pals, his entire way of life. That he had been traded like a baseball card. And that he now belonged to this tall, handsome man who looked at him with such hope and longing that it terrified him, even though he admired him and wanted more and more to be like him. Anton had skipped school a week later and taken two buses to go back to his old apartment, hoping to find his mam and convince her that she was making a mistake, only to return home to the Colemans that evening, exhausted and defeated. As time went by, David and

Delores had become his real family, and his real mother had become a phantom, a cautionary tale, an embarrassment.

He sank to his knees, the green bathroom tile cool against his body. He was everybody's son, but he belonged to no one. The three parents in his life had each betrayed him in his or her own way, and he had no idea how to weigh one betrayal against the other. Who had the better claim on him? Did he belong to any of these damaged people? He had no idea. Who would he be when he opened this cheap wooden door and walked back out into that small living room? He knew he had to come out of the bathroom at some point and face her, but he didn't know how. His face flushed as he remembered how he had mocked her a short while ago, the contempt with which he had looked at her. And of course, his lawyer's mind told him, there was always the possibility that he was misreading the situation, believing her too easily, not comprehending some fiction in what she was telling him. His father had been a judge, for God's sake, at the time of her imprisonment. David would know better than to defraud an inmate, would think a million times before setting up a clandestine meeting in a deserted office building. Wasn't he afraid that someone—a guard, a fellow inmate—would squeal? If Mam's story was true, David had risked his legal license, his profession, his family name, for the sake of—for the sake of what? Him? A young, ignorant boy who, more often than not, was moody, sullen, withdrawn?

It was all too confusing, the dimly remembered past closing in on him like a hand at his throat. With an effort, he struggled to his feet, bracing himself with a hand on the sink. He turned on the faucet again, splashed more water across his face, and glanced at the distraught, wild-eyed stranger looking back at him in the mirror. Who was this man? How long had he been here? He looked at his watch and blinked. How the hell had it gotten to be three o'clock?

He walked back into the living room to find her sitting where she had been when he'd disappeared into the bathroom. "You okay?" she asked, but her voice was distant, with none of the maternal concern she had exhibited earlier. He nodded and sat down heavily on the rocker. "The check," he began, as if resuming a conversation. "How come you didn't cash it?"

She smiled a wan smile. "Couldn't. Dangerous to give that much money to a junkie. I was only a couple years sober, remember? So I mailed it to my mom. For safekeeping. She said she would hold it for me until I moved back down here. Which I did, a few months later." She made a sweeping gesture with her hand. "This is your nana's house, you know. You lived here until you were one. But you're too young to remember."

"Is she dead?"

Juanita nodded. "Yes, baby. Five years ago."

He wanted to ask a million more questions, but he couldn't. He was beginning to feel a dangerous, grudging respect for the older woman that unnerved him. It was too risky, too hard, too confusing. He was almost thirty-five years old, mere months away from most likely becoming a governor, yet he was afraid to find out how his nana had died and how his mother had lived. Not wanting to know. Dying to know.

He felt a familiar wave of nausea, but this time he made for the front door. "Air," he said. "I need air."

She was about to say something, but he pulled the car keys from his pocket. "I'll be back," he said. "I need to make a business call." And before she could respond, he was on the front porch and down the stone steps and getting into his car. He backed out and drove down the gravel road past her house, not turning around to see if she was watching him. He went down the road as far as he could to ensure that he was out of sight, to where she couldn't even see the dust cloud his car made, and then he stopped. The heat of the afternoon assailed him, and even though his windows were down, he turned on the air-conditioning. He listened to the quarrels of the birds, heard the buzz of a bee hovering near the front of his car. Beyond this, silence, the green fields still and sleepy on either side of him. He rested his forehead on the wheel and shut his eyes. He thought of calling Katherine, but he knew that would only delay the inevitable. There was only one person in the world who could answer the questions churning in his mind.

CHAPTER THIRTY-FOUR

Anton debated briefly whether to call on the home phone but decided not to risk Delores answering. And so he dialed his father's cell phone, hoping that William would not pick up, as he sometimes did when his dad was resting. His wishes were answered when David answered on the second ring. "Hi, son," he said. "How'd the stop at the retirement home go?"

Shit. He'd forgotten that David had a copy of his campaign itinerary. "I didn't go," he said.

"Why not?" David asked sharply. "We need those folks to show up at the polls."

"I'm not there," he said. "I'm out of the state, actually."

"What do you mean?" He could hear the impatience in David's voice and then a forced levity. "You and Katherine go away to the city for a quick rendezvous or something?"

"I wish." He took a deep breath and then said, "No, Dad. Actually, I'm in Georgia. Sitting on a dirt road in the middle of a field."

There was a slight pause and then David said, "What're you talking about?" There was the slightest quiver in his voice, but Anton heard it—fear, dread, calculation—clear as a church confession.

He gripped the phone tighter, his breathing now shallow. "I'm in Georgia, Dad. Sitting outside her house. Visiting with *her*."

Another pause, brief but infinite. "I see." A sigh. "How'd you find her?"

Anton was about to explain about the letter—how he'd distrusted her immediately, how he'd flown south to shut her up. And then he thought, I don't owe him this. The explanations need to flow in the opposite direction.

"I found her," he said simply. "And she told me . . . the whole story." He heard David make a sound, but he kept talking. "And she showed me the photograph. And the check that Mom made out to her. She never cashed it. Did you know that?"

He heard David's gasp. "Listen. I don't know what shit this woman has been saying. I . . . She was your birth mom, dammit. So I decided to help her out. Get her situated."

"You gave five thousand dollars to a drug addict, Dad? What were you trying to do? Kill her?"

"Anton. I won't be talked to in this manner. I won't. Now, listen, whatever you want to ask, you ask me straight. Like a man."

Despite his anger, Anton felt a grudging admiration for the old man. Even after the heart attack, David was steel, pure steel. "Okay, then. How'd you manage to sneak her out of prison for that impromptu meeting?"

There was a painfully long silence, and for a wild moment Anton wondered if his father had hung up on him. He was about to say "Hello?" when David said, "I'm not doing this, Anton. I'm not subjecting myself to answering every charge that this woman is leveling at me."

Anton heard the admission of guilt. "Dad," he said, incredulous. "You could've lost your law license. You could've gone to jail. It wasn't just immoral what you did. It was illegal."

"Immoral? You're going to give me morality from a woman who

locked you up in an apartment for a week?" David scoffed. "Or have you forgotten that cold, hard fact, Anton? What we rescued you from?"

Somehow, the word "rescue" stung. It objectified him, made him feel like a charity case. "I didn't ask you to rescue me," Anton said gruffly. "I don't mean to be ungrateful, but—"

"Son." The distress in David's voice was genuine. "Where are we going with this? Hell, how did we get here? I don't want your gratitude, goddammit. I didn't do you a favor. I . . . we . . . I love you. I've never regretted a second I've had with you. Never taken it for granted, either."

Anton had not known it was possible to have so many conflicting emotions slash at you at once and still be able to breathe. He heard David's distress and it tore at him. He loved the man at the other end of the phone, worshipped him. He was close to Delores in ways that he wasn't with anyone else. Pappy was the only grandparent he had known, the only death he had mourned. But there was another claim on him that he was now aware of. He couldn't ignore this fact. And try as he might, he couldn't leave out the racial element. She was a poor, unsophisticated black woman who had been railroaded by a bunch of powerful white men. One of whom happened to be the man who had made his entire life possible.

"Anton," David said. "You still there?"

"I'm here." He gulped hard and then asked, "Did Mom know?"

"Of course not. She knew what I told her. And I'd prefer to leave it that way."

Anton nodded, relief coursing through his body. "So she wrote the check because . . . ?"

"Because I asked her to. To give your . . . that woman . . . a leg up. You know your mom. She'd do anything for anyone." David's voice took on a businesslike tone. "Look, it's hard to do this on the phone. In any case, you need to get back home, son. There's an election to be won, remember? This is the time to focus on the future, not on the past."

Anton shook his head. The last statement was so typically David. But then the image of the woman in the yellow cottage rose before his eyes, and he felt a deep reluctance at the thought of pivoting to the future. Not so fast. He knew how easily he would get caught up in the gears of the campaign from the moment he landed back home. How easily he and David would resume their normal relationship, how the lovely Katherine and the comforts of his life would blur the memory of the woman who had sat upright, without flinching, while he had falsely accused her of lying to him. He had been hero-worshipping the wrong parent, it turned out. The true steel was in the tiny girl-like woman who had battled drug addiction, poverty, false sentencing, abduction of her son, and God knew how many other injustices in order to arrive at the moment when her grown son had called her a liar.

Something flashed in Anton's mind right then, like a bright light, and he asked, "Does—did Uncle Connor know about this?" There was a long silence, and Anton felt the thudding of his heart reverberate through his entire body. "Dad?"

He heard the sharp exhale. "Of course. Connor was the prosecutor."

"Jesus Christ. It was a damn conspiracy. All because—"

"Anton. Stop being melodramatic. We were just trying to—"

"Why'd you do it, Dad?" he yelled. "I mean, Jesus H. Christ, it's lie after lie and deceit after deceit."

David lowered his voice. "What would you have had me do, Anton? Risked returning you to that woman? And the next time she decided to sneak off hunting for drugs? What then?"

Anton shook his head. "She's clean, Dad. She's been clean all these years."

David scoffed. "So she says. And in any case, hindsight is twenty-twenty. You know as well as I do what the recidivism rates are for crack-heads."

Anton flinched as if David had physically struck him. Crackhead.

That's how David saw his mother. As a statistic, a number, a data point. "You should see her, Dad," he said. "She's nothing like what you imagine. Just a good, decent workingwoman. The kind you've extolled in a million political speeches."

David grunted. "Touché. A low blow, but touché. Though let me remind you that even a junkie can hold it together for a few hours."

"She's not a junkie," Anton yelled. "And even if she were, nothing changes the fact that you stole from her. This is as bad a case of abuse of power as I've ever seen. You could be in jail for this, Dad." His voice broke. "And you lied to me. You lied. You told me she'd given me up. You lied."

"And for that I'm sorry. But I had no choice. You have to believe me." David's voice shook, but when he spoke again, his tone was urgent, pitched. "Goddammit, Anton. I'm human, too. I did the best I could, under very trying circumstances."

"You had no choice? Of course you did. All you had to do was follow the law."

David made an exasperated sound. "I couldn't. Don't you see? Because you . . . you were special. Such great potential. And I was the only one who could see it through. Hell, son, it would've been a crime, no, a sin, to have wasted that potential. No. Not in a million years. You were worth fighting for."

Anton smacked his hand on the steering wheel. "Don't. Don't make this about me, Dad. This was about you. What you needed." He closed his eyes because he was about to go where he knew he shouldn't, to that cold, wet, dark place where James lay in a grave. "You needed another child to love, Dad. I get that. After James . . ."

"Anton, you don't wanna go there. In any case, that's not true . . ."

"I mean, it's very sad what happened, but that didn't . . ."

"Anton, I'm warning you . . ."

". . . that didn't give you the right to . . ."

"Goddammit, you little prick. Stop," David roared in his ear. "What do you want from me? I've given you every fucking thing I've ever had. I'm about to give you the goddamn governorship of the fucking state on a silver platter. And you dare talk to me like this?"

Anton sat frozen in his seat. He could hear William's concerned voice in the background and David saying he was all right and to please give him some damn privacy. Anton felt a moment of trepidation. Dad had a weak heart, and Dr. Carlson had told them repeatedly that he was not supposed to get too agitated about anything.

"Dad, listen," he said. "Calm down. How about we talk when—"

"No, Anton, you listen. You want me to apologize for what I did? I'll only say this once, so listen up: I won't. I will never apologize for fighting to keep you in my life. Because guess what? You were worth it. You were worth all of it. And I will never apologize *to* you *for* you. Never."

Anton had been beaten by the better man. He knew this. Even with a bad heart and diminished strength, his father was still twice the man he was. Because right or wrong, David had conviction. Whereas he, Anton, sat in the car vanquished while his father growled in his ear, "Now put all this nonsense out of your head and get the hell back into town and get on with your life," and all he could do was reply, "Yes, sir." He hung up the phone and sat staring straight ahead, not knowing whether or not to drive back to his mother's house and, if so, what to say to her. He was acutely aware that he had failed in the most basic of tasks: getting David to apologize to Juanita Vesper for the grievous harm he had done her. She would not have even the smallest of civilities afforded to her.

Anton turned off his phone. He knew that David would try to call back or Delores would. He didn't want to talk to any of them yet, not even Katherine. After a few moments, he turned the car around. He would say his goodbye to the woman in the yellow house and then be on his way home. There was nothing more to keep him here.

CHAPTER THIRTY-FIVE

She was waiting for him on the front porch when he returned, watching him as he got out of his car and came wearily up the steps. She rose from the porch swing as he approached, but he motioned for her to remain seated and went and sat next to her. She shifted a bit and then reached over and took his hand in both of hers and placed it in her lap. It occurred to him that this was the first time his mother had taken his hand in hers in twenty-five years. He shook his head ruefully, then allowed his head to lean in to hers, and they sat there for what seemed to him like hours, and then she was shaking against him and he lifted his head to see the tears streaming down her face. "Mam, don't," he started, but that was a mistake, because all of a sudden her tears acquired a voice and she was making a keening sound that made his hair stand up. *If grief had a baby, she would sing like this.* The line went through his mind, and he was not sure if it was something he had heard before, a line from a song, maybe, or if it was his own. But he could barely complete the thought, because the woman next to him looked like she was going to keel over. She had released his hand and was holding herself from the waist and rocking as if she would fly apart should she let go of her body. And those terrible sounds kept pouring out of her, released to the air like a poisonous vapor, and he thought absently, How could this frail, small body have carried the weight of this? As if her pain were a living, physical animal that had lain curled up inside her until this moment.

Anton's senses felt dull, hazy, his default reaction in the face of other people's sorrow. When Katherine had sobbed at her beloved uncle Jeffrey's funeral, all he could do was pat her repeatedly on her back and say, "There, there. It'll be okay." His stilted, miserly reaction had led to one of their rare fights, with Katherine accusing him of compounding her loneliness rather than mitigating it. "It's like you disappeared," she'd said days later. "You were there, but you disappeared." And he had dropped his head in acknowledgment, knowing she was right, unable to explain to her how people's pain paralyzed him, how desperately he wanted to help alleviate it, and how completely he knew that he couldn't. It was one of the functions of being a governor that he was dreading, truth be told—the comforting of strangers after touring an area struck by a tornado or a flood or a school shooting, the glare of the TV cameras turning every interaction into a performance. Sometimes, even in the midst of campaigning, he would think that he was a politician better suited to an earlier age, say, during the Depression, when the voters themselves were more stoic and close-lipped about loss. Now, it seemed, a calamity was not a calamity until you tweeted it or spoke about it to Anderson Cooper in prime time. He had inherited none of Pappy's easy affability or David's intense charm; he was a technocrat, he wanted to fix problems and improve people's lives but without too much interaction with the people themselves.

"Say it, son, I beg you," Juanita was saying, and he blinked, pulling himself out of his disappearance, trying to focus on her.

"I'm sorry. What?"

"I am begging you. To forgive me for what I've done." He looked and saw that her hands were folded in a pleading gesture. Her pixie-like face no longer looked young; grief had given it a timeless quality, like one of those stone statues from antiquity. He stared at her in fascination, unable to speak, but this only made her sob harder. "You're angry with me, Anton." She sniffed. "I can tell. And I don't blame you at all. Not at all."

He reached into his pocket and pulled out a handkerchief and handed it to her. She took it uncertainly, and he gestured toward her face, and she wiped her eyes with it before handing it back. He held the damp cloth in his hand, thinking, I have my mother's tears with me. I will carry my mother's tears home with me, and I will have them forever. Something pinched at his heart then, and he said, "What happened, Mam? Why'd you leave me all alone like that?" And as he heard the question, he realized that he had waited a lifetime to ask it.

"Anton," she said urgently, her eyes searching his face, "you've got to believe me. I was planning on being gone for half hour. An hour, tops. But . . ." Here she stumbled, her expression wild. "I don't know what happened . . . I remember taking one hit . . . and then someone, one of the men in that house . . ." She stopped, shut her eyes, rocking slightly, her mouth moving wordlessly.

He wanted to end her embarrassment, say it was okay and she needn't continue, but his need to know was too great. "Did you think of me during those days?" he cried.

She didn't answer, just sat there with her eyes closed, whispering words he couldn't hear. He couldn't tell if she was praying or saying something to herself, but just as he was about to ask, she opened her eyes, reached over, and took his hand back in hers. "I was a druggie, Anton," she said quietly. "Your mama was a druggie. And I owed money to this guy Victor. He was my dealer, see? And so he kept me there in that house. To repay his loan. You get what I'm saying, baby? Every time I came to, I remembered you and I tried to leave. But those men wouldn't let me. And Victor would give me another hit and off I'd go. I lost track of time after the first few days."

It was the most exquisite pain, listening to his mother telling him that she'd been raped, prostituted off, but below that pain was relief. At last he was finding out the truth, no matter how stomach-churning that truth was. "I'm sorry," he murmured, and for the first time, he was sorry for her rather than for himself. For the first time, he was no longer the protagonist in his life's story.

They were quiet for a long time, and then she said, "I went to college for a semester, you know," a different note in her voice.

"You did?" he asked, wondering what had made her think of that.

"Yup. Community college. But then I got pregnant with you." She looked at him shyly. "It was a big scandal. Because of who your daddy was."

He looked away and into the yard, unsure how many more revelations he could handle in a day. He glanced back at her, but she was searching his face, and Anton knew she wouldn't continue unless he asked. "What happened?" he said gruffly.

"He was a white doctor who came to work at the county hospital. He was from Chicago. I used to go once a week to clean his house. He had a house right in town. He was older than me, by fifteen years, maybe. So I didn't ever think of him in that way. But—he liked me, Anton. Poor man, far from home, stuck among us black folks. And he was a kind man, too. Anyway, it pleased me that someone like him took an interest in me. You know? He was always asking me what I thought about this and that. What I wanted to be when I was older. Where I wanted to live. Don't nobody ever ask me this. Your nana—God bless her soul—she thought I was gonna live out here in Podunk forever. But he treated me like I was something smart. And slowly, I came around to him. And so it happened."

"I remember Nana," Anton said. "She came to visit us once, right?"

Juanita's face brightened. "You remember that? You cried for two days straight after she left." She sighed. "She asked me so many times to move back to Georgia. You see, she'd seen what my life was like up north—single mom, no man, working a shitty job, barely making it.

But I couldn't. You were one when we left Ronan, and I vowed never to raise you here. Folks here have long memories. And wagging tongues. That's why we got out in the first place. A mixed-race boy in a small town—forget it." She smiled mirthlessly. "That was before I learned that the North was just a different kind of prison."

"And my—The doctor? He just abandoned you?"

She shot him a puzzled look. "What was he supposed to do? Marry a skinny black ninny whose head was as empty as an old wooden trunk? He was a learned man. In any case, he took a job in Chicago just before you were born."

"Bastard," Anton swore under his breath.

Juanita looked shocked. "Bad luck to speak ill of the dead, Baby Boy. And that, too, your own daddy." She caught his start of surprise and nodded. "He died in 1989. Car crash. I heard from Nana. Her old doctor told her. Guess they were still friends."

All these screwed-up adults. He was just the end product of their stories, the tail end, an afterthought. So much had gone into making him—poverty, ignorance, racism—all of which would have made it impossible for an educated white doctor to be seen with a black country girl, even if he'd wanted to, even in the 1980s. And then another layer—the unwanted pregnancy, the loneliness of life in the North, the solace of a mind-dulling drug that made you forget the world would never belong to you. Really, it was as if history itself had conspired to deliver Anton into the arms of David and Delores Coleman. And he supposed he should be thankful for that deliverance, because an alternative fate would've meant that he'd be either on the streets or in prison or in a morgue.

He opened his mouth to ask more questions, because his hunger for his past suddenly seemed insatiable, when he was betrayed by another kind of hunger. His stomach growled loudly. And there was no time to be ashamed, because here was Juanita, brushing away the last of her tears, jumping to her feet, apologizing again, but this time for her poor manners, for not realizing that Baby Boy had traveled a long ways to come here and that he was probably starving. He tried shaking his head, but she was having none of it and was already hurrying into the kitchen. A moment later, he heard the opening of the fridge door and then the setting down of a few pots and pans. By the time he entered the kitchen, she was pouring some spices and flour into a bowl and rolling raw chicken into the mixture. "You remember your mam's fried chicken, baby?" she said, and then turned her back before he could lie and say yes. "I'm gonna make you my famous chicken. It's your nana's recipe. And I don't mind saying, folks come to Sal's from the next county over to get a taste of it. I make it every Thursday." She picked six large potatoes from a hanging basket and set them on the counter.

"You know, I really need to get going . . ." he began, but she shot him a look that made him stop. "Or we could just go out . . ." he attempted feebly.

"Out?" She laughed. "Nearest restaurant is eight miles up the road. This is the country, baby." She was girlish again, in her element in the kitchen, and Anton's heart skipped a beat at how beautiful she looked. "Naw, you just go back in the living room and take a nap on the couch. You must be so tired."

But the thought of being away from her was unbearable. "I'm okay," he said quietly. "Let me help."

"You wanna help? Here, peel these. I'll get the water boiling. I'll make you mashed potatoes like you never tasted. And collard greens. You like greens?"

He laughed self-consciously. "I don't think I've ever tasted those."

She looked stricken for a moment and then muttered to herself, "Of course you have. You just forgotten." She drew a pair of scissors out of the drawer. " 'Scuse me while I go pick some fresh ones from the yard."

WHEN THEY WERE done with dinner, Anton wondered if he'd eaten an entire chicken. He remembered eating at least four pieces, the last one to sate not his hunger but his mother's. It was as if, with every bite of food that she served him, Juanita was filling up with pleasure and pride. "This," he said, licking his fingers, "is hands-down the best fried chicken I have ever eaten."

Juanita beamed.

"If you opened your own restaurant up north, folks would drive in from New York to eat this."

She laughed that girlish laugh again. "Oh, Lord. I don't think my blood could handle that cold anymore," she said. "I got used to the heat down here."

They had already argued at dinner about the fact that he would be leaving tonight. She had looked stunned, then crestfallen, but now he took the opportunity to say, "Well, you'll have to come up for a visit after . . . after the election is over."

"After you become the governor, you mean." She clapped her hands. "Hallelujah. If someone had told me a year ago that my son would be governor, I would've asked 'em if they thought I just fell off a turnip truck." She looked deeply into his face. "You are a good man. Kind. I can tell. You will make a fine governor, Anton. I know."

He wondered how much she knew about Pappy, his family history, the weight that the Coleman name carried back home. He opened his mouth, but just then she said shyly, "And that young lady you are dating? What's she like? I saw y'all's picture in the magazine."

"Katherine? Oh, she's wonderful. Really smart. Generous. Beautiful." And then, because he felt obligated, "You'll meet her. Soon. When you, you know, come visit."

There was an awkward pause. Juanita rose from the table and picked up their plates. "We'll see," she mumbled. "You're gonna be plenty busy in your new job."

"If I win." He laughed.

She fixed him a look. "Of course you will win." She cleared her throat and sang softly:

> "And he will raise you up on eagle's wings
> Bear you on the breath of dawn
> Make you to shine like the sun
> And hold you in the palm of his hand."

The lump that formed in his throat mortified him. He stared down at the table, wrestling to control his emotions, and as if to spare him, she turned away abruptly. She put the dishes in the sink and ran water over them. When she spoke, her voice was gruff. "You best be getting back, son," she said. "It will start getting dark soon, and these are unfamiliar roads to you. Where did you fly into?"

"A small airport near Augusta." He rose and cleared his throat. "I flew in on a private plane."

Her eyes widened, but she remained silent. "Well," she said at last. "We have chocolate cake. I can pack you some for the road."

He nodded and watched wordlessly as she cut him a slice larger than he could eat. He used the bathroom again, and when he came out, she was waiting on the front porch, the paper bag with the cake in her hand. She was not crying, but her nose was red, and Anton felt his own eyes sting with tears. "Bye, Mam," he said, stooping low to hug her.

She threw her arms around him and clung to him. When she finally released him, she took his face in her hands and kissed it repeatedly. "I love you more than the moon loves the sky," she whispered. "You remember that. Anytime you see the night sky, you remember that"—and here she let out a cackle—"that there's a crazy fool in Georgia who loves you more than there are stars in the sky."

I love you, too. It would've been so easy to say those words, to let them slip out of where they were gathering in his mouth. But he didn't. Couldn't. In some dim way, he understood that if he said those words, he would break, that the ice that was encasing his body, helping him hold his shit together, would crack and shatter, leaving in its wake that dark, vulnerable place where he couldn't go. He had already had his entire known world turned upside down. This seemingly fragile, power-less woman standing in front of him, with her teary, beautiful face, her longing and her loneliness, her guilt and her shame, her weakness and her strength, her moon and her sky, held the power to destroy him. This much he knew.

And so he said, "I'll see you soon," and forced himself to pat her shoulder, turn and run down the steps, flashing her a smile and a wave as he got into his car, and then he gunned his engine and backed out of her driveway and sped down the gravel road until all that remained of him and his surreal visit was the dust cloud he left in his wake.

CHAPTER THIRTY-SIX

By the time he passed through the small town of Ronan and slowed down when he drove by Sal's restaurant, he was almost relieved to have left that small cottage behind. He felt his usual equilibrium, his practicality, settling back into him, and with each mile, the tearing, helpless feelings she had aroused in him were lessening.

Of course, there would be the fallout of this visit to deal with upon his return. He'd barely had a chance to absorb the extent of David's reckless behavior. He had no real idea how much Delores knew or suspected about what her husband had done and what he had risked. And then there was the fact that Uncle Connor had been complicit in Juanita's imprisonment. It was as though every adult he had trusted had behaved in the most contemptible of ways. Their education, their wealth, their liberal leanings, none of that had kept them from deceiving Juanita Vesper. In fact, it was precisely the opposite—it was their very privilege that had allowed it to happen. And he had to live with that. The next time David Coleman talked about the importance of raising the minimum wage, Anton would have to ignore what he'd done to an impoverished black woman. The next time Delores came home from her Planned Parenthood meeting, Anton would have to forget the five-thousand-dollar check that lived inside a manila folder in Georgia.

The next time Uncle Connor pontificated about reforms to the criminal justice system, Anton would have to forget how he had railroaded an imprisoned woman with a court-appointed lawyer.

A slow burn started within Anton, making his skull tingle. He blinked rapidly a few times but couldn't say whether it was to keep his tears at bay or to fight off the sudden fatigue that he felt. *Let him take his stupid governorship and stuff it.* The thought came into his head and was accompanied by its physical counterpart—almost immediately, the knots in his neck and upper back released, his grip on the wheel slackened, and a feeling of liberation swept through him. It would be so great to walk away from this campaign, to continue being attorney general, and later, to fade into anonymity, maybe someday run a small law firm. But before his body could even absorb what had happened, his mind betrayed him, flooding itself with notions of duty, responsibility, obligation, and honor. His grip on the wheel tightened as he looked for the signs to the freeway.

He decided to use his phone's GPS and remembered that he had not turned it back on since rushing out of his mother's house. As he had expected, there were several voice messages. One from Delores, one from David, two from Katherine, three from Bradley. Anton sighed, a feeling of revulsion gripping him. He turned onto the freeway, knowing that every mile was taking him closer to them, the people who had loved him, shaped him, molded him, as if he were a block of clay they had found by the roadside. He remembered how, in the early days, friends of the Colemans used to comment on how well adjusted their new boy was, how well he conducted himself, what good manners he had, and now he wanted to scream, And didn't any of you ever stop and wonder why? How bad of a mother could she have been, for fuck's sake, if she produced such a son? But then his lawyerly self took over. In truth, probably none of them had known about the rape, and without that knowledge, what she'd done was inexcusable. Now it was easy to admire Juanita Vesper's sobriety, the fact that she had beaten the odds. But back then, who could blame David Coleman for thinking he was—what was the word he'd used?—*rescuing* a child from a lifetime of neglect, terror, or worse? No, it wasn't fair that Juanita's one terrible error in judgment should result in a lifetime of punishment, but hell, that happened all the time, didn't it? Most people never got a shot at redemption. It was the way of the world, and what was Juanita Vesper's claim to go against this?

And so Anton rode along the dark highway, arguing with himself. The clock said 9:32. He knew he should call Brad back, if for no other reason than to make sure the pilot was available, but a wave of sleepiness assaulted him, and he pondered whether to spend the night in a motel and then make a fresh start in the morning. He began glancing at road signs to see if there was lodging nearby. He drove a short distance and then saw a sign that said, "Thomasville 12 miles ahead." Thomasville. Why did that sound familiar? He frowned, trying to remember, but couldn't connect the name to a news story. And then it struck him and his heart pounded. Thomasville. That's where she lived. Carine. That's what she'd written to him almost two years ago. He hadn't written back, afraid that Katherine would be hurt if she knew he was communicating with an old flame.

But now, seeing the road sign felt like divine intervention. He had traveled the same way earlier today. Why had he not noticed it on the way to his mother's house? He knew that the prudent thing to do would be to keep driving all the way to that little private airport and get the hell out of Georgia tonight. But he was bone-tired. And in any case, what would be the harm to contact Carine again, to maybe have a late-night coffee with her and then check in to a motel?

He drummed his fingers on the steering wheel, tempted to stop, agitated at the thought. Drive on, he told himself. Just pretend you never saw the goddamned road sign. Who knows if she's even in town? She could be on vacation, for God's sake. He decided to pull off at the rest area and get a coffee. Except for the trucks parked there, it was almost deserted. He pulled up to the building and then sat in the dark, staring at his phone. After a moment, he logged on to his email. He found her email but no home phone number. He glanced at the clock—10:02. He stared at her email, chewing on his lower lip, and then, on an impulse, hit reply. "Hey, there," he wrote. "You won't believe this, but I'm sitting at a rest stop just outside of Thomasville. If, by some stroke of luck, you see this in the next ten minutes or so, email me. If you're up for it, I'll buy you a cup of coffee."

He hit send, set his phone on the console, and got out. He used the restroom, splashed water over his face, then got a coffee from a vending machine. He knew it was stupid, but his hands were shaking as he walked back to the car and unlocked it. He set the coffee down in the holder before he allowed himself to check his phone. There was no reply. He blew out his cheeks, disappointed but relieved. Come on, Anton, he chided himself. You think she's sitting by the damn computer at ten o'clock on a Friday night? What are the odds of that? Well, it was better this way. Less complicated. No lying to Katherine.

He turned on the ignition and rolled out of the parking lot onto the freeway. Another road sign said he was now eight miles away from Thomasville. He'd picked up the phone to call Brad when the ping alerted him to a new email. He fumbled with the phone, almost dropped it, and died a hundred deaths in the second it took him to click on the mail. And there she was. "24 Magnolia Lane. I'll put on a pot of coffee. Come."

He let out a startled laugh, unable to believe his good fortune, her exquisite timing, the brevity of her email, the presumption and self-confidence that lay beneath it. But then he was uneasy, the fact that he was going to her home instead of meeting her at an all-night diner making it a little more complicated. The next second he remembered she had kids, chiding himself for not understanding that she couldn't exactly slip out at a moment's notice. And really, what was the harm in seeing an old friend? It seemed like providence—the fact that he'd read the road sign to Thomasville, then remembered that it was where Carine lived, and finally, the unbelievable odds that she had checked her email and replied when he was, what, a couple of miles away from her exit.

Seven minutes later, he was turning onto a quiet brick street with old-fashioned gas lamps. A street sign proclaimed it a historic district. The houses here were large, and almost all of them had flowering bushes and flower boxes in their windows. Anton whistled to himself. He hadn't given any thought to what Carine's neighborhood would look like, but he certainly wasn't expecting her to be living on this very bourgeois street. Perhaps this was her parents' home? Maybe, because she was a single parent, they helped support her? He would find out in a moment.

He pulled up to her house and debated whether to park on the street or in her driveway. As he sat there hesitating, the front porch light went on and the door opened. "Pull in," Carine yelled, though it was too dark and she was too far for Anton to get a good look at her. He turned in to her driveway, and even before he got out of the car, his chest filled with a warm happiness and he felt young again. He turned off the engine and sat there for a moment, grinning like a happy fool. But the next second, there was a pounding on the passenger window, and he looked over to see Carine's face, looking more beautiful than he ever could have imagined it.

CHAPTER THIRTY-SEVEN

Carine had changed a lot. She had not changed at all. She was a stranger. She was his close friend. She looked rounder, more maternal than he remembered, but she still had those sharp features that used to take his breath away.

Anton was staring at her and he knew it, but he couldn't keep his eyes off that face. He watched as she walked across her large white kitchen and poured two mugs of coffee. He watched her walk back to the granite island, knew he should help, but he couldn't move. He noticed that she had served his coffee black, had remembered, hadn't bothered to check, as if all these years had not gone by, as if his tastes couldn't have altered, as if they were still that boy and girl who had crossed Harvard Yard together that first time, already half in love with each other. And even if his taste in coffee had changed, even if he now took it with sugar and cream, would he have dared to say so? To challenge this lovely creature who sat next to him on a bar stool, who set the mug down and then patted his hand excitedly, saying, "Anton. My God, Anton. I can't believe this. Who would've thought?"

He remembered this feeling, this lightness, this joy, this inability to not smile. It was a thing young people enjoyed, and Anton realized with a thud that he had not felt this way in a very long time. Not, as a matter of fact, since he had left Carine. For years, all he had remembered were the arguments and the fights and the disagreements. But she had also given him this giddiness, this skipping, dancing feeling. He had thought it was his, but she had bequeathed it to him. He had been a serious boy and now he was a serious man. But he missed what he had been with her for that brief while.

"I'm sorry to barge in here like this," he said. "It just felt—wrong, you know, to not stop."

"I would've never forgiven you," she said. "But what brings you here? A fund-raiser or something?"

He lifted his shoulders in a dismissive way, not answering, looking around the room instead. "So . . . you said you have kids? Are they home?"

She nodded, still smiling. "They're asleep. I just put them to bed a while back and then got on the computer. First time all day."

"And you found me." He was aware how that sounded, a little flirty, but he didn't care.

"And I found you," she said, and did he imagine that her voice was a little husky? She opened her mouth to say something, but he interrupted: "So, can I see them? Do they look like you?"

She laughed. "A little bit." She considered his request and then got up. "Sure. But you've got to be quiet. They're light sleepers."

As they went up the stairs, he noticed she hadn't mentioned a husband. He was curious but decided not to ask. Because he wanted to sleep with her tonight. The realization hit him with such force that he actually gasped. She looked back. "You okay?"

He nodded, unable to speak. You're just tired and confused, he told himself. Just reacting to the weird day. You don't even know Carine anymore. And you have a girlfriend at home. Who is probably frantic with worry by now.

But there was a stirring in his stomach as they reached the landing, and it didn't go away when Carine took his hand as if it were the most natural thing in the world. "This way," she said, and led him to the nursery.

They stood in the doorway watching the two sleeping boys. "How can you tell them apart?" he whispered, and she laughed and shrugged. "A mother knows."

He nodded. "I guess." And then, "Although I can't believe you're a mom. You don't look a day older . . ."

She hit him playfully on the shoulder. "If only."

"No, honest. You look great." He swallowed, allowing her to see desire that was making his eyes bright. "Really great."

To his chagrin, Carine burst into silent laughter. "Upon my word, Anton. I do believe you're flirting with me. Me, an old married woman."

It was the gentlest of letdowns, but it stung. "You're married?" he blurted out.

She shot him a quizzical look and then pointed with her chin toward the bedroom. "Did you think the stork brought those two?" She laughed and then stopped, and her eyes widened. "Oh God. You thought—I get it. You thought I had kids on my own? Jeez, Anton."

"No, Carine. I mean, I didn't think anything. When you wrote, you never mentioned a husband." He knew he was blushing, and he peered down the darkened corridor. "Is he home? Your husband?"

She laughed again. "Mike? I wish. No, he's ten thousand miles away. In Afghanistan."

Anton blinked. "Wow. What's he doing there?"

Even in the dark, he could see her looking at him carefully. "He's stationed there, Anton. He's a medic in the army."

Suddenly, Anton longed for it to be midnight, for it to be another day, because this day held too many shocks. "You? You're married to a military guy? You . . . my God, you were the most anti-military person I've ever met. A total peacenik. What happened?"

He must've raised his voice, because one of the boys stirred, and Carine held up a cautionary finger to her lips. She watched her son for a second and then motioned Anton to follow her down the stairs. She led the way wordlessly, but this time they went into the living room, his earlier lust dulled by fatigue and awkwardness. Anton noticed how elegant the room was, the Oriental rug on the hardwood floor, the expensive-looking sofa where she motioned him to sit. Carine waited until he did, then turned on a floor lamp before settling in a rocking chair across from him. "So?" she said, a smile in her voice. "I've thrown you for a loop, huh?" She ran her hand self-consciously through her short hair.

He forced the same lightness into his voice. "I'll say. Carine Biya, campus radical, married to a guy in the military?" He waited for her to respond, but when she didn't, he asked, "What happened?" This time he was unable to keep the incredulity—and yes, the faintest tone of reproach—out of his voice.

Carine shrugged. "I fell in love," she answered simply.

A million thoughts scampered through Anton's mind. That's it? he wanted to say. You, the woman I put up on a pedestal, the woman so righteous in her political beliefs, whom I defended to all my friends even while I was secretly appalled by what came out of her mouth, you, that woman, that Carine Biya, turned out to be a mere mortal who fell in love like the rest of us, who threw it all away and settled into this bourgeois suburban life? Anton leaned back in the couch and closed his eyes for a moment. Apart from his father, Carine had been the person he'd admired most. Even when he'd disagreed with her, he had admired her for having the courage of her convictions, for the principles with which she seemed to live her life.

"Whoa, Anton," Carine was saying. He opened his eyes and saw that she was sitting forward in her chair, a worried frown on her beautiful face. "Jesus, man. What the hell? You're acting like I told you I went and married Osama bin Laden."

"That would've surprised me less." The words shot out of his mouth, and he thought he must have looked as shocked as she did. They stared at each other for a moment and then she giggled. "You son of a bitch," she swore, and then they were laughing madly, and for the first time since he'd gotten there, the air between them turned easy and friendly.

"Sorry," he spluttered, but she shook her head. "Was I really that bad?" she asked, and he rolled his eyes. "Terrible," he said. "You were incorrigible. You were Malcolm fucking X."

She hooted with laughter, then rose in a swift motion and walked across the living room. She picked up a photo frame and walked toward him, wiping the glass on her blouse as she did. She handed it to Anton. "This is Mike," she said. "This is my husband."

The picture that had formed in Anton's head ever since Carine had announced she was married was that of Denzel Washington, and so he felt a jolt of surprise when he saw the man in the picture. Mike was white. He was a good-looking guy, he'd give her that. Thick dark hair, a strong jaw, and warm gray eyes peering from behind rimless glasses, a thoughtful look on his face. Without the military fatigues, Mike could've passed for a humanities professor. Anton forced a smile onto his face. "So this is Mr. Right, huh?"

Carine took the picture frame out of Anton's hands. "It is," she said, and it was as if there were a blush in her voice.

"How long will he be away?"

She made a face. "Who knows? He's on his fourth tour."

Anton rubbed his face, feeling a creeping sympathy. "Thought we were supposed to be out of that mess years ago," he muttered.

She shrugged. "Sometimes I wonder if it will ever end." She fell silent and he felt compelled to say, "It must be really tough. With the kids and all?"

"He was home for a week about a month ago. That was good. And my parents live twenty minutes away. That's a huge help."

"Your parents," he said. "How are they?" He frowned, remembering something. "Your dad still goes on those overseas trips?"

"Not really. He's getting old." Her face brightened. "That's how I met Mike, you know. He was volunteering at the clinic in Haiti when we were last there. He's a physician's assistant."

"Really? That's cool," he said, not knowing what to say but thinking, *If you'd married me, you would've been the wife of a governor. Instead, here you are, in a suburban home, the mother of two children, the wife of a man who is ten thousand miles away.* It was amazing how the currents of destiny had taken them to such different places.

As if she'd read his mind, Carine said, "But enough about me. What about you? You're not married, right?"

He laughed, but it rang hollow to his ears. "Me? God, no." He said it as if she'd asked an absurd question.

"But you have someone?" Carine's voice was gentle but persistent. "A sweetheart? I think I read that in the article?"

"I do." And then, seeing that she wanted to know more, "Her name's Katherine. She's a human rights lawyer. We've been going steady now for—Gosh, it's been over two years."

"But no wedding bells on the horizon?"

Why was Carine suddenly sounding like his mother? What was it with happily married people that they felt the answer to all of life's problems was marriage? Did she even know that he was about to become the youngest governor of his state? Wasn't that accomplishment enough? "Well," he said, "it's hard to run a political campaign and plan a wedding at the same time."

"Oh, but that's great," Carine said, misunderstanding him. "Congratulations."

"Congrats? Jeez, Carine. You're as bad as my mom." His grin took the sting out of his words. "I—we—Katherine and I don't have a date planned, for chrissake. I haven't even asked her yet." All the while thinking, Does she even care that sitting in her living room is the man who could be governor?

Carine smiled warmly. "Your mom," she said. "How is she?" There was not a trace of wariness in her voice, as if she had no recollection of her last disastrous meeting with Delores.

"She's good. She's great."

"And your dad?"

He felt a heaviness in his heart at the thought of David, their earlier conversation coming back to him with vivid ferocity. "He's okay. A little frail. He's never been the same since he had his heart attack . . ." He trailed off.

There was a short silence, as if they were both thinking about David and his mortality, and then Anton heard himself saying, "Actually, I've had a very strange day today. You'll never guess why I'm in town."

"Wasn't it for a fund-raiser or something?"

He pulled on his right ear. "I wish. No, actually, I came to see . . . her. My birth mom. She lives around here. Out in the country. Just outside of Ronan. Do you know where that is?" He didn't wait for her response. "It's kind of funny, really. That both of you—that the two of you, my mom and my former . . . you . . . live less than two hours from each other." He stopped abruptly and stared at the floor, suddenly teary, the events of the day catching up with him.

"You met her?" Carine said sharply. "Today? Oh, wow. Anton. That's huge. But why now?"

He forced his eyes upward to meet her gaze. "She wrote to me. There was an article about me, and she saw it. So she wrote to me. Turns out it was just to say hello, like." He gulped and forced himself to go on, feeling like he was confessing something. "But I didn't know. I thought that maybe—perhaps, you know, since I was running for governor—I thought that she—"

"You thought she was blackmailing you or something," Carine interrupted. Her voice was flat.

He nodded. "Yes. Yes, I did. And so I slipped out of town this morning. And met with her." He heard the tremor in his voice and couldn't quite account for it. God, he was tired, really tired.

"Oh, Anton." Carine rose from her chair and came to sit down next to him on the couch. She took his trembling hand in hers. "Oh, baby. What a mess. I could've told you she wasn't after anything."

His hand felt cold, dead, in hers. "How could you know?"

She turned to face him, and for the first time since he'd gotten here, the look in her eyes reminded him of the old Carine. Not the fiery old Carine who mouthed off whenever he was being hopelessly conventional, but the Carine who sometimes looked . . . disappointed in him. "I just know," she said at last. "How could she hurt you? How could a poor black woman living in rural Georgia go up against . . . someone like you?"

He flinched, hearing what Carine was too polite to say: To Juanita Vesper, Anton Coleman may as well be a powerful white man. Ordinarily, this wouldn't have necessarily registered as an insult, but today, his feelings bruised by David's deceit, he resented the association. "Well," he said. "Paula Jones was a nobody, too. But she almost destroyed a president."

Carine's eyes were watchful, her voice gentle. "Yes. But Paula Jones wasn't Bill Clinton's mother. A mom would never deliberately hurt her child, Anton."

He sat still, blinking back the tears that burned in his eyes. "You're right. Turns out I misread the situation."

Carine squeezed his hand. "So it went okay? The visit? I can't even imagine what that would feel like—for either one of you. How many years had it been?"

How many years? Too many. "I was nine when I last saw her," he said. "So it's been a long time."

"And how was the reunion?"

He looked back at her, his brain processing her question, unsure how to answer. Had it gone okay? It had, in fact. He had liked Juanita, and none of his fears about her had been realized. But he had learned something about David that had shaken him to his roots, that had made his whole life with the Colemans seem as if it had been built on someone else's back. Carine was looking at him, expecting his answer, when his phone rang. The ring sounded loud in the silent room, and as if on cue, he heard a tiny voice call from the upstairs bedroom, "Mom?" He mouthed an apology to Carine as he silenced the phone and saw that it was Katherine and that it was past eleven-thirty. "I have to take this," he whispered, getting onto his feet. "Hi, baby," he said.

"Anton? Where the hell are you?" Katherine's voice sounded close, as if she were in the room with him.

"A good evening to you, too," he said, stalling for time, trying to gauge the wisdom of answering Katherine's inelegant question truthfully. He glanced over at Carine, saw that she was leaving the room, and was relieved.

"It's not funny, Anton. We were getting worried," Katherine said. "Brad said he hadn't heard from you since morning. He's apoplectic. So are you on your way home or not?"

He sighed. Facing all of them—and yes, to his great surprise and sadness, he associated Katherine with *them*—was the last thing he wanted to do. He knew this as surely as he had ever known anything. "I'm gonna spend the night here, okay, baby?" he said. "I'm exhausted. It's been a very long day."

"Where are you?" she asked again.

"I pulled off the road," he lied. "And I'm gonna check in to a motel in a few minutes."

Katherine exhaled. "Okay. That's probably a good idea. You've got to be dead-tired." She cleared her throat. "So, how'd it go? With your mom?"

He shut his eyes. "It's a long story, honey. I'll tell you when I'm home. But it went pretty okay."

"Oh, good. I'm so relieved. So what time are you coming home to-morrow?"

He hesitated, unsure of what to say. Because the truth was, he wasn't ready to say goodbye to Carine yet. He'd check in to a nearby motel tonight, and then—if she wasn't tied up tomorrow—he wanted to come back to this pretty house for breakfast. To meet her kids. To tell her about his birth mom. He didn't know when he'd ever see Carine again, and now that he knew she was happily married, he felt safe being alone with her, didn't feel like he was cheating on Katherine. He would have to explain everything to Katherine when he returned home, of course, and he knew he was digging a trap for himself by lying to her now, but he couldn't do any better tonight. Not when he was too tired to think straight. Not when Carine could walk back into the room at any min-ute. Not when there was a pretty good chance that Katherine would freak out at the truth.

"Well," he began, but there was a voice at the other end and he heard Katherine say, "Here, you talk to him," and then he heard Brad's voice, hot and urgent in his ear, "You dickhead. Where did you disappear?"

Despite himself, Anton began to laugh. "I've been gone one freakin' day," he said. "You guys are acting like I've gone AWOL or something."

He expected Bradley to come back at him with a soft curse, but there was nothing. "Hello?" Anton said cautiously. "Brad?"

"Listen," Brad said, "you get some rest tonight. I'll try and fend off your mother and the press for a few more hours until you get your ass back into town tomorrow. But if you still want me to run your god-damn campaign, you better start picking up the phone when I call. Or you can find yourself a new manager. Now go to bed, asshole. And for your sake, I hope you have the sense to pay for your room with cash."

"You should've listened to me when I told you to spread the word we were leaving town for the weekend," Anton teased and then waited for Brad to cuss him out. But there was no response. Anton stared at his phone in disbelief. They had both hung up on him? He was a grown man in his thirties and he hadn't earned the right to take off for one day with-out them tracking him like a dog on a leash? He had never heard Brad so bent out of shape, not even when Anton had kept flubbing his lines during the practice session for the first debate against Johnny Newman. He felt a sudden dread at the realization that his life would only get more con-strained if he became governor. Hell, if even Brad and Katherine couldn't appreciate why he sometimes needed to disappear, what hope was there for the media and the public to be more forgiving? He felt a heaviness clamp down on him. I don't want this, he thought, I can't live like this. But the thought was so treacherous, so much a negation of everybody's efforts on his behalf, that he dismissed it as abruptly as he had allowed it to seep into his mind. You're tired, he said to himself. Just go find a motel and everything will seem clearer in the morning. Hell, you can be home by tomorrow afternoon if you catch that plane in the morning.

He went out into the hallway and saw that Carine was sitting by herself in the kitchen. She looked up when he walked in. "Everything okay?" she said.

He nodded. "Yup." He rocked on his heels, the reason why he'd re-ally stopped by here tonight dawning on him. "Listen. I know it's late. But—something happened today. I mean, something else. Something I found out. I . . . I just need to process it with a friend. If you're too tired, I'll under—"

"Anton." Carine gave an exasperated hiss. "Stop talking in riddles and come sit down. What is it?"

He told her. All of it. Including his conversation with David in which the older man had refused to apologize. Anton could see the tears glinting in her eyes when he got done, but she sat there, not moving, staring silently at him. "It's unbelievable," she whispered at long last. "It's not possible." She shook her head as if to untangle the knot of images forming there. "So what're you going to *do*?"

He shrugged, meeting her eyes, resenting the pity he saw there, but forcing himself to not look away. "Nothing. What can I do? There's nothing to do. He's my father. It's not like I can disown him. You know? I mean, I'm still in shock, but I know that he meant well." He stifled a yawn. "Tonight I'll check in to a motel. Get some sleep. And tomorrow I'll get up early and take the plane home. Or meet you for breakfast and then go home."

"That's it? You'll just put it behind you? You can do that?"

Now he heard the anger in Carine's voice, and it made him half wish he hadn't confided in her. "I'll go see her," he mumbled. "After the election."

"Ah, the election. The friggin' all-important election." Before he could reply and tell her how many people had worked their hearts out for him to win, she swung her legs around and hopped off the stool. "And don't be an ass about going to a motel," she said. "I just made up the guest bedroom. While you were on the phone."

He stared after her dumbly, his resentment at her dig tempered by his gratitude at her matter-of-fact friendship and hospitality. He knew spending the night here would complicate things with Katherine—and he realized he didn't care. He really didn't want to be alone in a motel tonight, not after the kind of day he'd had. The thought of spending a little more time with Carine cheered him. Already the sharp lust that he had felt for her when he'd shown up was easing into a deep affection, blunted by the fact of her marriage and her obvious love for her husband. And it was this knowledge that made him feel right about replying with a simple "You did? Bless you."

She eyed his duffel bag. "You bring any PJs with you? Or I could loan you Mike's."

He shrugged. "Nah. I didn't think I was gonna spend the night in Georgia. But I'll manage. Don't worry."

She looked like she was about to argue, but all she said was "Okay. This way." She led him to a small but beautiful room with an attached half-bath and sliding doors that opened into the backyard. "The boys get up early," she warned. "So unless you want two wild seven-year-olds jumping on your bed in the morning, you best shut your door." She pushed him toward the bathroom. "Go get ready for bed. I'll come in and check on you in a few."

He brushed his teeth with the new toothbrush she'd put out for him, washed his face, untucked his shirt, and slipped into bed. He fought sleep as he waited for her to return, inexplicably feeling a childlike anticipation at the thought. Just as his eyelids were closing, she came back in and sat at the foot of his bed. "What do you want for breakfast tomorrow? We have eggs, cereal—"

He shook his head ruefully, cutting her off. "I'm rethinking it. It's best if I leave early. My campaign manager thinks I've gone rogue. I'll just grab a coffee on the way."

Even in the dark, he felt her stiffen with disappointment. "Okay," she said briskly. "Whatever."

He reached over and took her hand and squeezed it. "I wish I could stay longer. I feel like we hardly got to talk about you. I'm sorry."

"Don't be. I lead the world's most boring life." She sighed. "I love my life. But sometimes . . . being alone with the kids . . . it's always nice to see old friends."

They sat in the dark holding hands, and Anton felt a warmth start in his chest and make its way down into his belly and then, slowly, into that dangerous place. And Carine must have sensed it, because she pulled her hand away from his and got up. She bent over and kissed him on the forehead. "Good night, sweet boy," she whispered. "What a terrible day you've had. Get some rest."

Anton drifted off to sleep with a smile on his lips. Sweet boy. Only Carine could pull that off. She had called him sweet boy as if he were one of her kids. Or as if she were Juanita Vesper. They were lovely, these Georgia women. Warm, tender, as if they had been shaped by the loamy, rich southern soil that had nurtured them. He wanted to nestle in to them, cover himself with their richness, their blackness. And then the blackness was over him and he fell asleep, Georgia on his mind.

CHAPTER THIRTY-EIGHT

He opened his eyes the next morning and found himself looking into the dark brown eyes of a solemn boy sitting next to him on the bed. "Well, hello," he said, but the boy didn't respond and kept looking into his face as if trying to memorize it. In that short time, with the sun pouring into the small room and the boy's upturned face still as the moon, Anton felt transported into a different dimension of time and space. This boy could've been his son, he thought, if he hadn't broken up with Carine. This sweet, serious face could've belonged to *his* child, and there could've been countless Saturday mornings of waking up to such exquisite sweetness. If this had been his routine on weekends, he could've kissed the boy without asking permission, could've cupped that light brown face with his large hand and felt the pride and pleasure in the simple gesture. He shut his eyes for a moment to imagine this, but what he saw, improbably, was Juanita's face, beaming with pride as she looked upon her grandchildren. He hurriedly opened them again, smiled at the face next to his, and said, "What's your name?"

"Shay."

"Hi, Shay. Where's your brother?"

The boy looked at him shyly. "I don't know," he said.

Anton tossed off the covers. "Let's go find out, shall we?" He slipped out of bed, glanced at his watch, and groaned when he realized the time. So much for good intentions. He was obviously going to get off to a later start than he'd planned, and would have to deal with Bradley's wrath. But first he had to turn his attention back to the boy, who was asking him something. "What's that, buddy?" he said.

"Are you Santa Claus?" the boy repeated.

"Am I—*what*?" Anton let out a guffaw. "Why . . . what makes you think that?"

The boy cocked his head. "Ralph said you came down the chimney."

"Ralph's your brother?"

"Yeah."

Anton tousled Shay's hair. "Let's go ask him, then."

They found Ralph in the kitchen with Carine, who was making pancakes. "Ho, ho, ho," Anton said as he walked in, and Carine raised her eyebrows.

He shook his head. "Never mind. It's an inside joke." He bent from the waist to shake hands with Ralph, who hid behind Carine. "You been a good boy, Ralph?"

Carine shot him a puzzled look and then gave him a quick peck on the cheek. "Good morning. I didn't know whether to wake you up or not. You were sleeping so soundly that I didn't have the heart."

He made a rueful face. "Can't remember the last time I slept in. The weather here is messing with me."

"This place is in your blood, boy, it's in your blood." Carine smiled as she brushed past him to open the refrigerator. "You hungry?" she asked.

He was. Ravenously hungry. The two boys watched in fascination as he ate the two fried eggs and three pancakes on his plate and then drank a tall glass of orange juice. Carine nibbled on some toast, a bemused look on her face. "You're right," she said. "Georgia agrees with you."

"I figured since I'm Santa, I got to be fat," he said, winking at the boys.

Carine looked from one to the other. "What're you talking about?"

"Oh, it's our secret," he said. "Right?"

The twins shuffled in their seats and giggled. "You're not Santa," Ralph drawled. "You're Uncle Anton. And you're nice."

Anton laughed, but he felt a sting in his heart. Uncle Anton sounded so distant. Carine looked up. "So you gotta leave soon?"

He nodded and Shay squealed. "I don't want him to," he cried.

"Yeah. Me, neither. I want him to stay," Ralph said.

"Hey, hey. Behave," Carine said, wagging her finger at them. She turned toward him. "Sorry. They don't usually act like this. I think they just miss their dad."

"Don't be. I'm flattered. They're . . . they're beautiful boys."

"Thanks." Carine spoke gently to the twins. "Uncle Anton lives far away. He needs to get home, kids. Maybe next summer we can go see him . . ."

"I want him to come see my play," Shay screamed.

"Me, too," Ralph wailed.

Anton frowned, looking at Carine. "What play?"

She shrugged dismissively. "Don't worry about it. It's just a local theater group they're in. They have a performance this evening."

"I'm a lollipop," Shay yelled.

"And I'm a cheese."

Anton had never felt the joy of having children fight over him; even the knowledge that they simply saw him as a substitute for their father didn't diminish his pleasure. He wanted to spend some more time with these kids. Carine's children.

"I'll go to their play with you," he said quietly. "I'll stay an extra day. If you'll have me."

Carine's eyes widened, and for a moment, she looked like she would argue with him. But her face softened, as if she'd read something in his eyes. "If you won't get into trouble, we'd love to have you. The concert is at five."

Shay did a cartwheel on the tiled kitchen floor in celebration, while Ralph simply high-fived Anton. "You've obviously wormed your way into my children's hearts," Carine said wryly, and although he replied with a self-deprecating "Yeah, I'm a one-day wonder," Anton glowed with pleasure.

She eyed him critically. "Tell you what. Either we go out and buy you some clothes this afternoon, or you slip into Mike's bathrobe after your shower and let me wash what you have on."

He stayed alone in the house with the kids for a couple of hours while she drove to Penney's to buy him a pair of jeans and a shirt. After the boys went to take their afternoon nap, he wandered around the house, feeling more at home in this warm, sunlit house with the African wall hangings and paintings than he ever had in his minimalist condo with its strange blend of expensive artwork and IKEA furnishings. He looked for things to fix, his way of thanking Carine for giving him this respite from his life. He would pay a heavy price for the callous disregard of his responsibilities back home, but each time he remembered David's treachery, he felt a fresh outrage that threatened to destroy everything associated with his father. And so he paced, making a mental list of chores he could perform, ignoring the fact that he hadn't turned on his phone, dreading the assault of voicemails and texts that he knew awaited him.

He was fixing a leaky faucet in the guest bathroom when Carine returned home. He met her in his bedroom, the wrench still in his hand. He gasped when she entered the bedroom with boxes piled high. "I only gave you, like, sixty bucks. What's all this?"

She set the boxes down on his bed. "They had a great sale. I got a little carried away," she said. "I'm sure you can use the shirts on the campaign trail or something."

He smiled ruefully. "I wish," he said.

"Huh?"

"We have this guy on the payroll. He's some sartorial expert. He decides what I wear on the trail."

"You're kidding, right?"

He shook his head. "I wish."

Carine opened her mouth and then shut it. She stared at him, those dark eyes probing his face. Then she smiled and pointed to the wrench. "I didn't know you were handy."

He knew she was changing the subject, and he let her. He didn't really want to explain the state of modern campaigning to Carine. He smiled back. "I've picked up a few skills over the years," he said vaguely.

An hour before they were to leave for the concert, he texted Brad. "Coming home tomorrow," he wrote. "Sorry. I just need a few days away to think. Will explain everything when I return. Can you let Katherine know?" He knew what he was doing was cowardly, unfair, and potentially fatal to his campaign and to his relationship with Katherine, but at the moment, going to a concert to see two little boys dressed as a lollipop and a piece of cheese seemed like the most important thing in the world.

So that when Carine said to him on the drive, "What if someone recognizes you?," he could smile broadly and say, "I really don't care." And mean it.

MIKE CALLED FROM Afghanistan on Sunday morning, and Carine excused herself to take the call in the bedroom. A few minutes later, she called for the boys to join her, and Anton could hear them squealing with joy, jumping up and down as they told him all about their play.

Hearing their chatter interrupted by "I love you, Daddy," Anton felt like an intruder, a man with his nose pressed against the window of someone else's happiness. The contentment that he had felt during the play and the ride back here vanished completely. Carine's home was a borrowed sanctuary, he knew, but was his real life back home anything more than that? Out of the blue, Anton remembered an evening at the Cape when he was a teenager. The sun had set, and he and Pappy were out on the front deck, watching the dark, stormy waves, when a lone gull flew across the water. "The ocean looks lonely tonight," Pappy had murmured, but Anton had thought: At least the waves have each other for company; the poor seagull is truly alone, and his heart had ached with a reciprocal loneliness. Standing by himself in Carine's kitchen, Anton remembered that seagull. In order to block out the happy murmur of their conversation, he began to rinse the dishes in the sink from last night's pasta dinner.

Carine was glowing when she reentered the kitchen ten minutes later. "Everything all right?" he asked politely.

She stood on her toes and kissed his cheek. "Yes. Mike says hi."

"You told him. About my being here."

"Of course. Why wouldn't I?"

He heard what she was saying—that he was no threat to her marriage. And that she had reassured her husband of the same by not keeping the visit a secret. He felt his cheeks flushing as the differences in their approaches became obvious to him. "He sounds like a good guy," he said vaguely, aware that Carine was still looking at him.

Her eyes were bright. "He is. The best."

Anton nodded, and as the silence stretched awkwardly between them, he went back to rinsing the dishes. Carine began to chop the spinach for the omelets she was making. After a few moments she said, "So what's the plan for today? You need to head back?"

He considered the question. Even if he left soon, it would be late afternoon to early evening before he got home. He imagined walking into his modern, sterile condo, and his heart sank at the thought. Katherine would probably come over, but then there'd be the inevitable questions about where he'd been and what his mother was like. And he knew he wasn't ready for the questions. He needed time, time and a healthy distance to process what Georgia had done to him. And Brad would do what any good campaign manager would—he'd ask Anton to compartmentalize, to put aside all of the turmoil, until after the election. A week ago, he would've agreed with his friend, would have considered it the professional, responsible, adult thing to do. But now he knew the truth—there were no adults. There were just tall children stumbling around the world, walking pools of unfinished hopes, unmet needs, and seething desires. The unsuccessful ones ended up in asylums. The ones who learned to masquerade those needs became politicians. No, his reluctance to return home today was so strong, it felt oppressive, like an overcoat two sizes too small. He wasn't ready to move from the detonation in his life to figuring out with Katherine whether they should order Thai or Indian for dinner.

He kept his eyes on the soapy water in the sink. "I was thinking of staying another day," he mumbled. "Unless you want me gone?"

She reached over and turned off the kitchen faucet. "Anton," she said, her eyes searching his face, "you can stay as long as you want. You know that. But what's really going on? Are you simply avoiding your dad?"

He bit his lower lip. "I'm tired, Carine. I've been working really long hours. This is a good break, that's all."

She nodded. "Of course. Well, honey, as you can see, the boys love having you here. Stay as long as you want." She reached for a pod of garlic from a jar to his right. "The boys have a playdate at a neighbor's house at four o'clock. I'll be gone for less than ten minutes to drop them off. Think you can stay out of trouble that long?"

He smiled his gratitude. "I think so."

"Good," she said. "Now get me six eggs from the fridge and beat them for me, would you?"

"Yes'm."

ANTON WAS LYING in the lounge chair in the backyard, a newspaper draped over his face to protect it from the sun, when Carine got home from dropping off the boys. She came up to him and removed the newspaper, and the light from the sun was so fierce that he squinted as he looked up at her. She had on a white cotton dress, and her dark skin glinted in the sunlight. "You look gorgeous," he said before he could stop himself.

"Why, thank you," she said lightly. "You, on the other hand, will look like a boiled tomato unless you get out of this heat."

He laughed and allowed her to pull him out of the chair. She led him into the kitchen, still holding his hand, and let go only to open the refrigerator. She poured two tall glasses of lemonade and handed him one.

"Wow," he said, smacking his lips. "How'd you learn to make that?"

"How'd I learn to make lemonade?" Carine fixed him with a baleful look. "Shit, Anton, even my kids know how. Didn't your mama teach you?" Her hand flew to her mouth as soon as the words had left her mouth.

He grinned to show her he wasn't offended. "No. She didn't. Though ask me how to fill a crack pipe and I'll show you."

He had meant the words jokingly, but they came out bitter, and his voice, harsh. Carine stared at him for a moment and then turned away.

"Hey," he said, reaching for her wrist. "That was a joke."

"I didn't say anything."

"You didn't have to. You have the most expressive face." He waited for her to respond, but she simply made her way into the sunroom. He stood dumbly in the kitchen for a second, sensing her disapproval but unsure what had caused it. Then he followed her and sat on the couch beside her. "What time do the kids come home?" he asked.

She shrugged. "Around eight, I guess. They're eating dinner at Mary's."

He lifted up her wrist with his index finger and then let it drop onto her lap. "You wanna go out for dinner? I'll buy."

She opened her mouth, closed it, shook her head as if having an argument with herself, glanced at him, and then opened her mouth again.

"Good God, Carine." He laughed. "What is it? Spit it out." Despite his laugh, there was a tightness at the base of his throat.

"Nothing. It's just that . . . I was thinking. I mean, being a mom myself." She turned to him, her dark eyes filled with a light he could not name. "Are you still angry with her, Anton? Even after knowing what really happened? Do you think you'll ever be able to forgive her? I know there's nothing my kids could do that would make me disown them. But is the opposite not always true? Is it possible for you to walk away from her forever? Anton?"

He stiffened, not liking the judgment he heard in Carine's voice. Most of all, he didn't appreciate the intrusion of reality on this brief idyll, with the endless moral and ethical questions that he was made to confront each time he thought about the woman he'd left alone in the yellow cottage. He was tired of atoning for other people's mistakes, he really was.

"It's complicated, Carine," he said, unable to keep the patronizing note out of his voice.

But she was having none of it. "What's complicated? Whether you love your birth mom or not? That seems like the easiest question in the world."

The easiest question in the world. That was the whole problem, the dilemma he had grappled with his entire life. His analytical mind was an asset when it came to figuring out the constitutional questions that came before him, but the easy questions about love and commitment rendered him mute. This was why he hadn't proposed yet to Katherine. Why he had left behind an impoverished woman to whom he was the sun and moon and stars. His public record on women's rights was impeccable. His personal record, not so much.

Something tore in Anton's chest then. He stared at the tiled floor, unable to look up, feeling his Adam's apple bob up and down. He sensed that Carine was looking at him, but his gaze felt rooted to that spot on the floor.

Carine took his hand in hers and held it. "You know what I don't get?" she said softly.

"What?" he whispered, his voice hoarse with shame.

"How you bear it."

He forced himself to raise his head and look at her. "Bear what?"

"You. How you bear being you." Carine bit down on her lower lip, and for a second, her eyes looked apologetic. Then they were bright again. "How do you do it, Anton? This . . . self-control. This weird composure. Don't you ever want to just let it all out? I don't get it."

His mouth went dry, but he managed to croak out a laugh he didn't feel. "What're you talking about, Carine?"

"I'm talking about the fact that you met your birth mom for the first time in God knows how long, and what did you do? You just left her. Hello and goodbye. You walked away after spending a few hours with her. Even after you found out the truth about her and your . . . dad, you left her, like this was some dinner party you'd attended and you didn't want to overstay your welcome. And now you're getting ready to go back—to what? A job you seem to dread? A woman whose phone calls you've been ducking for two days? What are you going back to, Anton? But most of all, I want to know this: How do you keep up the facade? Why are you not falling apart, man?"

He was vaguely aware that behind the rhetorical question there lay an insult, a damnation of his entire way of being, but he couldn't muster up the outrage that he knew he ought to be feeling. He felt pinned, speared into place, by Carine's eyes. And he was rattled by what he saw in those eyes—not insult, not a desire to injure, but concern. And genuine puzzlement. And so the moment dragged on as he tried to constitute a response, a flippant comeback, maybe, that would lighten the suddenly serious mood in the room, but his mind felt sluggish. The next second his focus shifted from Carine, and he became aware of a thin cord of pain that wrapped around his heart, his throbbing, breaking, splintered heart. For two days he had fought to cover up the memory of the devastation on his mother's face as he'd taken his leave, a devastation that he was responsible for. He had scuttled out of her house and into Carine's home, Carine, who had been blissfully welcoming. He had covered up his own pain at the abrupt rending of his time with his mother by his anger at David, by his stealthy avoidance of Katherine and Brad, by his horseplay with Carine's boys. The last two days, as furtive as they had been, had been a throwback, as if he were still that innocent Harvard boy in love with his fiery, impetuous girlfriend. But to cling to that privileged innocence now was to crawl back into his pristine white world, back to a time when the forces of betrayal and corruption lay on the outside and not within his own family. His entire life had been called into question by the arrival of Juanita's fateful letter, and yet here he was, sitting in Carine's home, pretending otherwise. How could he blame David for taking what didn't belong to him when he, Anton, didn't have the sense to hold on to what was his for the taking? Why was it that the two times in his life when he had been offered the love of a black woman, he had spurned them both? What was he running away from? More to the point, what was he running toward? A political office that would make him the most powerful man in the state? Hadn't he already seen—experienced—what that kind of power did to a man? Wasn't it high time to really figure out how much of his life was his choosing?

Carine's face had grown blurry, as if from behind a windshield on a rainy day. He heard her say, "Oh, sweetie, oh, baby," and looked down to see her darker hand covering his own, and as he stared at it, confused, the first of the tears streaming down his cheeks landed. The instant he became aware of the tears, he tried to suck them back in, actually tightened his stomach muscles as if he could reverse their humiliating journey, but he remembered what Carine had said about his self-control, his amazing, superhuman, no, subhuman, monstrous self-control, and he felt his whole body go slack, and then he cried like he hadn't cried in decades, not since—not since . . . since Pappy died? No, he had been teary but—here was that word again—controlled at the funeral, they all had been, David putting an affectionate—or was it a cautioning?— arm around Anton's shoulder at the very moment he was about to lose it, and he had read the gesture correctly—they were Coleman men, they were in the public eye, there were reporters and photographers at the funeral, dammit—and never let the bastards see you sweat or cry or bleed in public. No matter what. So, no, he had not cried at Pappy's funeral, no, he would have to dig deeper, go back further to find a time, and now it comes back, comes back with a swoosh, and holy God, just the memory of it makes his throat and chest feel raw, hollowed out—it was the day he had skipped school and gone searching for her. Her. His mother. His beloved, cracked mother, who, he knew even back then, despite everything that they told him (and when had he stopped knowing it?) had sinned but was not a sinner, who would've sacrificed her life for him. (And if he knew that, why did he ever stop believing in her love for him?) It was on that day, after the two bus rides to the housing project, after the frantic pounding on the door, after the hairy man in the red shorts who answered the door and looked at Anton blankly when he asked for her, after he swallowed his pride and went over to his neighbor Maurice's house to ask Maurice's mom where his own mom was, after he realized that Mam was still in jail, that she wasn't coming back to him anytime soon, probably, after it dawned on him that there would be no easy slipping back into his old life with Mam, that he would have to return to David and FM, after dread coiled around his chest, and he ran out of Maurice's home and flew down the three flights of stairs and into the open air. He made his way behind the thicket of bushes that grew near the left side of the building, where drug deals went down during the evening, he knew, but luckily, at this hour there was no one, and he crouched behind the bushes and cried, holding himself from the waist as he rocked and cried, making himself smaller and smaller, as if to burrow into the earth. And as he cried, he felt his tears extinguishing the flame of hope that he had tended and kept burning all this time. He had been a good son to her, faithful, loyal, he had not allowed himself to be seduced by the abundant food and the soft mattress, the piles of gifts they'd bought him for Christmas, even the pride he felt at his growing popularity in school. But it all amounted to nothing, ashes at his feet.

Then, after a long time, he had stopped crying. The boy who rose from behind the bushes was a different boy than the one who had hid behind them. There was something a little hazy in his eyes—in fact, he himself was a little hazy, as if an invisible cartoonist had rubbed away some part of him and filled in the rest with scribbles. But he didn't know it then. At that time, he was simply hunting for something tangible—and he found it in the silver quarter in his pocket. Enough to make a phone call to FM, to let them know where to come find him so that they could lead him—he choked a bit over the word but steadied himself—home. To their big, luxurious mansion where the memory of a face that would remind him of himself would never again haunt him. Where the wild, dangerous anguish that had seized him just a few minutes ago would not have to be faced again, replaced as it would be by a cool, controlled demeanor. Where he would never again have to take two buses to reach home because limos, taxis, and planes would be waiting for him wherever he went. Never again would he be the son of a single mom whose greatest damage to him was the fact that he felt responsible for her, as if he were the adult and she the child. Not when there was a two-parent family waiting to claim him, to enshrine him, to hand him his patrimony on a silver platter. Anton kicked savagely at a stone in the dust as he headed for the pay phone. By the time he saw David's familiar car snake down the side street an hour later, he had already said goodbye to all of it—the rude, impudent boys who had made fun of his good clothes as he waited at the bus stop, the shabby-looking woman who had shuffled up to him wanting to know if he was "Juanita's boy," the brooding, dark brick buildings that he once thought of as comfort and now wished to never enter again. How wrong he had been, romanticizing this squalor, pretending that he had been in exile the whole time he had slept on clean sheets in a soft bed. Now he knew the truth—this was the true exile. He would never forget it.

And here he was in Carine's sunroom, remembering it all, the herculean, otherworldly effort with which he had stopped crying that day and made the phone call. How, when he went to bed that night, surrounded by the stuffed bears they'd bought for him, he still felt something was missing, and it was only hours later that he knew what it was: the dream of unification with his mam that had lulled him to sleep for over two years. Once again he had felt his chest begin to heave, but this time he had stopped himself, pulled his own body back from drowning.

Drowning. Carine was watching him, her brow knitted with concern, and he wanted to stop this ridiculous crying, but he was as helpless as a wailing infant. What on earth did she say that resulted in this? Anton asked himself. Hell, what his political opponents had said about him was a million times worse, but nothing, no breakup with a girlfriend, no academic failure, no political setback, had resulted in this total loss of control over his emotions. Poor Carine looked like she was ready to dial 911 for help. He twisted his lips into what he hoped was a smile. "I'm okay," he gasped. "I'm sorry."

She squeezed his hand. "Don't be," she whispered. "Keep crying. It's good for you."

This time his smile was genuine. "Only you, Carine," he said, "would encourage someone to cry. Everybody else tries to get you to stop."

"Crying's good for the soul. I do it at least once a week."

He turned his head to face her, the tears beginning to dry on his face. "I never do. Not since—" And he found himself telling her the story of going to find his mom.

After he was done, she spoke at last, her voice awash with compassion. "Anton. What are you going to *do*? I mean, your whole life has been fractured, no? Are you just gonna, you know, soldier on? Pretend like the last few days didn't happen? *Can* you?"

He was about to nod, say yes, tell her that there was no choice, there was an election to win and too many people were counting on him and he would settle up on his personal life after November, when he thought: In whose voice am I going to say these things? Brad's? Dad's? Uncle Connor's? He jumped, as if singed by the matchstick flare of his anger. He blinked at her, processing this revelation, unwilling to speak until the anger either extinguished itself, tamped down by the winds of duty, obligation, and responsibility, or blew up into a bonfire that would destroy his old life. He waited as if he were a disinterested party, curious to see which direction the wind would carry the fire, as if the decision were someone else's to make.

As if the decision were someone else's to make. There it was, in a nutshell. The laziness, the timidity, the caution. He would make a lousy governor, if this was who he truly was or allowed himself to be. He would also make a lousy son. This was where the legendary Coleman self-control had brought him. All the king's horses and all the king's men. A fine Harvard education and this was where he had ended up, a directionless, paunchy prince with no kingdom of his own. No wonder he was mindlessly rushing his way back to David. Without the daring, impetuous, and yes, brave man who had shaped his life, who was he? He had long ago accepted that without David, he never would have had a political life. But now a more urgent existential question nagged at him—without David, would he have any kind of a life at all?

He wanted to find out. The voice within him was small, no more than a murmur. But Anton heard it, and he heard it as the loudest sound in the world. He wanted to find out. Who he was outside the shade of the branches that grew from David's tree. He knew—had been taught—how to be David's son, heir to a political destiny. He had that part down pat, to the extent that he had waltzed his way up to the doorstep of the Governor's Mansion. But did he know how to be a poor woman's son? Did he know how to right the grievous wrong that had been visited upon her? Did he know how to be worthy of the pride she felt in him, since she was unaware of what a frightened, prissy, ineffectual man her son truly was? Was he man enough not to be ashamed of Juanita, of her country ways, her imperfect grammar, which was sweet as spring water to him but which, he knew, would register as ignorant on the ears of his people back home?

Something moved inside Anton's chest, and for a moment it felt physical—not painful, really, but a physical sensation, like an extra heartbeat. Then he recognized it. It was joy. Joy bubbling within him, its edges laced with fear but not the paralyzing kind of fear, not fear that made you afraid to look or move. The right kind of fear, the kind a man feels before he jumps off a cliff into startlingly blue icy-cold waters and knows that it will be all right, because mid-fall, he will learn to fly. The kind of exhilarating fear that pulls joy along in its wake. He was about to jump off a cliff. He couldn't really see the way after that, but it didn't matter.

He leaned over and put his arm around Carine. "Thank you," he said, and he knew his voice was different, more confident.

"For what?" she said, her eyebrows raised.

He kissed her on the cheek. "You'll understand that I can't stay to-night," he said. "You'll explain to the boys?" And he was on his feet, brushing past her.

"Wait. Anton. Where're you going?"

He turned his head to look at her as he headed out of the sunroom and into the bedroom to grab his things. "Home," he said. "I'm going home. I'm off to see my mam."

CHAPTER THIRTY-NINE

He phoned Katherine minutes after he got on the freeway. He let her swear at him for a minute, call him irresponsible, selfish, and a few choice names, and then he interrupted her. "I have to tell you something. Actually, I have to tell you everything, Katherine. But you can't hang up on me until I'm done. Even though you'll want to. Can you promise?"

She almost broke her word when he told her about the two days he'd spent with Carine and her sons, even though he emphasized the presence of the two young boys. He heard her sharp intake of breath and spoke fast, telling her about Carine's husband and explaining that he'd lied only because it had been too difficult to say it all on the phone right then. She gasped again when he told her what David had done and about the uncashed check. "If what you're saying is true, Anton, that's criminal. That's a criminal offense."

"It's true," he said simply. "It's all true."

"But why?" Katherine cried. "I mean, he could've adopted any kid that he wanted, for God's sake."

He pretended to be insulted. "Excuse me," he said. "A great kid like me doesn't come around every day, you know."

There was a stunned silence, and then Katherine said, "I can't believe you can even joke about this. I mean, I'm in shock."

He was immediately contrite. "I'm not. Really. I'm still processing it. Honestly, I feel like someone's beaten me on the head with a baseball bat. I mean, my God, Katherine. This is a man whom I adored. Adore. And that's the reason why I couldn't rush home. I need some time—and distance—to process what I've found out. Do you understand?"

There was another silence. "And did Carine help you . . . process it?" Katherine asked carefully.

He heard the hurt in her question and shook his head impatiently. "I did talk to her," he said. "But babe, you gotta understand—the reason I could talk to Carine was precisely because she's not close to the situation. And that's exactly why I couldn't talk to you. Because I needed an objective listener, and she . . . Carine . . . well, she's not in love with me. So she could be dispassionate. Whereas you . . ." It was sounding fake to him, like some bullshit line a cheating husband fed to his wife, and he wondered if Katherine was hearing it the same way. He sighed. This was not a conversation to be had while they were several states apart. On the other hand, he appreciated her resilience, her toughness in abiding by her promise and not hanging up. She was lovely, Katherine, and he was suddenly sure he wanted her in his life for a long time to come.

"This is very difficult," he said quietly. "And doing it long-distance makes it harder. I'm sorry. But I didn't want to lie to you another minute. I know it's asking you for a lot, Katherine. I know how this looks. But—"

"Where're you now?" she interrupted.

He exhaled, knowing he was about to drop another bombshell on her. "Driving back. To her. To my mam."

"I was hoping you'd say that," Katherine said, and he slackened his grip on the steering wheel. He had been unaware that he had been gripping it that hard.

"You were?" He felt his eyes fill with tears and was about to blink them back when he remembered what Carine had accused him of. He let them roll.

"Of course. You need to spend time with her. Do you have any idea how long you'll be away?"

He mulled over her question, and even though he was still crying, he smiled. He felt his chest expand and fill with lightness. "Katherine. I have no friggin' idea. I don't know what I'm gonna say to her or what we'll eat for dinner tonight or where I'll sleep. All I know is I'm gonna fling my arms around my mam and hug her senseless."

He heard the smile in her voice. "That sounds like a plan." Then her voice grew serious. "But what're we going to do about the media, Anton? Come Monday they will be circling like vultures. Brad's going to go crazy trying to keep them at bay."

His chest constricted again at this reminder of his real life. "I know," he said miserably. "I don't think Brad's ever going to speak to me again. It's just that . . . the thought of campaigning is just beyond me right now. I'm sorry I've left you guys a mess to clean up. I have no clue what we'll tell the media."

Katherine's voice was cool, thoughtful. "What if we tell them the truth?"

Anton grimaced. "The truth?"

"Not all of it, of course. Just that your long-lost mom reached out to you. And you went out to see her. And are now spending a few days catching up."

It was brilliant, really. The truth. Not the whole truth, naturally, but enough of it. A simple, elegant way out of their dilemma. "Brad can't tell them where I am," he said, warming up to the idea. "No details at all. I don't want the press crawling around her place, messing up her life."

"Fair enough." Katherine was quiet for a moment and then asked, "Anton. What is she like?"

A feeling of pride swept over Anton. He grinned broadly. "Mam? She's pretty cool, actually. You'd like her, Kat." And even as he said those words, he knew it was true. Katherine would be able to see past Juanita's lack of education and poor grammar to her quiet, heroic core. It would take some time, but the two of them would grow comfortable around each other.

"If she's anything like you, I'm sure I will."

He swallowed. "You're the best, you know that?" he said. "If the roles were reversed, if you'd spent the last two days with an old boyfriend, I don't know if I could've forgiven you as easily."

"Anton," she said quietly. "Love is not love without trust."

He fell silent, thinking of what she'd said.

"Hello?"

"I'm here."

"Okay, well . . ."

"I love you, Kat," he said. "And I really hope to spend my days with you."

"Honey. If this is some kind of a lame long-distance marriage proposal . . ."

He laughed dutifully. "No. It isn't. But we need to talk when I get home. I have so very much I need to tell you."

"I think I like this new Anton."

"From now on, this is the only Anton you'll see. I promise."

CHAPTER FORTY

He drove down the same roads that he'd driven down just two days before, but this time everything was different. The sky was hazier today and his windshield dirtier, but to Anton, everything shone brighter. His body pulsed with awareness, felt prickly with sensation, as if now that he'd acknowledged his mother's sorrow, he was finally in tune with the sway and thrum of the entire universe. But was that really what he'd done, acknowledged his mother's pain? Or was it simply that for the first time, he had entered the dark cave that he had always been afraid to explore—his own heart? What that heart wanted, what it ached and longed for, he had never allowed himself to know, but now that he had walked through its chambers, he was flooding it with light at every step he took. If he didn't accomplish another thing in his life, there would be this.

What're you gonna do when you get to Mam's? he asked himself, but his imagination led him only as far as climbing up the porch steps and knocking on the front door. What happened after that was a canvas as blank as the sky above. And unlike on his first trip to his mother's home, when he'd showed up bristling with purpose, he was content with not knowing.

His phone rang, and he glanced at where it lay on the passenger seat, and his heart sank. It was Dad. He knew he shouldn't pick up, because if anyone in the world could make him reverse his course, it was David, but a lifetime of habit prevailed and he answered. "Hi, Dad," he said.

"You're going back? To her house?" David's voice was so close and urgent in his ear, it was as if he could feel the breath, and Anton jerked the phone away and put it on speaker instead. "Anton? Is that what you're doing?"

Despite his growing anger, Anton marveled at the impetuous quality in the older man's voice. David was not someone who gave up without a fight. This was what Pappy had bred him to be—a scrappy fighter. He had tried to do the same with Anton, but what he'd produced instead was a deferential, obedient son.

Until now. And suddenly, Anton heard it, the tremor behind the arrogance, the loss of control, and the fact that David had no clue how to win back that control. His son was six hundred miles away, speeding along a freeway that would take him back to his dark past, into the shadows that David had prided himself on rescuing Anton from. There was nothing in David's arsenal that could help him understand the choice Anton was making. In the split second before he answered, Anton understood this, and the knowledge made his voice softer when he replied, "Yes, Dad. Katherine spoke to you?"

"No." David's voice was curt, and again Anton heard something—a trace of hurt—and knew that Katherine had refused to speak to him. "I heard it from Brad."

"News travels fast up north," he said, not trying to hide the amusement in his voice.

There was a short, angry silence. "You think that's funny? May I also remind you that 'up north' is where you're running for governor? Unless . . . unless you've decided to throw that away along with everything else?" This time the wobble in David's voice was so distinct that Anton felt a pang in his chest. For a moment he saw it all from David's point of view—the horror of the past rising up, acquiring fangs and claws, and bloodying their present, and then the truest horror: Instead of beating it back, Anton was suddenly, improbably joining forces with it and blaming him, *him,* David Coleman, who had done everything that a biological father would do, who had given Anton a great education, unconditional love, who had shared his wealth, who, most of all, had conferred upon this ungrateful boy his illustrious family name and had rescued him from a life of poverty and mediocrity. All to have it end up in a pile of ashes, because ultimately, ultimately, the pull of blood, the tug of—say it, *say it*—of blackness was too compelling. When Anton had turned his car around and begun driving toward Juanita Vesper's house, he'd been heading toward everything David scorned and feared—the rural South and its untidy poverty, disorder, and squalor.

But here was the rub. Anton couldn't think of David as just another privileged old white guy. Because for every radiant memory David carried of him, Anton had a correspondingly sweet memory of his father. Of the man who'd been so patient when he had stumbled, but who had instilled in him the kind of confidence that had served him well in his adult life; who had cried tears of joy the day they had formally adopted him, who had been a source of guidance and advice and inspiration on every matter in his life, large and small. David had been a monumental presence in his life, a linebacker who had sheltered and protected Anton so that he could keep his eyes focused on the fifty-yard line, and only the most unforgiving of men would allow the revelation of his one terrible sin to tarnish every other golden memory.

"What am I throwing away, Dad? All I'm doing is spending some more time with her."

"To what end? Don't you think you owe the voters something more than your hiney?"

The question was so vintage David that Anton had to suppress a laugh. He waited until the impulse passed and then said, "Dad. This is a woman who has suffered a lot." His voice trembled a bit. "Who . . . has had a grave injustice done to her." He bit his lip, suppressing the urge to say more, reminding himself of David's heart condition, reluctant to wound the older man, but also wanting to make it clear that David was not off the hook. Not by a long shot. "What you and Uncle Connor did, Dad . . . I still can barely understand it. And it's going to take me a long time to forgive you."

David made a sound so harsh, so bitter, that it took Anton's breath away. "Guess I should've known," he said.

"Known what?"

"Pappy used to say blood is thicker than water. It always wins, blood."

Anton felt a slow burn creeping onto his cheeks. "What does that even mean? You think I'm siding with my—my birth mom—because of blood? How convenient that must be for you, Dad. It lets you off the hook completely, doesn't it?"

David made that same ugly sound again, a combination of laughter and throat clearing. "And how come you don't hold her responsible, huh? For what she did? A grown woman leaving a young child trapped alone in a room. Do you know what the goddamn temperatures were that week?" David's voice rose. "It was ninety-five fucking degrees inside that goddamned apartment. *That's* what I rescued you from, Anton. I rescued you from hell. From a—" David coughed, a loud, jagged fit that went on and on. "Water," Anton heard him whisper, and the next moment there was a disturbance, and then Delores's voice, cool and firm. "Anton? Sweetheart? What's going on? Will someone please tell me?"

Her voice held such concern and bewilderment that Anton's chest felt warm, as if she were once again applying Vicks to his chest the way she would when he was a boy with a cold. He was about to answer when a car passed him on the left, the driver leaning on the horn and glaring as he passed. Anton must've been weaving across lanes, he realized. On an impulse, he pulled onto the shoulder of the highway in order to focus on the call. "Hey, Mom," he said wearily, dreading her reaction if he had to tell her something she didn't know.

"Honey. What's going on? Why's Dad walking around the house like he's seen a ghost?"

Anton closed his eyes and then opened them. "Because he has, Mom," he said. And proceeded to answer her question.

There was a long, stunned silence after he was done, and just as it was beginning to feel unbearable to Anton, Delores said, "You have to answer one question honestly. Will you be able to forgive him, Anton? Will you be able to forgive us?"

The question was so purely Delores—compassionate, humble, intuitive—that Anton began to cry.

"Darling. Anton, baby. Don't. Please don't. I can't bear it. What we've done." And then Delores was crying, too.

"But you didn't . . . you didn't do anything wrong, Mom," Anton said. "How could you have . . ."

"Oh, but yes, I did." Though Delores's voice was weak, Anton heard the iron in it. "That day when he told me that poor woman . . . your . . . mom . . . had asked to be relieved of her legal rights. I knew . . . I knew something wasn't right. It was too—convenient. Too easy. And yet I didn't push David too hard. I didn't dare. He looked—so happy. You made him so happy, Anton." Delores's voice cracked. "And he had been so unhappy for so long. After James died. It was like watching a dead man come back to life, with you in the house." Delores stopped abruptly, and it killed Anton to imagine what she looked like in that moment. He imagined her sitting on the cherry rocker beside the phone stand, hunched with grief, dabbing her eyes, trying to control her voice and her emotions in case someone—William, probably—was nearby.

"Where's Dad?" he asked.

"Not in the room," she answered. "I don't know. And at the moment, I don't care."

He felt a moment's gratitude at this linking of arms, even though he knew what it cost her to go against David. "Don't be too hard on him, Mom," he said. "I—I know Dad meant well. I do get that."

"Don't. Don't do it, Anton."

"Do what?"

"What you always do. Don't make excuses for him. He's not a saint, Anton. And he's not a superman. Even though he's always wanted you to believe this. He's just a man. A good man most of the time, but just a man. It's time you start seeing this, baby."

"Mom, I—"

"And you're a better man than he is. You're . . . kinder. Softer. Maybe you get that from her. Your . . . mom. You certainly didn't learn that warmth from us."

He hated what she was doing, this self-flagellation, almost as much as he'd hated David's unapologetic bravado a few minutes earlier. "You're the warmest person I know, Mom," he said.

Delores made a sound like she was spitting up a bitter pit. "Me? I'm six generations of Yankee, son. I think my father hugged me exactly three times in my entire life. I inherited that legendary New England reticence. We were all so obsessed with who was and who was not 'our kind' that we bred all the humanity out of our bloodlines." And Delores was crying again.

"Well, you let *me* in," Anton said, trying desperately to help.

Delores sighed. "We tried. We really tried. And Anton, one thing you've got to believe me when I tell you—we never felt that we were doing you the favor. We always knew the truth: that it was you helping us."

"That's not what Dad said," Anton said quietly.

"Ignore him. He's like an insane person right now. He doesn't even know what's coming out of his mouth, Anton. The fact that you're not out on the campaign trail is driving him nuts. You must understand."

Why was she talking to him like he was a distant relative who had to have things explained to him? They're both getting old, Anton thought. Dad's illness has prematurely aged both of them. "I know, Mom," he said. "I know. And I'll be home soon, I promise."

"What are you going to do?" Delores asked, and again there was this distant politeness, this formality lacing her words, as if she had already decided that Juanita had the better claim. "When you see her again, I mean?"

"I'm not sure. I honestly don't know. I just . . . want to spend some time with her." He wanted to add, And I never would've imagined how much resistance I'd run into to keep me from doing this very modest thing.

"You should bring her back," Delores said. "With you."

"Bring her where?"

"Home. Bring her home. With you."

"And where would she stay, Mom?" he said carefully.

"You have a nice condo. Or. She could stay here. With us."

The snort escaped before Anton could control it. "You want to put Dad into an early grave, Mom?"

"I see what you mean." He could hear the smile in Delores's voice. But then she continued, improbably, "But you said she's been sober now for—how many years? And I bet she's a very nice lady."

He shook his head, smiling at the when-hell-freezes-over vision of Juanita Vesper sitting at the table in David and Delores Coleman's well-appointed dining room. He heard the clanking of the heavy soup spoons, saw the startled, eager-to-please smile on Delores's lips as she strove to make conversation, the quizzical look David would cast Anton's way each time Juanita said something country or unsophisticated. He could almost picture it—the burning, acidic feeling in his stomach every time Juanita made a social gaffe, the puff of pride when she said something unexpectedly clever and David shot him an astonished look.

Anton kept his eyes closed after he hung up with Delores, promising to phone her later that night, and continued to imagine the scene around the dinner table. William would probably draw Juanita out of her shell, so that her tight, awkward smile would loosen a bit around the edges when she spoke to him. Brad would treat her with his usual egalitarian, breezy charm, and she would blossom under his teasing. But she would remain shy and quiet around Katherine, casting appraising looks from below hooded eyes when she thought Katherine wasn't looking. And Katherine would squeeze Anton's hand under the table every time Juanita said something that made the others respond with soft, appreciative chuckles.

Anton was smiling to himself when the rapping at his window caused him to open his eyes. He turned his head and saw the window blocked by a uniformed state trooper. Muttering a soft "fuck" to himself, Anton rolled down the window, involuntarily running a hand through his hair. He craned his neck and looked up into a broad red face. "Hi, Officer," he said, forcing a brightness into his voice that he didn't feel. "I just pulled over to make a phone call."

"Registration and driver's license." The voice was flat, slightly nasal.

"I need to explain something," Anton said. His voice sounded strange, high-pitched to his ear. "The car belongs to a friend of mine. So it's not in my name, okay? I'm visiting from up north, actually. I'm just here on—"

The gray eyes went hard. "I said, registration and driver's license."

"Yeah, yeah, sure." To Anton's mortification, he found himself fumbling as he reached for his wallet. The few times he had been stopped and frisked by the cops when he was a teenager, his family name had smoothed out any potential rough spots. Here, he knew exactly who he was—a lone black man with an out-of-town license in an expensive car that was not registered to him. Here, on a strip of highway in the middle of rural Georgia.

He watched his license disappear into the large beefy hand and sat staring ahead as the cop removed a flashlight and peered into the car even though it wasn't dark. His mind was racing, anticipating what would come next—permission to conduct a search of the car—and whether he should allow it or not. He was out of his element here, a stranger in a strange land, and all his earlier affinity for the land of his forefathers had flown out of the window and was lying in the dirt at the side of the road. The small, narrowing eyes of the patrolman told him exactly who he was—he was a northerner, he was black, and he was guilty. Of what, he wasn't sure. But he was pretty sure it didn't matter, that on the side of a deserted highway, innocence would be only a formality.

Get a grip, he said to himself. Think. Tell him you're the fucking attorney general back home, for fuck's sake, if you think that will help. Although it could make matters worse. The uppity Negro and all that.

He was aware that he was inexplicably indulging in the worst racial stereotypes of the white southerner, but given the initial signs, he was not wrong. He mentally cataloged the clues: the curtness with which he had been asked for his license. The lack of pleasantries and the lack of "sir" that had followed the command. The unnecessary intimidation of the flashlight search of his car. No, he had not imagined the hostility in the patrolman's posture, the presumption of guilt.

Anton waited with growing anger and dread as the officer went back to his patrol car to call in the license number. He had not lived the life of the average black male in so long that he had gone soft, lacking the sharpness that he would need to call upon now. He wanted to nip this incident in the bud, even if it meant accepting a traffic violation ticket, although what the cop would list as his offense, he hadn't a clue. That was what he should've done, dammit, asked the man immediately what he was being questioned for. But the officer's posture had been so curt and intimidating that Anton had meekly handed over his license.

It came to him as he sat there waiting. How often had an incident

like this occurred in his mother's life? How many such insults and hu-
miliations had she endured? And how had she dealt with them? Had
she smiled and cowered, as he had? Or had her eyes blazed with anger, the corners of her mouth turned down with scorn and hatred? As
he remembered her large liquid eyes, the girl-like face, Anton's heart
pinched with regret. How had she done it, kicked her drug addiction
and stayed sober in a world that seemed designed to break down women
like her? A world where perhaps the sanest response was to lose yourself
in a drugged stupor? What an iron will she must possess, what pools of
courage must lie behind those gentle brown eyes. And the worst part
was, her reward for a lifetime of self-discipline and hard work was so
paltry. Pappy and David had worked hard, and so did Anton. But their
efforts had such enormous payoffs—good salaries, wealth that repro-
duced itself, luxury cars, beautiful homes. What had Juanita Vesper
earned in exchange for kicking a drug habit, for twenty-five years of
sobriety, for decades of working in a small, hot restaurant kitchen? A
free lunch hurriedly eaten in between customers. A small house on the
outskirts of town that had been left to her by her blind mother. A car
that ran but could stop any day. A solitary, almost reclusive life. No
extravagant habits, no eating out, no trips to Europe. Did she even have
health care? He had no idea. Carine was right. How did he bear it? How
did he bear being the thoughtless, self-absorbed prick that he was? How
had he not collapsed, how had his bones not cracked under the unbearable weight of his selfishness?

   He knew that such thoughts would not help his situation, that they
might make him combative when the officer returned, but without
knowing it, he was sitting taller in his seat. In his job, he had put away
hardened police officers for corruption, had faced off against members
of the Mob and powerful high rollers on Wall Street. He was not going
to be intimidated by an asshole patrolman with a red face and a southern drawl. Anton tapped his fingers impatiently on the steering wheel,

and then struck by an idea, he dialed Beau Branson's phone number, careful to leave the phone sitting on the passenger seat.

"BB speaking."

"BB, this is Anton."

"Anton. You run away with my plane? Where the hell—?"

Anton faked a chuckle. "Yeah, man. Can't say I blame you. I'll explain everything when I return. And I'll make it right financially, okay? But BB, listen. I have a problem. I've been pulled over by a state trooper who may be suspicious about me driving a car not registered in my name." He heard his voice tighten and hoped that Beau would pick up on the gravity of the situation without him having to spell out the obvious.

"Well, fuck," BB interrupted. "Did you tell him who you are?"

"No. Not yet. He's—He didn't seem like he was in any mood to listen. He's running my license right now. But I . . ." Anton looked around wildly, trying to find an identifying road marker to let BB know where he was. "I'm northbound on Route 25. About an hour away from a town called Thomasville. And I need to know—whose car have I been driving?"

He finally had BB's attention. "Anton. Are you feeling—unsafe? Dude, what'd he pull you over for?"

Anton shook his head impatiently. "I don't know. I'm hoping he'll just give me a ticket and I'll be on my way. And he didn't. Pull me over, that is. I had pulled over to take a phone call from my mom. And next thing I knew, he was up my ass."

BB let out a low whistle. "Man. It's another world down there, isn't it? The South."

Anton didn't want to get into a goddamn political conversation right now. "BB," he said desperately. "I'm telling you my location just in case. But mostly, I need to know whose name the car is registered under. In case he asks."

"The car? Hell, I don't know. My secretary arranged it. Probably a company car. We do business in Atlanta, right? It's probably under Branson Industries."

Anton looked in the rearview mirror and saw the trooper exiting his vehicle. "He's headed back this way, BB. I should hang up. Can you make a few calls to find out and get right back to me?"

"Sure. I'll be in touch."

Anton hung up without saying goodbye, looking out of his side mirror as the trooper's bulky frame filled it. He rolled down the window again and was relieved when the man handed his license back to him. "You didn't tell me you were attorney general, sir." The voice was still gruff, distant, but it was obvious that an olive branch was being extended. Anton had not misheard the note of deference.

"You didn't ask my occupation," Anton said lightly, draining the slightest hint of hostility or indignation from his voice.

"You here on business, sir?"

Anton's right hand gave an involuntary flutter, but he steadied it immediately. "You could say that," he said in a noncommittal manner. The "sir" was encouraging and Anton took solace from it. Now the best strategy was to get out of here before too many questions were asked.

They both spoke at the same moment, and Anton stopped, indicating with his hand that the trooper—P. Flynn was the name on his badge—should go first. "Oh, sorry," the man said. "I was just asking, so the car belongs to a friend?"

Anton swallowed hard, uneasy at this turn in the conversation. He stared out of his windshield for a second and then came to a decision. "Yes. But it may be registered to his company." He forced himself to look Flynn directly in the face, straining his neck to look up. "I made a call to my friend," he said, aware of the small muscle throbbing in his jaw. "While you were—checking my driver's license in your cruiser. I gave him my location and asked him to call back in a few minutes with information about who the car is registered to."

He noticed with satisfaction that Flynn took a step away from the car. "That won't be necessary, sir," he said. "I've—Everything checked out fine. We're good."

The relief Anton felt was so palpable that his upper eyelid twitched in celebration. "Am I free to go, then?" he said, the authority back in his voice.

"Absolutely." Flynn gave a small, tight smile that nevertheless softened his face. "Have a good day, Mr. Coleman."

Anton waited until the trooper was back in his car before clicking on his turn signal, waiting until the lane was completely absent of traffic before getting back on the highway. He drove the speed limit for the next eight miles, until he was very sure that Flynn was nowhere near him. It was only then that he became aware of his ice-cold hands and feet and the throbbing in his neck from where the muscles had stood at attention for the whole encounter. The fear that he had felt was wildly disproportionate to what had actually happened. He had not even had the presence of mind to ask Flynn how he'd found out who Anton was. But even as his mind told him that the whole thing had not been such a big deal, his body gave him a different answer. What he had felt was a primal fear, something coded into his DNA, the fear of a black man pulled over by a cop on a stretch of road in Georgia. A black man. That was exactly who he was in this godforsaken place. In New England he was scarcely aware of his skin as he went about his daily life. It wasn't like he was ignorant of the fact that cops back home routinely racially profiled black kids. Or that black men around the country were still prey. Trayvon Martin. Eric Garner. Michael Brown. The names were etched into his consciousness. But it had always been easy to put distance between himself and the Hoodie. The Cigarillos. The Overweight Guy choked like a dog on the streets of New York by a pack of cops.

Those black men didn't drive a Lexus. They did not have skin the color of copper, they did not make the cover of *People* magazine, they hadn't been to Ivy League schools, they didn't speak with a posh accent. And yet all this meant nothing to Trooper Flynn, who had eyed him with the same scorn that Anton had shown convicted felons and drug dealers. Trooper Flynn, who had just handed Anton one of the best lessons about his place in history that he'd ever learned.

He imagined telling David about this encounter, how the older man's jaw would clench at the thought of some ignorant prick cop mistreating his son like this, how he would mentally comb through his Rolodex trying to think of whom he knew down there in Georgia who could haul this trooper's sorry ass into the office and chew him out for disrespecting the governor's son. And yet this same man, who would be more upset than Anton over the trivial, routine incident, could not see his way to apologize to a powerless black woman whom he had robbed. Yes, that was what David had done, he had robbed Juanita Vesper of her one singular possession, and given that she was serving a needlessly long prison sentence at the time, it may as well have been at gunpoint.

Anton thought of what Delores had suggested—bringing Juanita back home with him. And he replayed over and over what David had said about never apologizing to him for what he had done. To his enormous surprise, he found himself agreeing with his father. David was right. He did not owe Anton an apology. At Carine's house, tears streaming down his cheeks, Anton had remembered the housing project where he'd lived with his mother. Over the years he had forgotten the details about the bleakness of his early life. But what he remembered now was the boredom. The tedium of poverty. A tedium whose only antidote, whose only disruption, came from a gun burst of violence, of an unexpected scream shattering the quiet of a Sunday morning, or a stream of loud obscenities wafting from the streets at midnight. Maybe that's why Mam used crack, Anton thought, to handle that tedium. He remembered how the energy in the apartment used to change when she had those people over. Even though she'd lock him in the bedroom so that he would not witness her using, he could hear the thud of the music, the sudden peals of laughter, the voices getting louder and higher. For the most part, it hadn't frightened him. Rather, he found it reassuring, because it proved that there was more to their lives than soul-wrecking jobs and occasional visits to fast-food restaurants.

He wouldn't have survived the boredom. Anton knew that now. In order to not succumb to it, he would've joined a gang. He had been a good boy, quiet and polite to his elders. But he was also intelligent, and that intelligence would have been his downfall. Some resourceful neighborhood drug dealer would've figured out how to make that brightness work for him. And Mam would've been able to protect him less and less, the crack eating away at whatever maternal protective instinct remained. No, David was right. Between being groomed by a shrewd dope dealer and rescued by David and Delores, there was no doubt that he had hit the jackpot.

It wasn't Anton's forgiveness that David needed to ask for. It was Juanita's.

He was so struck by this thought that he almost drove past his exit. He saw it too late, slammed on his brakes, and yanked the wheel to the right, going over the striped lines to get on the exit ramp. For a split second he couldn't bear to look in the rearview mirror, as if he expected Trooper Flynn to be right behind him. But the sun was low in the sky and the road deserted. Anton pulled into the parking lot of the first gas station he saw and once again called up the directions to his mother's address. If he didn't run into any traffic along the way, he would be there in about twenty-five minutes. He smiled with pleasure at the thought of climbing up those porch steps, his footsteps lighter this time, his eyes unclouded with hostility and suspicion, and of the look on her face when she opened the door and saw that it was him. Him. Her son. Come for her again.

And what then? he asked himself as he drove down the two-lane road. What'll you do? Sleep on the couch tonight? Will she be okay with that? The giddy feeling deserted him for a moment as he considered the logistics and the inevitable complications his reentry into Juanita's life would involve, but then he thought: First things first. First I'll take her out to dinner. To the most expensive restaurant in the county. He sighed, the very thought of ordering a bottle of a good red soothing him, but then he remembered that she was a recovering addict. No, he'd have to do without alcohol tonight. And what if you run out of things to say to each other? he thought. What if you find her to be, you know, *limited* in her vocabulary or interests or general knowledge? The thought depressed him. But then he remembered the proprietary way she'd called him "Baby Boy," the way she'd looked at him, looked *through* him, and he knew: He had a mama he could be proud of. What Juanita Vesper knew, what she had lived through and experienced, he could only read about in books. No, the danger was exactly the opposite—that he would disappoint *her*, that she would see through him and realize that he was made of cotton and straw, an empty suit lacking vigor and conviction. When she asked him why he'd returned, for instance, what would he say? That he'd had a change of heart? Or would he credit Carine for asking a question that had made him see what he'd been too blind to see on his own?

One thing he knew for sure he would tell his mam: the recently surfaced memory of when he'd returned to the housing project to find her. She had earned that story and its meaning—that her son had not forgotten her after two and a half years of living in luxury. That he had been willing to give it up just to move back into the dingy apartment with her. That in his deepest, darkest hour, in the hour of his abandonment, when he believed that she had forsaken him, he had sought her out.

Anton drove along in this manner, alternating between a chest-pounding excitement and a sobering dread. It was all too soon, too fast, too unexpected. This was to have been a quick trip to a new place—the South, so deceptively soft and beautiful, with its rich bloodred earth and magnolia trees and wildflowers growing alongside the highway—but it had become a different kind of journey. As long as Anton had known him, Pappy had had a big hand-painted sign hanging in his home office that read, "Know Thyself." Anton had claimed the sign after Pappy had died, and it now resided on the floor in his own apartment. He had always intended to put it up, but as with so many things, he had not gotten around to it. That small procrastination, easy enough to explain away in his busy daily life, now assumed symbolic meaning. He had been raised by people whose creed revolved around Know Thyself, a family steeped in the wisdom of its secular saints, Emerson and Thoreau. Anton had no doubt that his father knew himself, even if it meant acknowledging the black stain on his own heart. Because, for all his flaws, David was a complete man, someone who knew exactly what he saw when he looked at himself in the mirror.

As did, Anton suspected, his mam. You couldn't have twenty-five years of sobriety without knowing thyself. It was obvious in the clearness of those brown eyes—Juanita Vesper did not owe the world anything and did not expect that the world owed her a thing. Not a single thing. She had repaid her debt to society by sacrificing her proudest creation. No matter how modest her life, no matter how pinched and narrow her circumstances, when Juanita laid her head on the pillow at night, she knew that everything around her belonged to her. She had paid for all of it with her own flesh and blood.

Anton massaged the spot that throbbed in his temple. There was no way to recoup the years they had spent apart. Perhaps it was just as well, to have not witnessed the ugliness of her recovery—the withdrawal symptoms, the shakes, the tremors, the relapses. The slow return of light to her eyes. What would his life have been like if he had been returned to her after her time in prison? They undoubtedly would have lost their subsidized apartment, shabby and claustrophobic as it was. Would he have continued at the same school, where the teachers themselves spread the virus of discouragement and defeatism to their students? Would he have ever met someone like David, who believed in him, who was alternately encouraging and firm but whose very sternness was propelled by a belief that no matter what level of excellence he demanded from Anton, the boy was capable of delivering it? For a long time, Anton had loved Delores more, felt more comfortable around her, because she was easier on him. Delores was like Mam in that regard, soft, undemanding, loving. And he had desperately needed that after his abrupt parting from his mam. But it had taken David's mix of sweet and sour, his glowing with pride and his glowering with disappointment, to drive Anton to achieve all that he had.

In some horrible way, he understood why David had done what he had. He also understood that the passage of time and its retrospective gaze could lengthen the shadows of an original deed and give it a more monstrous shape. The men who owned slaves were thinking about their cotton yield that year, and how to protect their wives from the roving eye of *that particular Negro*, and not about original sin. Anton had always believed that the great fatal flaw in Marxist theory was that it had never accounted for actual human behavior—the yawn, the stretch, the shrug, the looking away. And that was exactly what David had done. He had not battled with complexity, had not tried to figure out a way to remain a presence in Anton's life after his mother was released from prison. What was unforgivable was not that David had wanted Anton to remain in his life or even his conceit in believing that he knew better than anybody else what was in the boy's best interest. It was that he'd taken a shortcut and exploited Juanita's situation. It was the oldest story in the world—the ends justifying the means.

The late-evening Georgia sky was throwing up streaks of murderous, ludicrous color. The color entered the car, turning Anton's face and hands golden. He lowered his window, hoping for some evening cool, but the air was still heavy with heat, and he raised it again, escaping into the artificial coolness of the air-conditioning. He drove through a small town and then on an open stretch of road with fields on either side. Next he saw a few cows, and later, a few horses dotted the landscape, their bodies dark and vivid against the green fields. He passed a marsh, wood storks rising and fluttering in the distance, and the sight was so magnificent that he slowed down to watch. A little while later, he saw a patch of purple coneflowers that made him suck in his breath. Georgia, in its tender, maternal beauty, drew him in her embrace again, softening the memory of his encounter with Flynn. He remembered what Juanita had told him about moving north when he was a year old. Had Nana encouraged or resisted her migration? Had Mam thought about it much, how she would cope in a new place where the snow covered the ground for five months out of the year? What she would miss and what she would be happy to forget? Had she considered what it would be like to live with Betsy, who had just gotten a clerical job at the Higbee's department store and who herself might not want too many reminders of her old life? What had it been like for this young woman, who'd had sex with an older man but had never tasted alcohol, who had just finished a semester of community college but had never seen the inside of an airport, who was about to leave her mother and the only home she'd known, to move to another city that she hoped would be kinder to her bastard son than the small, cruel place she was leaving behind? It hit Anton hard, how much of her story he didn't know. How much catching up they had to do. This was why he was going back to her, to learn more of her story.

As for his own story, how much of it would he share? What would he tell her about Carine? How would he describe his relationship with David and Delores? Would it hurt or please her to know that he was the soft spot in their hearts, that they loved him as much as she did? Could he confess to the princely comforts of his life without insulting hers? Did he dare tell her that he probably spent more on books and dinners out than she earned in a month? Was David right? Would their blood tie prove to be thicker than the acute class differences between them? There was so much he didn't know. But he was going to find out. In the end, that was the best thing he could say about himself—that he was ready to find out. At long last, he was willing to be a son. Oh, he had been a son to David and Delores, of course, had shone for them and made them proud. But what Juanita would require from him would be harder. Because what she would require was honesty, an absolute lack of pretense. Carine was the only other person in his life who had required this degree of nakedness from him, and he had dumped her. But Juanita was in his life now. And he could no more dump her than he could chop off his own hand.

Suddenly, he wanted all of them, wanted to gather them up—David and Delores, Juanita and Carine and Katherine, Uncle Connor and Brad—and place them in an orchestra that would play the music of his life. He wanted to leave out none of it—not the trombone, not the cello, not the cymbals or the violin. Synthesis. He needed a fusing together of all the strands of his life: past and present, black and white, poor and rich. He had lived for so long with pieces of his life missing, and as he drove through downtown Ronan and past the diner where his mother worked, it came to him what he must do, what he had come here to do: take her back with him. For a little while, maybe. Or for a long while. That decision, along with every other that she would make from here on out, would be hers. That much, he was sure, he could give her, the ability and the means to make her own decisions.

He stopped at the only red light in town, and as he sat there, he saw it: Sometime tonight, he would propose it, maybe over dinner, maybe when they'd returned home and she was preparing the couch for him.

Come with me, Mam, he would say. Now that I've found you, it would be unbearable for me to leave you again. It would destroy me not to have you in my life. And I do have to go back, because I have a race to win. I wouldn't care so much for myself, but you see, there are a lot of people who are counting on me. There are kids who dropped out of college to work on my campaign. There are old ladies in nursing homes who have sent me five dollars each month. And here's the thing, Mam. I think I have it in me to be a good governor. You know, people always want their politicians to be father figures. I won't be. But what I think I can be is a damn good son. A responsible heir, a sober custodian of what belongs to them. Because it ain't my state or my dad's. It's theirs. And you know who reminded me of that, Mam? You did. It's knowing that I can learn to be a good son to you that gives me the confidence to think I can do this job.

Anton smiled to himself as he drove past the fields that his forefathers may have tilled, and toward his nana's house.

★　　★　　★

As Anton makes the sudden sharp turn onto the gravel road that leads to his grandmother's house, the sun is beginning to protest its dying. It shoots its anguish into the sky, sparks of gold and orange and a lurid purple. The melodrama of the sky contrasts with the placid, dark green fields. The Lexus inches along the gravel road, not wanting to miss the driveway that leads to the house. Anton turns left onto the driveway, and the first thing he notices is absence. The absence of Mam's car. His heart sinks a bit, following the trajectory of the sun. He peers out of the windshield and notices the house is dark. She's not home. She's not home. It's almost eight o'clock on a Sunday night, and she's not home. He kicks himself for not having stopped at the diner, but she had told him that her shift ended at five-thirty. And surely she wasn't working on a Sunday night.

Well, nothing to do but wait. She could be anywhere, really. Gone to the movies. Gone to an evening church service. Visiting one of Nana's friends at the hospital. He steps out of the car and stretches his stiff back, pulling his arms above his head, flattening his palms so that they appear to hold up the weight of the sky. The gravel crunches under his feet as he walks toward the house in his expensive calf-leather shoes. He takes the porch steps in one stride, and even though he knows she's not home, he knocks on the door. There is no sound or movement. He waits for a moment and then heads back down from the porch.

Out in the yard, he listens to the sound of the quiet. It is loud, deafening, and for a moment, unbearable. And then his ear sinks into it and it pleases him. As does the sight of the powerless sun, vanquished at last, dimming in the horizon. Now, finally, there is a breeze, and it brings with it welcome perfumes from the honeysuckle growing in the yard, and from the other flowers, flowers he doesn't know the names of but suspects that his mother does. He unbuttons the top button on his shirt and bends his elbows as if he's doing the chicken dance in order to air out his damp armpits. He opens the door of the car to get in, but the seductions of late evening win and he shuts it again. He leans against the vehicle, his legs crossed at the ankles, and waits. His right foot digs into the gravel, sending up a small puff of dust that settles on his shoe. He taps his toe, following a rhythm he is unaware of. *Tap tap tap. Tap tap tap. Tap.*

He is unaccustomed to waiting, unaccustomed to being idle, unaccustomed to being undistracted by cell phones or computers or events and people competing for his time. He is not used to being entranced by the scent of flowers, by a sky that is fresh out of a Turner painting, by a breeze that is ruffling his hair, a breeze whose tickle he feels deep inside his chest. His rising, swelling chest.

He has never felt this at ease in the world. Here, alone, outside his mother's home, he is content to wait. Wait for her to return home, his mam, his blood, his future. Because it is true. Together, they will script his future. He almost laughs out loud at the man he was just earlier today—the cautious, timid straw man who fretted about being caught by the media, who was shackled to the burdensome pillars of duty and obligation, so utterly different from responsibility, which is freely chosen. He listens to the footsteps of the approaching dark, and he sees now how the orchestra plays in the natural world, how effortless the coordination of wind is with sky and sun and dusky fields. This is what he wants for himself, all the elements of his life coming together. And if he has this wish granted occasionally, here and there and now and then, he will still be the luckiest of men.

And so Anton Vesper Coleman waits. Under a darkening sky. Outside his mother's house. Leaning against his car. With one foot tapping a melody only he can hear. *Tap tap tap. Tap tap tap.*

Tap.

ABOUT THE AUTHOR

THRITY UMRIGAR is the author of six novels—*The Story Hour, The World We Found, The Weight of Heaven, The Space Between Us, If Today Be Sweet,* and *Bombay Time*—and the memoir *First Darling of the Morning.* A journalist for almost twenty years, she is the winner of the Nieman Fellowship to Harvard and the 2006 finalist for the PEN/ Beyond Margins Award. The Armington professor of English at Case Western Reserve University, Umrigar lives in Cleveland.